Still Bullish
on
America

A MEMOIR

To Joan, to Drue and Rod, to Kelly and Charlie, and to generations yet to come

Still Bullish
—on—
America

A MEMOIR

—— by ——

WILLIAM A. SCHREYER

FIRST LIMITED EDITION

ISBN 978-0-615-29816-0 (PAPERBACK)
ISBN 978-0-615-27931-2 (HARDBACK)

Contents

Preface

Some years back, several of my colleagues at Merrill Lynch suggested that maybe I should write a book. I had just completed forty years at the company, including nearly a decade as the CEO, and it was a logical thing to do.

We started that project, and I had some good stuff. Then I got thinking about it. I said, "You know, I never read Jack Welch's book; I had no desire to." I read Don Regan's book and, as much as I appreciated Don, I got bored with it halfway through. "Face it, Schreyer," I thought, "you'll probably get bored reading your own damn book!" I had no strong desire to complete it, so we dropped the project for about fifteen years.

What made the difference were the grandchildren. I was really so fond of them, they were such great kids, that I just thought it would not be fair if I didn't at least share as many of my thoughts as I could with them about my own life, as well as my philosophy of life, of business, of religion. Of anything I wanted to talk about. And what better way to do that than by putting it in book form?

It's not my objective to produce a *New York Times* bestseller. This is meant to be a private book for the family primarily, and a few close friends at the most. So I consider this not a book for its own sake, but a recording of things important in my life that would be interesting to the grandchildren and, in the years ahead, to their kids. That's all. Nothing more complicated than that.

One of the things that I hope comes through is how much I have enjoyed my life. It would be a hell of a thing to spend eighty years, roughly, and be miserable. And there're a lot of people who aren't happy unless they're miserable. We could all name names, but we'll keep that for a separate book if we have to.

Someone once said that writing a memoir is like peeling an onion: The deeper you go into the layers, the more pungent it gets. My objective is not to draw tears or draw blood; I feel no need to settle any scores, or "set the record straight." The fact of the matter is that I've enjoyed the competition in life and the business of life; I've enjoyed all that goes with it. I have no regrets about anything that I've ever done, about whom I've been involved with, so forth and so on.

While I have mentioned many people in this book who have been important in my life, I know there are many others not included in these pages. I want to assure all of these dear friends that the omission was unintentional, and I'll get to you in my next book!

My good friend Dr. Charles Sanders, whom you'll meet in these pages, suggests that this book ought to start like every good "Texas fairy tale": *Son of a bitch, you're not going to believe this one!* I don't know about that, but I do know the ideal ending: *To be continued.*

It's been a great road, and still is. We just can't go quite as fast as we used to, that's all. I still like fast cars, of course, but I know I don't have to go quite as fast in those cars as in the old days. It's great to have those memories, though. Memories of fast times, fast friends, a lot of laughs, and a rich and rewarding life. Something greater than that I could not wish for anyone.

William A. Schreyer
Princeton, N.J.
January 20, 2009

Still Bullish

——— on ———
America

A MEMOIR

——————————— by ———————————

WILLIAM A. SCHREYER

CHAPTER 1

"Still Bullish on America"

For those who have worked hard and earned the privilege and responsibility of leadership, there inevitably arrives a moment of truth.

Most of the time it comes out of the blue, when you least expect it. There is nothing you can do to prepare for it, except to rely on the instincts and skills that you have spent a lifetime developing. This is the moment that can make or break your career. And I don't want to seem too grandiose about it, but it also can define your place in history.

My defining moment was two moments, really—a double whammy. It was the year 1987. I had been elected CEO of Merrill Lynch two and a half years earlier; it had been an eventful period. I had recovered from triple-bypass heart surgery, picked my management team, assembled a good board of directors, and begun to put my stamp on Merrill Lynch's business strategy.

The year got off to a reasonable start. We were well along in shedding our real estate business, our two-sector, Capital Markets and Consumer Markets structure was working well, the markets were strong, and we were making good money. But late one spring afternoon, that all came crashing down. I was in my office in Princeton after attending a Schering

Plough board meeting, when the phone call came.

It was Dan Tully, the executive I had picked to be president and chief operating officer. "Are you sitting down?" he asked me.

"Yes," I replied. "What's the matter?"

"Bill, there's only one way to tell you this, and that's to tell you."

"OK, let's have it."

"It looks like we've got a two-hundred-million-plus loss on our hands."

That got my attention. I was alarmed, to say the least, but I also knew how important it was for me to stay calm. I told Tully to gather up as much information as he could and we'd get people together in the morning to sort it out. I sounded more relaxed than I felt, and I imagine that was also the case with Dan. We both knew we had a big problem on our hands. I went home and had a good, stiff drink.

As the years have passed and I've reflected on that phone call, I've often thought that I know how the Soviet Premier Mikhail Gorbachev must have felt when the phone rang and the fellow at the other end said, "Comrade, we've got a little problem at the nuclear plant down in Chernobyl." This was my Chernobyl.

When we sorted out all the details, it turned out the loss was closer to twice what Tully had originally indicated—$377 million on a pre-tax basis. It was in an exotic form of mortgage-backed securities known as IOs and POs. I had another name for them, but it's unprintable.

Mortgage-backed securities represent pools of home mortgages that Wall Street packages into liquid securities and trades in the marketplace. It was a growing business at the time, and we wanted a piece of it. The Street—ever adept at unbundling risk and finding new ways to trade it for potential profit—further refined mortgage-backeds into IO, or interest-only, and PO, or principal-only, securities. As the names suggest, the IOs represent only the value of the interest portion of the underlying securities, and the POs only the value of the principal portion. They trade differently in different interest rate environments.

We had hired a young trader from Salomon Brothers named Howard Rubin to be in charge of the mortgage-backed business. He had a degree from the Harvard Business School and by everyone's reckoning was an immensely talented trader. Someone told me later that like many traders he loved to gamble; in fact, he was such a good card-counter in blackjack that the casinos had banned him.

As we pieced the details together, we learned that Rubin was long on POs as interest rates started going against him. In a classic gambler's move, he decided to "double-down" and buy more, under the assumption that the direction of rates would soon reverse and erase the losses. Only it didn't happen. We had trading limits, but Rubin exceeded them. He went so far as to hide trading tickets in his desk, so his superiors had no idea of the firm's true exposure before it all came crashing down. Now we had a big mess to clean up.

From the vantage point of 2008, when losses by financial institutions in a global credit crisis are running into the hundreds of billions, $377 million may not seem like a lot of money. But at the time it was one of the largest losses, if not *the* largest, ever reported by a Wall Street firm, and it happened on my watch. Since it was material to our earnings and balance sheet, we had to publicly disclose it promptly, which caused our stock to take quite a hit. The retail system was up in arms, demanding to know how something like this could happen (and, by extension, if Schreyer and Tully knew what the hell they were doing).

Howard Rubin, of course, was fired immediately. He later went to Bear Stearns and, as far I know, had an uneventful career. I guess old Ace Greenberg, the CEO there and a pretty shrewd character, figured the guy wasn't going to make the same mistake twice. How ironic that twenty years later, Bear Stearns would be destroyed by its own reckless exposure to an even more exotic set of securities backed by mortgages and other debt obligations.

One of the first things I did was personally call all the directors to let them know what had happened and assure them that we were getting our arms around it. Then, much as Don Regan had done with me during the Hunt Silver Crisis (more about that later), I put Dan Tully in charge of the situation.

He handled it well. When we got word that morale on the debt-trading floor was devastated, he went down there and was visible. He set up a desk so people would know he was on the scene. He dealt with the people responsible until we got the thing under control.

At one point, he had me come down and talk to the entire floor. I said, "Am I upset about it? You're damn right I'm upset about it. But the only question now is, how do we deal with it? We suck it up, do what we have to do, and make sure we have the right controls in place so it won't happen again."

Of course, we had all the other constituencies to deal with, too. We had to deal with the press. We had to deal with our competitors. (Fortunately, they didn't try to take advantage of it. Not all of them, but most of them.) We had to deal with our board of directors, who were responsible for making sure we were running the place properly, not hiding anything, keeping everything upfront. It was a pretty intensive scene for a few weeks.

As was so often the case during my life, the counsel I received from Bill Rogers, a former U.S. attorney general and secretary of state who had joined our board shortly after Merrill Lynch went public, was invaluable to me during this period. As a director, he agreed to lead a review of the entire situation along with Irving M. Pollack, a former member of the Securities and Exchange Commission. They did a thorough postmortem on what had happened and what we should do to make sure it wouldn't happen again. Bill had performed a similar function for President Reagan when he headed the national commission that investigated the explosion of the space shuttle *Challenger*. He was truly one of our nation's great statesmen.

At the height of the crisis, right after it hit the papers and everyone was in full cry, I received a little note from my beloved Uncle Wilk—Elwood Wilkins, a close friend of my dad's who had married my mother's sister. Uncle Wilk was a role model for me in many ways. He sent me a short poem:

When things go wrong
As they usually will,
And your daily road
Seems all uphill

When funds are low
And debts are high
When you try to smile
And can only cry

And you really feel
You'd like to quit,
Don't run to me,
I don't give a shit!

I showed it to Dan Tully and we both got a good laugh out of it. Good old Uncle Wilk. He reminded me once again how important it is never to lose your sense of humor when the going gets tough, or to take yourself too seriously. Take the situation seriously, but not yourself.

The fact of the matter is that in any large organization you cannot always protect yourself from every person who is going to pee in the pool. But if everyone's more alert and looking for potential problems much more carefully than they were in the past, then you've got a better chance of protecting yourself. And that was the outcome of this particular episode.

Though it wasn't a hell of a lot of fun, there was a genuine silver lining to the mortgage-backed securities loss: I found out who among our executive team I could really count on in a crisis. And we put stronger and more effective controls in place on our trading floors. Both would prove invaluable just a scant five months later on October 19, 1987, when the stock market experienced its second-largest single-day decline in American history.

By the middle of October, stock markets around the world, which had performed strongly in the first three quarters of 1987, were starting to get jittery. On Friday, October 16, the Dow dropped 108 points—at the time, a record. The next day I was over at my friend Charlie Sanders's house to watch the Penn State-Syracuse football game. During the game a *New York Times* reporter tracked me down for a little interview about what I thought was going to happen in the markets on Monday. I kept it pretty vague because I really didn't know what the hell was going to happen, and anyway, a doom-and-gloom prognostication by the chairman of Merrill Lynch could become a self-fulfilling prophesy.

Syracuse beat Penn State soundly that day. I said to Charlie, "This is a bad indicator. This does not look good for Monday." I was mostly kidding, but half-serious. Sunday night, New York time, the markets opened in Asia and dropped sharply. We were in for a bumpy ride.

Monday morning, before the market opened, all of the heads of the major firms met over at the New York Stock Exchange at the request of the exchange's chairman, John Phelan. As an exchange vice chairman, I had a prominent seat at the table. Phelan said it looked like we'd be in for a pretty wild market that day, and put the question on the table: Should the exchange close? Should we just stop trading if it gets too heavy? I can't remember a single person who wanted to take that step. The view was that if we did close the exchange, when we reopened it would be much, much worse. It would send the wrong signal—that something was really wrong.

I got back to our headquarters—we had just moved in

6

earlier that year to our new buildings in the World Financial Center—and called together Dan Tully and a few of our other key people. I wanted to make sure that whatever happened, we would be ready from an operational standpoint.

The market opened sharply down and just got worse from there. We watched it drop before our eyes on the quote machine in the conference room. By the time the market closed at four that afternoon, the Dow Jones Industrial Average had dropped 508 points. It was, for a single day, the largest point decline in history and the second-largest percentage decline, exceeded only by that earlier Black Monday in October 1929, the day that ushered in the Great Depression.

That was a terrible time for America. Banks failed, people lost their life savings, millions lost their jobs, and it took over a decade for the economy to recover. But 1987 was different from 1929; many protections, such as federal insurance for bank deposits, had been put in place, so history was not likely to repeat itself—exactly. Yet none of us had ever lived through a market crash of this magnitude before. We were facing the unknown, and the thought weighed heavily on our minds: Were we on the threshold of another period of prolonged economic recession or even depression?

How would our clients react, and our employees? Then there was the question of our own personal wealth—which had taken a big hit that day, at least on paper.

One of the first things that any leader must do in a crisis is attempt to gather the facts. Before you can make any decision, you have to try to separate fact from fiction, reality from rumor. It was a fact that the market was dropping violently. The key question was: *Why?* If we could answer that, it would go a long way in helping us determine our actions in the days ahead.

We turned to our experts in the securities and economic research department for help. Bob Farrell was our chief market analyst at the time. At Columbia University, he had studied under the legendary Benjamin Graham, the father of value investing. Bob spent hours that morning poring over his stock market charts, trying to decode what was happening. Other of our analysts were experts on the fixed-income and credit markets. They turned a sharp eye to what was happening with bonds, which in fact were holding up pretty well.

Alan Greenspan had just taken over as Federal Reserve chairman, and he was not going to make the same mistake his predecessors had made back in 1929. He sent a signal that the Fed was prepared to flood the market with liquidity.

There was a fair amount of concern at the time over what was known as the "twin deficits"–foreign trade and the federal budget–and U.S. officials had recently engaged in some saber rattling with the Europeans over currency valuation. These factors notwithstanding, our experts soon came to a consensus: They did not see the kind of fundamental economic deterioration that warranted a sell-off of this magnitude. The economy was basically sound, and what we were seeing was a classic panic–an emotional selling spree based on unfounded fears. (We later found out that this selling was exacerbated by computer programs that were supposed to help protect big investment portfolios but in fact had the opposite effect.) Calm and reason were two medicines the country needed a big dose of. This would become the basis of our message in the days ahead.

I felt our team had a head start and I told them so. We had just come through the crucible of the mortgage-backed trading loss, and as a result were prepared to handle the much bigger crisis that was now upon us. I knew that as the firm that "brought Wall Street to Main Street," Merrill Lynch would need to step forward and communicate with the public. What we did and said would have a big impact.

The first message was to our own people, the account executives–today they call them financial advisors–who had the most direct relationships with our millions of customers, advising them and helping them manage their finances. We sent out a wire to the troops signed by Dan Tully and me. We reaffirmed our confidence in the economy and financial markets, assuring them that Merrill Lynch was financially strong and had the wherewithal to deal with the situation. Later we put our money where our mouth was, announcing that the board of directors had authorized a buyback of up to five million additional shares.

We urged our people to counsel our clients to take a long-term view and, wherever possible, avoid selling at distressed prices. We made these internal communications available to the news media and they were widely quoted, including, prominently, on the front page of Tuesday's *Wall Street Journal,* which noted in a subhead to its main story on the market crash that "Some Stay Bullish."

I stayed in close contact with the stock exchange during this entire period. My good friend, former U.S. Senator Howard Baker, who had succeeded former Merrill Lynch CEO Don Regan as the White House chief of staff, called the exchange at one point on behalf of President Reagan, asking if there were any plans to close. The rationale against closing was explained to him, and the White House was comfortable with that. Later in the week the exchange did decide to close a couple hours early for a few days, just to allow time to process and clear the huge volume of trades. If they couldn't handle the processing, it would have been a big problem.

We were a day into the crisis when I found myself in a meeting with Larry Speakes, who had recently left his position as press secretary to President Reagan and joined Merrill Lynch as our communications head, and his chief deputy, Paul Critchlow. Paul had been press secretary to Pennsylvania Governor Dick Thornburgh during the Three Mile Island nu-clear accident, and knew a thing or two about managing a crisis.

Merrill Lynch had previously purchased some commercial time during the telecast of the World Series, then under way between the St. Louis Cardinals and the Minnesota Twins. It was clear that running our regular commercials was not an option in the middle of the biggest market disruption in nearly sixty years. Speakes and Critchlow presented me with a radical proposal. They wanted me to tape a new commercial—a message from Merrill Lynch—that I would deliver to a nationwide TV audience.

The idea intrigued me, but I had my concerns about it. No Merrill Lynch chairman and CEO had ever gone on TV as the company spokesman, and whatever I did would be exceptionally visible. I pondered their proposal. Was it the right approach? If I was going to put my reputation and my career so publicly on the line, I wanted them to be damn certain it was the right thing to do.

Finally I said, "OK. I hear what you're recommending. Now, I want you to go away for one hour and think this through very carefully—and I mean carefully! If you come back in an hour and still tell me you think it's the right thing to do, then I'll do it."

Something like fifty-nine minutes and fifty-nine seconds later they were back in my office. "Bill, we want you to do it." We cleared time on my schedule to tape the commercials that afternoon at our in-house television studio. Our advertising director, Charlie Mangano, set about making the arrangements required to switch the old spots with the new ones.

Critchlow swung into high gear. Operating as he would in the closing days of a tight political campaign, he banged out some spots—simple, straightforward messages that we would later dub "straight talk." He worked closely with his sidekick Jim Wiggins—Wiggs—also a former Thornburgh press operative and a fellow Penn Stater who would become my collaborator over many years on speeches and other projects, including this book. Paul and Jim batted a few word changes back and forth, and we were ready to go.

We were on our way over to the studio when my chief

legal counsel, Steve Hammerman, got wind of the project. Steve was naturally cautious and very protective of me. He started phoning over to the studio to put a hold on things. Larry and Paul dodged his calls.

The market remained turbulent throughout the week, but did not drop below Monday's low. On Thursday night, October 22, 1987, as millions of Americans tuned in to watch the Cards battle the Twins at Busch Stadium in St. Louis, they saw a fellow named William A. Schreyer appear on their TV screens, along with the words "A Message from Merrill Lynch." This is what I said:

I'm here for some straight talk about the stock market. It's important to everyone. It provides capital that creates jobs to make America grow.

Emotions can run high during market turbulence, just when reason should prevail.

We are confident in the markets. We've stayed active in them for all investors.

America's economy is the strongest in the world, with great ability to bounce back.

At Merrill Lynch, we're still Bullish on America.

This commercial and two others that we did had an enormous impact—exactly the effect we had hoped for. Merrill Lynch's bullishness in the face of a perceived market disaster quickly penetrated the national consciousness. You know you've hit a populist nerve when you become the subject of editorial cartoons. The cartoonist for the *Pittsburgh Press* drew a two-panel caricature of President Reagan. In the first panel the cartoon Reagan says, "The fluctuating market has serious economic implications. I better arrange a meeting with my financial advisors." In the second panel he picks up the phone: "Hello...Merrill Lynch?"

The commercial wasn't the only national television I did that week. Peter Jennings, the ABC anchorman, asked if I'd do a live, remote interview with him from the New York Stock Exchange. I was nervous going over there. Not about the questions–I knew I could give answers about what was going on. No, I was afraid that the earpiece they give you would fall out, and I'd look like a total jackass in front of 50 million Americans. Fortunately, that didn't happen.

On Friday afternoon I flew down to suburban Washington to appear on public television's *Wall Street Week,* at the time one of the most widely watched programs about investing and the markets. The other guest was Sir John Templeton, the legendary mutual fund investor, who also delivered a message of profound optimism.

The famous host, Louis Rukeyser (a Merrill Lynch client, by the way), opened his interview with a zinger of a question directed at me: "Bill, why didn't you warn your clients that this would happen?" All I could do was answer truthfully: "Because we didn't know." The fact of the matter is that no one can predict an irrational market panic. All you can do is advise your clients how to be prepared for it by being appropriately diversified, and how to react once it happens. That we did exceptionally well.

I went home, had a couple of well-deserved pops, and spent a relatively uneventful weekend. Then, on Monday, October 26, one week after the crash, the unthinkable happened. A distraught client entered one of our Miami offices, shot and killed the office manager, Jose F. Argilagos, seriously wounded a financial advisor, then killed himself.

This client had been trading heavily on margin and was wiped out when the market tanked. It turned out he had been part of the Federal Witness Protection Program and had assumed an entirely new identity. How are you supposed to fulfill the regulatory obligation to "know your client" under those kinds of circumstances? That was when morale hit a low point. Jose's death really hit home for me. After all, I was a former office manager myself.

In the days and weeks that followed, Merrill Lynch operated in an exemplary fashion. We extended office hours so that we'd be more available to our clients, published thoughtful research, recommended market reforms that could temper some of the mechanisms that had aggravated the sell-off. Some good stocks were selling at very attractive prices, and at the end of the week of October 19, based on our advice, our clients had snapped up some bargains; they were net buyers of equities over those five days. That's the "buy low" part of successful investing.

Several years later, I was at "21" one day having dinner with a big client and his wife, a French woman. She loved the 21 Club and was celebrating her fiftieth birthday there. Walter Cronkite, the legendary CBS anchorman, came in with his wife and sat a few tables down. I had met Cronkite three or four times, but he was hardly a close friend. As they were getting ready to leave, he came over and I introduced him to our friends.

"Bill," he said, "I just want to tell you that your going on television back during that big crash week was one of the greatest things I've ever seen in my life. It stopped the whole thing. It had tremendous impact."

I'm starting to feel ten feet tall, sitting there hearing this in front of my friends. Then he said, "I'm just glad I retired. I'd hate to have to compete with you." To hear that from the broadcaster who had earned the nickname "The Most Trusted Man in America" was gratifying indeed.

A few days later I was back at "21" having lunch with Bill Rogers and Dan Tully. I'm still kind of pumped up, so I told them this story. They said, "Yeah, yeah, yeah. That's what he said? Aw, come on."

In walks Cronkite. Bill Rogers said, "Well, let's find out, Danny." He waves to him, and Cronkite comes over, and we're all chatting. Bill said, "You know what Bill just told us you said about his TV commercial?"

"That's exactly right, and I meant every darn word of it," Cronkite said.

"There, fellows," I said. It really was fun.

Somebody asked me if, during that wild week in October, I'd wished I'd taken early retirement and escaped the whole mess. "Are you kidding?" I said. "All my life I've been in this business. I eat it, breathe it, sleep it. And not to be in the middle of one of the biggest events in financial history would have driven me crazy."

More than any personal satisfaction, I truly believe that the way the firm handled itself during this period, in the interests of our clients and the American public, was one of the finest moments in Merrill Lynch's history.

There would be many more memorable moments in my life and career, but none quite so memorable as the "Crash of '87." And in many ways, I had been preparing for it my whole life.

CHAPTER 2

The Screaming Angel

It all began on January 13, 1928. My father sent a telegram from the Western Union office in Williamsport, Pennsylvania, to my mother's next older sister, Helen, with whom she was very close, and her husband, my Uncle Wilk. They were on the high seas, heading to Panama for my uncle's first international assignment as a construction engineer. To save money, Dad kept it short: "Baby born. Mother's features, father's fixtures. Regards, Bill." That was his way of letting them know that a baby boy had come into the world, to be christened William Allen Schreyer.

I'm not sure what time of day I was born; I'd have to make it up. But years later, my father told me he remembered that I had been conceived on the night of the Jewish Charity Ball at the Lycoming Hotel in Williamsport. He and Mother stayed at the hotel that night even though they lived in Williamsport, because it was a great party! So that makes me acceptable to all faiths.

My father was William Linn Schreyer. His parents were Allen Schreyer—that's where I get my middle name—and Emily Rissell Schreyer from the Rissell branch of the family. Allen, my grandfather, worked for the Pennsylvania Railroad. He got tuberculosis, went out to Montana to recover, lived a couple more years, and died when Dad was just a kid. My grandmother sort of raised the two kids by herself—my dad and his older brother, Charlie. Did a great job.

My grandmother was quite a character. She was Lutheran, and for a while she lived with us. There was really never a problem, never a fuss. But she used to cheat me at Parcheesi. She'd roll the dice, say, an eight, and then tap out "One, two, three, four, five, six, seven, eight." But it was usually nine or ten spaces on the board.

I would say, "I caught you cheating, Nana." And she would say, "I did not!" Anyhow, she was quite a woman.

My mother's maiden name was Engel, Elizabeth Engel. Engel means "angel" in German, and Schreyer means "screamer." So I was known as the screaming angel, though much later, my wife, Joan, would find a few rare occasions to debate the angel part.

I never knew my mother's parents—they died when she was quite young. She was the thirteenth of thirteen children, and I was born on January 13, so that's why I think of thirteen as my lucky number. I've often said that I don't get into a lot of debates about birth control, because if my grandparents had stopped at an even twelve, I wouldn't be here today (though Joan claims I would have found a way).

With that many kids, the older sisters always took care of the younger sisters, and there were more girls than there were boys, which probably was better, because boys really aren't good at that sort of thing.

Aunt Anne was the matriarch of the family. As the oldest, she had charge of the family. A very strong woman. When I would drop in for a visit, she used to send me down to the basement to bring her up a bucket of coal. She never married until late in life, and that didn't work out too well. They ended up getting divorced.

At any rate, I was an only child, so obviously my mother had gone to the other extreme. I never had big arguments about whether or not I should have brothers or sisters. I kind of liked being an only child.

I also remember, on my mother's side, my Uncle John and Uncle Jacob. John was the oldest and was a Remington Rand typewriter dealer in Williamsport. Jacob was also with Remington Rand, in the shaver division. He was the first national sales manager for Remington Rand Electric Shaver, and he gave me one for my sixteenth birthday, which thrilled me to death, because I was just starting to shave.

That same weekend, I was walking by the guest bathroom and I heard him swearing. I said, "What's the matter, Uncle Jake?"

"Bud," he said—that was my nickname then, Buddy—"these things are the greatest things in the world to sell, but they don't give you a shave worth a damn!"

I've been asked where my nickname came from, but I'm not exactly sure. My parents didn't like "Billy," so to avoid confusion with my dad, who was Bill, too, they started calling me Buddy. Maybe it was taken from a first cousin by the name of Bud Engel.

Both my paternal and maternal ancestors were from Germany. They immigrated probably in the 1700s and settled in the Williamsport area. Mother's family was from the southern part of Germany, the Munich area, where most of the Catholics are from. Dad's family was from up north, probably the Frankfort or Düsseldorf area, where the Lutherans were popular. That was my basic, boyhood understanding of German history.

I have a lot of great memories of the relatives—the uncles, aunts, and so forth—from when I was growing up. My father's older brother, Charles, was a brilliant, self-educated man. He studied Latin and Greek; he was really a scholar. He could have gone to college, but he stayed at home to make money and take care of his mother. He was a town leader, involved in all the civic activities. He was a deacon in the Lutheran Church and president of the West Branch Bank and Trust

Company in Williamsport, the largest of the three banks in town. He had two daughters. Both are dead now, but we kind of all grew up together.

Uncle Charles looked a little like Dwight Eisenhower, and he was a very gentle man. A man of great dignity, with a quiet, warm sense of humor. He and my father had an extraordinarily good relationship.

Also on the Schreyer side of the family, I remember two great-aunts, Aunt Nell and Aunt Bess. Little League baseball began in Williamsport in the 1930s, and they play the Little League World Series there to this day. Aunt Bess never missed a Little League game. She was a retired office worker for the Pennsylvania Railroad, never married. They played the ball games at a park half a block down from her house, and she and her sister would go over every afternoon and see all those Little League games. She went to the World Series when they started having it, and continued going until she died. She was something, too.

Uncle Todd Rissell, God rest him, was one of my heroes. He was Director of Athletics out at Thiel College in western Pennsylvania, and also had a very successful tile business. My mother didn't want me to play football, and one day I heard her talking to Uncle Todd.

"Would you have a talk with Buddy?" she asked him. "He really would like to play football, and I just don't want him to."

And he said, "Well, you're smart. I would encourage him to play tennis, golf, and swim. If he does all three of those, he could do them until he's ninety years old, and it's something he could use socially and have fun playing, too."

So that's what he told me. And I didn't forgive him for that for years, until I saw I wasn't tough enough to play football at Penn State, and that his recommending lifelong sports was pretty damn good advice.

On my mother's side, she was probably closer to Aunt Helen than she was to any of her other sisters. Aunt Helen was number twelve and my mother was number thirteen among the Engel siblings. When Mother was dating Dad, if the story is correct, Dad suggested to his friend Wilk that he might want to have a date with Helen. And of course he did.

Uncle Wilk's full name was Elwood Kempton Wilkins. Typical New Englander, typical Maine guy, a Congregationalist and proud of it. After he proposed to Aunt Helen, he was transferred down to Florida, and they were going to get married there. Aunt Helen took the train down, of course. Normally the train never arrived on time, but for once it was actually ten minutes early getting into the station. Because Uncle Wilk had figured it would be in as usual, forty-five minutes late, he didn't think there was any rush to get to the train station. Meanwhile, Aunt Helen was cooling her heels. She was so mad that she was ready to take the next train back home. Uncle Wilk finally pulled up and they got in the car, and he found a priest who married them.

He was head of construction for Ebasco Services, and after Florida, he and Aunt Helen went to Panama. Then they went on to Mexico and then China. So they had a great life traveling for Ebasco.

My parents eloped, too. Uncle Jacob, the older brother in my mother's family, set them up to be married by a Catholic priest in Wilkes Barre, Pennsylvania. It was just easier to do it that way, given that my dad's mother was a serious Lutheran and my mother's people were Catholic. We've had a lot of fun over the years kidding about that momentous trip to Wilkes Barre. Someone would always joke, "There may be another good reason why someone would go there, but I can't think of it right now."

Uncle Wilk's international lifestyle was a great influence on me, as was his dry sense of humor. I remember one time having lunch with him at a country club he belonged to in Westchester County outside of New York City, and I'll never forget he said, referring to the club, "They want me to be president. I don't really want to be president, for cripes sake."

As we were walking out to the parking lot to get to his car, I noticed him shaking hands with everyone and patting the little kids on the head. When we got to the car I said, "Hey, Uncle, you really don't want to be president? You sure are running for office pretty hard."

He said to me, "Bill, you little bastard, you noticed that, huh?"

The club was half Catholic and half something else, and after he won the election, he gave a little speech. "I want you to know I have nothing against any race, creed, or color. I just happen to prefer Congregationalists. And if I find one more, there will be two of us in this club!"

I used the same line after I took over the Metropolitan Region at Merrill Lynch. Just about everyone was either Jewish or Irish Catholic, and I told them that was fine with me, but I just happened to prefer German Catholics. "And if I find one more of those..." I got a laugh out of the crowd with that one.

Dad and Uncle Wilk used to love to play jokes on Mom and Aunt Helen. After coming back from an assignment in Texas, Wilk the Congregationalist, Helen and Mom, who were German Catholic, and Lutherans Dad and Uncle Charles were all having cocktails. And so Dad asked Uncle Wilk—they had planned this thing—"Wilk, you enjoyed Texas and everything down there? How do they treat the Catholics down in Texas?" And Wilk said, "Oh, about the same as the coloreds and Jews, as long as they behave themselves."

Well, my mother and Aunt Helen could have killed both of them, because they knew that they'd been set up. But back in those days, religious and ethnic humor was an acceptable way of life. It was fun. Today everybody has to be politically correct and nobody can have fun about who you are and what your background is. And while we may have used slang in a good-natured way to describe people's racial or ethnic background, I learned very early on that bigotry or discrimination was just stupidity, period.

I went to first grade at the Samuel Transeau School. It was about three blocks down from where we lived, and bordered on the tougher section of town. It was a nice little school. We were not in a wealthy district by any means—there weren't many wealthy districts in those days.

I started when I was five, and I was the youngest and probably the smallest kid in the class. There was a clique from the tough part of Williamsport run by a guy named Ed. They surrounded me one morning during recess out in the back of the school. They were about to beat me up, and this guy Ed was urging the others on.

Then around the corner came a wonderful guy—African-American—who was big and tall. He came over and grabbed Ed and said, "You touch this kid and you're gonna deal with me."

The next morning we went out for recess. The guy who had saved me had the ball, the bat, and the catcher's mitt. He said, "Hey, Buddy, you want to pitch or you want to hit?" I said, "Well, I'll hit today." From then on, he always made sure I got the bat first, or whatever I wanted, and these other kids were afraid of him. I never had any race-relations problems with anybody after that; this guy was my hero. He went into his family business, as I recall. They had a nice diner type of operation in Williamsport.

We lived at 921 Park Avenue. It wasn't Park Avenue in New York, but it was a nice street back in those days. I lived in a two-family house. We were on the left, upstairs and downstairs, and the people who owned the house lived on the other side. Dad was working at the West Branch Bank and Trust Company in 1929, when the Crash came. He had been doing pretty well, but then he got wiped out.

We had an empty lot next to the house and we played all the sports–football, softball, and so forth–there. The grade school was just three or four blocks away, so it was easy to get to. Junior high school was a few blocks up the other direction– all public schools. I was glad I didn't go to parochial school because I was afraid of the nuns!

Actually, with my father being Lutheran and my mother Catholic, she didn't want me to go to parochial school because she was afraid it would just make the division a little deeper. I'd go to what was called catechism after school, once a week at the church, which the nuns would teach. You'd learn the basics. I'd go to Mass with my mother every Sunday and occasionally to Lutheran services with my father if he chose to go that week. He'd say, "You're covering me. I can stay home and do my homework from the office."

In earlier times, Williamsport had been one of the lumber capitals of the world, and when I was growing up you still had furniture manufacturing and a lot of small industries of all kinds; Lycoming Motors had a plant there. There was considerable unemployment during the Depression, but somehow people stuck together and would help other people if they possibly could.

I remember the great flood of 1936. The Susquehanna River overflowed its banks and we had three feet of water in our living room. We went out and stayed with Uncle Charlie, whose place looked down over the valley where the flood came. "Up in the hills," we called Uncle Charlie's place. We stayed out there until our place was cleaned up.

❈

Everybody knew everybody else in grade school. I was a pretty good student, but there were two classmates, a girl named Helen Louise Pechter and a guy named Ford Turnable, who were always at the top of the class. They would vie for number one or number two, and I'd try like hell to compete with them. But I was strictly third or fourth, never made it to one or two. That was a competitive thing with me. I remember it very well.

The art teacher had a little problem with me because I couldn't draw anything worth a damn. Let's say I'd have to draw an apple tree or something. Well, I'd draw the apples. Then I'd have to put a thing with an arrow saying A-P-P-L-E so she would know what it was. I was never very mechanical or very artistic.

Another thing I was not was a poet. I remember I had an English teacher named Miss Wendell in high school. She didn't just preside over a class, she ruled. I'll never forget one time when we were supposed to create our own poem. I went home at night and was really struggling with it, so my father said, "Why don't you give her something like this? A play on words":

Am her gone, is her when?
Has her left I all alone?
Us could never go to she,
They can never come to we.
Alas, it cannot was.

I thought, "Gee, that's terrific." So I turned it in. The next day when I got my paper back, I got a zero! I said, "Well, Miss Wendell, why did I get a zero? I thought it was pretty clever."

"It was," she said. "It was particularly clever when your

father did it in the same class thirty years ago!" So her message to me was: Even if it's lousy, do your own.

Like many American boys, my first job was delivering newspapers. I delivered the *Williamsport Sun* door-to-door. You would get a bunch of papers and put a sling around your neck, and you'd throw a paper up to the door or hand it to someone when they came out.

It was pretty pleasant except during the cold months, when you'd have to wear those gloves with half the fingers cut so you could pull out the papers. Anyhow, I'd get paid three dollars every two weeks, so I got a buck and a half a week to deliver those papers. I had about 120 houses that I had to cover, so it wasn't a high-yield income-producing job to say the least!

I'll never forget it, though. One neighbor had a dog who always accompanied me around on the tour. It was a little dog, but a tough little guy. There was a chow that would come out from one of the houses, and you could be scared just looking at him. So the chow would growl and start to come down the steps, and this little dog, a cocker spaniel, would go after him and chase him back up on the porch. He was my protector. It's a lot of fun remembering those days. That was a good life.

I was active in high school during the years of World War II. One of my friends and classmates was a great comic and a serious actor, with a really good sense of humor, and one day we came up with the idea of having bond rallies—getting the kids to buy war bonds or stamps. You got a $25 bond but would buy it for $18.75—the difference was the interest you got at maturity.

So, to entertain the rally, we started a little act called Gallagher and Sheen, after a famous vaudeville act in earlier years. We sang a long comical song with lots of verses, each ending with the refrain, "Thank you, Mr. Gallagher. You're welcome, Mr. Sheen." It was a pretty cute act. We were a big hit as a comedy team.

My stage partner later went on to become an actor professionally, and died too young. He was a very talented guy. In fact, he was elected the lead in the senior class play, *The Man Who Came to Dinner,* the famous role that Monty Woolley created on Broadway. I had a supporting role, playing a character named Dr. Bradley.

The night of the play, as I was backstage putting on my makeup, a girl in the cast came in, visibly upset. She said, "President Roosevelt just died."

I made what, from the perspective of sixty years, was clearly an inappropriate wisecrack, something like, "Good, that'll make for a great performance tonight." She was justifiably horrified.

But I was a teenager, and you see, I was anti-Roosevelt. I was brought up to be anti-Roosevelt. I felt bad afterward, but not that bad, because all is fair in love, war, and politics. That was the night that Roosevelt died, and it was the night of our class play. Funny how you remember those little things.

My lifelong affiliation with the Republican Party came naturally to me. I grew up in a house where my father was with Merrill Lynch and his older brother, Uncle Charles, was president of one of the banks in town. And Williamsport itself was a pretty conservative town. Every night, as a kid growing up, I heard my father and Uncle Charles talking on the phone about how Roosevelt was ruining the country. Politically speaking, in their view Roosevelt was a bad guy.

And so it was, as a matter of fact, in our neighborhood. It was a strictly middle-class neighborhood that was probably 80 percent Republican. Oh, a couple of Democrats lived nearby. One was a family with a French name. Delightful people. But they were Democrats. So one of the tricks at Halloween was, we'd sneak over and put WIN WITH WILKIE stickers on their car bumpers and windshields. Finally the family raised so much hell with my father, he told me I'd better stop doing that.

So by the time I got out of high school, there was no question about my political orientation. And I carried that right on through Penn State and life in general. I just never saw the light of the liberal left. I always saw the glory and justice of the capitalistic way, the free-enterprise system. God bless America and the free-enterprise system, where everybody is given an opportunity to compete and excel.

We had political groups within the high school. The Democrats had theirs and the Republicans had theirs. And you can guess where I was. It was all good, fierce competition. It was never as nasty as it is in Congress today. That's for sure. But it was hard-hitting. Hard-hitting, but fair. The left would try to make you look like you were against the little person. But hell, we were *all* little people. We all wanted to do well in life at whatever area we wanted to get into. So we believed in fiscal responsibility, the profit system, the marketing of products and ideas, and so forth. And the other side always wanted to have the government involved.

We came up through the WPA, the Work Projects Administration, and all that well-meaning stuff, but we always felt that the private sector could do more for the country than large government could. And the world's still arguing about that. Nothing much has changed. You'd think something would have changed after all these years.

So many of my values were shaped during those years of my childhood. I think I'd much rather grow up in a town like Williamsport than in a town like New York City. You get lost in the crowd in a big city. Williamsport was just the right size. You didn't know everybody in town, but you knew everybody you could possibly want to know.

Through my regular attendance of Mass with my mother, and through her influence, religion became an important part of my life. When she was growing up, my mother lived diagonally across the street from the Church of the Annunciation, the Catholic church that was known as the Irish parish, and where we ended up going regularly when I was a kid, but she went to school out at St. Boniface, the German Catholic parish way out on the hill. She had about a two-mile walk to school every day, even though there was that Catholic church right across the street. But the Germans, Italians, and Irish had their three separate churches in town, and she was identified with the German side.

She was religious in the sense that she wouldn't miss Mass. If she could physically handle it, she would go to church. And she always said her rosary—but very privately; she didn't flaunt it. Though my dad was Lutheran, in all the years that we were all together, there was never a religious argument of any kind.

My mother was a marvelous woman, very warm and loving, with a beautiful sense of humor. She and my father made a great couple in the sense that she could kid him and he'd kid her, and they were always a delight to be around at parties. If I wanted to sit down and have a talk with my mother about anything, it was never a problem; she was such an understanding person. She loved life, smoked too many cigarettes maybe, but she finally gave that up. That was a sign of the times in those days, to always have a cigarette when you were having a drink and socializing.

She always let you know if you were doing something she didn't think was right, but we had a great mother-son relationship. One thing we had in common was that we both enjoyed my father so much. It was not a complicated life growing up. Even though it was during the tough economic times of the thirties and forties, there was always joy and fun in the house.

My mother had her first medical challenge before I went off to Penn State, when she was diagnosed with breast cancer. It was back in the early days when they took care of it the old-fashioned way. But she recovered from the surgery and handled it like a trouper. She never let it really get her down. She stayed in pretty good health until she had problems later on. But all things considered, she lived a full and happy life, into her mid-seventies, well after my dad had died at fifty-three. She missed him a great deal—we both did—but she had a lot of good friends and family in Williamsport.

People ask me if I was frightened as a young man by the illnesses that affected both my parents. You just do a lot of praying when you have things like that. You have no place else to go, so you go to your knees. Fortunately, someone up there seemed to like me, because they both lived longer than might have been the case.

Both of my parents influenced me in so many ways, but I have to say that back then and to this very day, nobody has had a bigger influence on my life than my father.

CHAPTER 3

The Greatest Man
I've Ever Known

I'd still put my father at the top of the list of anybody I've ever known. He had a great way with people. A man once said to me, "You know, your father sees you on the street and when he says, 'Hello, how are you, Joe?' he really means it. He really wants to know how you are."

He was one of the greatest "people persons" I've ever known. Even though I was close to my mother, I was really much closer to my father, on a man-to-man basis. He gave me wonderful advice, and I have nothing but great memories of him.

He had a tremendous sense of humor. He could tell the raunchiest off-color joke to a group of old women and have them roar. He didn't do that very often, but the point was, he could make anyone laugh. He just had a quick and wonderful and very attractive sense of humor.

I remember one day my mother said to my father, "Now, Bill, Father Flanagan" (or whoever it was) "is coming by for a visit this afternoon, for a little coffee or tea. All I ask is that you behave yourself. Just behave yourself."

He said, "Betty, I won't do anything to embarrass you.

Why would I? You really hurt my feelings that you would even think I might do that."

So that afternoon the priest arrived at the door. I was upstairs, and I heard Mother greeting him. He came in, and she went out to the kitchen to fix something, and Dad started talking.

I heard Dad say, "Father, have you heard the story?" And I said, "Uh-oh," and snuck to the top of the stairs to listen. And it was a story about a little Irish girl going to confession.

She said, "Father, I've committed adultery."

And the priest said, "Was it against your will, my daughter?"

And she said, "Oh no, Father, it was against the china closet. Now, Father, it would have done your heart good to hear the dishes rattling." The priest roared.

Here's another example of his humor. Many years later, we were at the country club in Williamsport, and Dad and I went to get the girls a little after-dinner drink or something, one of those sweet concoctions we drank in those days.

Anyhow, we were sitting at the bar waiting, and the guy next to us, who was not a member, was using foul language. Finally he turned to Dad and said, "Do you have a men's room in this firetrap?"

And Dad says, "Yes, just walk down the hall. Second door to the left, you'll see a sign that says 'Gentlemen.' But don't pay any attention to that, you son of a bitch. Just walk right in." The guy went down the hall and never came back.

One of the great, lifelong lessons I learned from him was the use of humor to make a point or defuse a potentially difficult situation. In Williamsport in those days there was a police captain by the name of Ray Fedder. He was Irish, with red hair, and the way he carried himself when he walked down the street, you just knew he had to be police—he had that way about him.

One day Mother had dropped Dad off at work and was driving back home. She'd stopped at a traffic light downtown, and when the light changed, she didn't see Officer Fedder crossing the street—he was in the blind spot, where the windshield and door met—and she hit the gas. She missed him by about an eighth of an inch, and he just stood glaring at her as she drove by.

When she got home she called Dad, all shook up. "I wouldn't be a bit surprised if Ray Fedder comes to see you and says I almost killed him," she told him. "I just didn't see him."

Dad told her not to worry about it. "I'll handle it if he comes in."

Sure enough, about twenty minutes later, Dad looked down the hall and saw Officer Fedder coming in the front door. He went out to greet him and said, "Ray, what did you do to Betty? You scared the hell out of her this morning!"

"I scared the hell out of her?! She damn near killed me." He was really ticked off and he wanted to let Dad know it, but they both ended up laughing about it because of the way Dad handled it. His humor took a tense situation and totally defused it.

❋

Dad had gone to college at Bucknell in Lewisburg, Pennsylvania, for a year. Then World War I started and he went into the service for a short period of time before the war ended. He never went back to Bucknell.

He was working at the bank in 1929 when the historic stock market crash came. Like many people at the time, he had been trading on margin and was deeply in debt to the bank. I'm not exactly sure of the amount, but it was probably on the order of $100,000—a great deal of money in those days.

He could have declared bankruptcy and not paid off those debts—a lot of people did—but he wouldn't do that. He was a man of total integrity, and there was no way he was going to take the easy way out.

I never knew this until afterward, but it took him until 1950 to pay off his last note. It took from 1929 to 1950—all through the thirties and forties. He made that payment every month, and then he died two years later, in 1952, at age fifty-three. And all he had was a Merrill Lynch group insurance policy, worth about $30,000.

When he left the bank, he became the Williamsport branch manager for a stock brokerage, Granberry & Company. This was acquired by Fenner & Beane, which later became Merrill Lynch, Pierce, Fenner & Beane, and then still later, Merrill Lynch, Pierce, Fenner & Smith. So this was my first connection with Merrill Lynch.

It was a four-man office, and I keep a picture of it with me in my own office to this very day. In the picture, my dad is standing next to the girls who worked in the office—Dad always got next to the girls!—and there were the four brokers. One of the fellows had gone to Bucknell. It was a great little office. And back when I was growing up, I knew exactly what I wanted to do when I was older, because I spent a lot of time there.

The clients, people with accounts, would come in and sit and watch the ticker tape, watch the markets. So, in a small town like Williamsport you developed an easy rapport with the customers. And they enjoyed seeing a young kid come into the office.

I first started working there part-time in high school—for very little, I might add. I think they paid me three bucks a week or something. A girl a year ahead of me in high school was working there, too, as a board marker—putting the share prices that were wired from the New York Stock Exchange up on a chalkboard. So I'd help her.

The supply room was behind the board. On Saturdays, after the market closed at noon, we'd go back there to help with the supplies. One day my dad opened the door and caught us playing kissy-face.

So he said to me, "OK, it's time to go home." When we got in the car, he said, "You're fired."

I said, "What do you mean? Why, Pop?"

He said, "You never fool around in the office."

I protested, "We're just good high school friends."

But he would have none of it. "I'll let you know when you can come back to work. You can come back when you can convince me you can behave yourself."

He let me cool my heels for a month. She was a nice girl, but he had caught us necking there in the office, and that, I learned, wasn't the thing to do. And I've been strict about that sort of thing my entire career.

In high school, everybody had to write a senior class paper, and my topic was the New York Stock Exchange. I got a lot of information from New York on the history of the exchange.

I'll never forget a partner from the Philadelphia office who used to come to town, Ed Dempere. He was everybody's idea of how a Wall Street broker should look—beautiful blue suits, and he always wore a white carnation in his lapel. He had flowing white hair and a voice with a lot of resonance; he was just a handsome man. He'd talk to me about the stock exchange and the business of Wall Street. My father liked the business and it sort of got into my blood, and Mr. Dempere would come along and nudge me further in the direction I thought I wanted to go. So by the time I went off to Penn State, I knew I wanted to be with Merrill Lynch.

Dad didn't yell or lecture, but he had a wonderfully effective way of influencing me and pointing me in the right direction. One day he caught me smoking out in the backyard with a couple of the older guys in the neighborhood—they were a year ahead of me in school or something.

When I walked in, he said, "Hey, Joe."(He called me Joe College.) "I see you tried cigarettes. Well, I guess this is the first one."

I said the big boys thought it was time I learned. And he said, "Well, if you're smart, you won't smoke."

I said, "Pop, you smoke. As a matter of fact, you smoke Camels, the strongest of all."

He said, "I'm hooked. I'm absolutely hooked on the stuff. I love it. But if you're smart, you won't let yourself get hooked."

Dad had a heart condition. His first attack was when he was thirty-six, and his last when he died at fifty-three. After Camels, he later smoked Parliaments and, you know, Kools or something like that, with filters. He said they weren't worth a damn. But he had been a heavy Camel smoker for years. I'm convinced that was what caused his heart condition—or at the very least aggravated it.

When Dad had his first big heart attack—I think it was the second attack, but the first big one—I saw the doctor come downstairs after he finished examining him in the bedroom. He went into the dining room, and I saw my mother close the glass doors. I sat there and watched through the doors as the doctor told my mother what the problem was.

She never got excited for any reason at all. She was pretty level headed. But that day I saw her start to cry.

Then I remember running outside the house, and I ran for what must have been three or four miles, down to the nearest Catholic church. It happened to be the one that we attended. I went in there, and I've never prayed harder.

I was still quite young. And I prayed so hard that the good Lord would save Dad. I was so close to him, and I just couldn't imagine that God wouldn't listen, wouldn't let Dad recover from the heart attack.

Well, he did recover for a time, and if his heart condition bothered him or frightened him, he did his best not to show it. In those days most homes were heated by coal. Many had coal furnaces in the basement and a single vent above the furnace, on the first floor. And whatever heat got upstairs, it just came up by natural convection—pretty primitive central heating compared with what we've got today.

Anyway, Dad, with his heart condition, would say, "Bud, you're going to have to shovel the coal. The doctor says I shouldn't shovel coal."

I said, "I think I can do it."

But I bitched about it, and he said, "It's either you or your mother. Now, who do you want to do it?"

I said, "I'll do it, Pop. Just forget about it." So I shoveled the coal for him and put it in that furnace.

He never, ever had to spank me for any reason. (Well, maybe once. But we'll get to that in a minute.) The only thing I ever wanted to do was please him. I just admired him and respected him and loved him so much.

But…I could be a little bit of a rascal at times, too. There was a couple who lived next door, across the lot between our house and theirs. Doc and Mamie Crise. He worked with Dad at the bank and they were good friends. They never had any children. So I would spend a lot of time over there.

Mamie was a great cook. My mother was a good cook, but she couldn't bake worth a damn. She'd make a pie, but it wouldn't be the same as Mamie's pie. Her cake wouldn't be the same, either. Like I said, Mom was a very good cook—she could make sauerkraut and pork that still makes me salivate when I think about it, all kinds of things—but she wasn't a baker.

One of Dad's favorite pies was lemon meringue. Well, Mamie would call over and say, "Bill, would you like a lemon meringue pie? I'll make one for you folks." And Dad would say, "Call me when it's time to come over."

So one day we went over to get the meringue pie and visit a little bit. And then as we were crossing the lot to come home, my dad carrying the pie carefully in front of him, I had a stick or a shovel in my hand, and I took a whack at it for some reason. A totally impulsive action. Didn't think I'd hit it, I guess. But I did hit it, and it flew up in the air and right down, upside down.

He said, "You little son of a bitch." And he chased me into the house. He went by the cupboard and he reached in and pulled out a yardstick. By then I was running up the steps and he was running after me.

Bang! He hit me hard enough to break the yardstick, and I laughed. He kept coming after me. Then I ducked underneath the bed, because I knew he wasn't about to crawl under there. He said, "You come out of there, you little blankety-blank." That was the only time in all those years that I saw him really get mad at me. It was about that lemon meringue pie. What a funny guy.

The Crises were great neighbors. They told my parents, "We're glad Bud visits. We like to have him come over here. By the way, he is really quite a scholar."

Dad was incredulous. "He is?"

"Yeah, we subscribe to *National Geographic.* He studies those magazines all the time."

Well, Dad knew damn well why I was "studying" the *National Geographic.* That's where they showed the bare naked women. Those black girls in Africa. That was the forerunner of *Playboy.* At least it was the only place we kids could see pictures like that.

Dad reacted with his characteristic humor and good nature to my high school basketball career—or should I say, lack thereof. He had been an all-state basketball player. He was good. The coach at the high school had been on his team, and he expected me to be as good as my dad.

So I went out for the team. One day we were playing one

of the local schools, Lock Haven High School. I got in at the end of the second period; halftime came, then I started the third period.

In the heat of battle, I stole the ball away from the Lock Haven guy, dribbled down the floor, shot the shot. It didn't even touch the rim, it swished right through. I scored two points! Only one problem: They were for Lock Haven.

That was the end of my basketball career. My dad had been watching from the stands and thought it was kind of funny. But his old pal, the coach, didn't think it was funny at all. He benched me, and afterward, chewed me out.

And I said, "Coach, first of all, I heard what you said. I made a mistake. But I don't like the way you've handled this," and I quit. I walked out of the place.

He tried to get ahold of me the next day. I told Dad, and he said, "Ah, screw him! You don't have to play basketball for him. Don't worry about it. You never really liked the game that much, anyhow."

"Not really," I admitted. "I played because I thought you wanted me to."

It's funny, thinking about it all these years later. But oh God, that was probably my most embarrassing moment at the time.

Then there were the times—infrequent but memorable— when we went to church together. Dad, the Lutheran, would go every few months, and he'd take me with him, after I'd been to Mass with my mother in the morning. The minister was a handsome, tall man whose twins, a boy and a girl, were in my class in high school.

Whenever I went into the church, why, the first thing the pastor would do was look down and spot me with my dad. Then he'd say, "I want to thank young Bill Schreyer for bringing his father to church today." Of course, the whole church knew I was being raised Catholic. Back in those days, there was quite a difference. But it was never a problem. I got a big round of applause, and everybody made a big deal out of it. We had a lot of fun with that.

I can't imagine not having some sort of religious faith. Life wouldn't be as full as it is by having it. But I have never tried to merchandise or sell my religious convictions—it's a personal thing. I don't care if your religion is Catholic, Lutheran, or Jewish, it doesn't make any difference.

Somewhere along the line I learned about the power of prayer. I've never gone in and asked for material things. It's always, "Just let me do the best I can," or something like that. And that's worked out pretty well. So even now, knowing that my dad died at fifty-three, I figure I've had twenty-five years' bonus—or more.

I've enjoyed my religion, and Joan has enjoyed hers, too. I think she's probably made me a better Catholic and I've made her a better Episcopalian because we're both stubborn. Deep down we both maybe think that one is a little bit better than the other one.

My close relationship with my dad continued even after I graduated from high school and traveled fifty miles west to Penn State. In 1945 there was still gasoline rationing. They gave you coupons—A, B, or C. C was the best, for doctors who needed the gas. Dad had B because he was a bond salesman at the time—a U.S. government bond salesman at Merrill Lynch. Which didn't really have much to do with anything, but B meant more gasoline, and more gas meant that he could make the trip to State College.

There still was food rationing, too. And we had a butcher who was a big commodities speculator. A woman, Mrs. King. She'd barely meet the margin calls, getting the money in at the last minute. And I said, "Dad, she's going to kill you if you keep dealing with her." But she was a nice lady, and whenever he wanted to get some steaks and stuff, she would never even ask for the food coupons. She just gave him the steaks.

So he'd come up to the fraternity house where I was living

my freshman year and bring some steaks. This was a big deal back then, and of course, the guys at the house thought he was great. He'd bring a case of beer along, too. Sometimes he'd get to telling stories and having a beer with everyone. It got so he was more popular in the fraternity house than anybody there. Those were the good old days.

Other times, I would take three or four of my fraternity brothers back home to Williamsport. They were all older guys, like Bill Douglas, who was a Marine Corps pilot, and Gilbert Dante Zuccarini, who was a Naval pilot. He thought he looked like Clark Gable. We reminded him he looked more like Jerry Colonna—the pop-eyed, mustachioed comedian who worked with Bob Hope—than Clark Gable. The guys loved coming down to my house, and they would double up and we'd have a great time.

When I was at home during those later years in Williamsport, I'd come in at night, and tiptoe upstairs. Because of Dad's heart condition, my parents had separate bedrooms in the last four or five years before he died. He'd use the guest bedroom because he had trouble sleeping and would stay up late reading. Mom would be in their original bedroom, and I would just get past the door and I'd hear her say, "Bud! Kiss me good night!"

So I'd go in and give her a quick peck. Whether I'd had one beer, or two Canadian Clubs, or maybe just a Coke, she would say, "Whew! You've been drinking!" She always said that. She didn't want me to think I could get away with anything.

I'd say, "Oh, just a little, Mom. Good night, good night."

Then I'd go by my dad's bedroom and he'd say, "How you doin', Joe. C'mon in!" So I'd go in and he'd say, "Who'd you have a date with tonight?"

"Oh, Mary Ann Egan," or whoever it had been with.

He'd say, "How'd you make out?"

I'd say, "We had a good time, Pop. We had a good time."

He'd say, "I'll bet you did!" He didn't want to miss any of the action. He always got a kick out of things.

❋

Dad had a simple philosophy regarding Merrill Lynch. He said, "If New York leaves me alone, I'll leave them alone." He didn't like to go to the home office for anything. He did it as infrequently as he could get away with.

After Penn State I entered the Merrill Lynch training program, and one of those days, I remember walking with him on the streets of New York. His heart condition had gotten worse by then, and in those days, not like now, all you could do was take nitroglycerin. He slipped these pills underneath his tongue, and I'd get mad at him, because I really didn't want to admit that he had a problem.

That day, as we were walking down the street, I saw him slip a pill in his mouth, and I said, "They're probably just a bunch of soda pills or sugar pills they're giving you. You don't need that stuff."

He said, "You think so? Put this under your tongue." He handed me one of his pills and I put it under my tongue and I thought it was going to blow my head off. It *was* nitroglycerin. It just opened your blood vessels up.

(P.S. Here it is all these years later, and instead of taking a nitroglycerin pill today, I have to use a nitroglycerin patch–developed by a couple of professors from Penn State. In the morning after a shower, I'll put on a fresh one. Actually Joan does it because I never can get the damn thing on. And so I'm taking the modern version of nitroglycerin, while he took those pills. But now they have other medications as well, all kinds of stuff.)

I'd completed the training program and started my first job in the Merrill Lynch office in Buffalo–that city that would play such a big role in my life and career–when Dad died.

We always talked to each other every Saturday, and we would compare notes about the business at the Williamsport office and at the office in Buffalo. We just talked about anything we wanted to talk about. But this particular day, we talked four times. I called him in the morning as I usually did, and then he called me back around noon, and then he called me again later in the afternoon, and he called me that night before I went out on a date with Joan.

Why did he call me four times that day? Did he have a premonition that his life was on the verge of ending? I will never know the answers to these questions, though I do recall that after the second call, I was privately concerned, but I kept it to myself.

When we got back to Joan's house after going out, the phone rang and she answered. "It's Uncle Charlie calling," she said, and I took the phone from her.

He said, "Well, your dad had his last heart attack, and he's gone." He handled it as nicely as he could and encouraged me not to come that night, but to wait til the next day. He assured me there was nothing to do, that my mother was OK.

In those days I wore a religious medal around my neck. When I hung up, I was so mad at God that I ripped that medal off. Just tore it off and threw it across the room. I was really angry. How could God do such a thing to me? Particularly since He knew how close Dad and I were, and I always was going to miss him. All this stuff goes through your mind at a time like that.

The next day, I went to Mass at a Jesuit church in Buffalo headed by Father Jim Redmond, who was a terrific guy. And we had a nice visit, a nice talk after Mass. He helped a lot.

Years later, on May 13, 1987, when I was chairman and CEO of Merrill Lynch, I went back to Williamsport for a dedication ceremony when they named the building where the Merrill Lynch office was located the William L. Schreyer Building, after my father. I was just so proud. We ran a wonderful ad in the local paper, and I have a framed copy hanging in my beach house.

Recently a friend whose family roots are also in Pennsylvania told me of inheriting his grandfather's Bible. He discovered a handwritten aphorism, probably dating from the 1920s, inscribed inside the front cover:

Lose money and lose nothing.
Lose health and lose something.
Lose character and lose everything.

I think of those words in relation to my dad's life. He lost money, and he lost health. But he never lost character. It remained straight and true throughout his life, and it inspires me to this day.

CHAPTER 4

The Penn State Years

I graduated from high school in the spring of 1945, just as World War II was ending in Europe and the GIs were starting to come home. For college, my dad wanted me to look at Bucknell, which was located thirty or forty miles down the river from Williamsport and which he had attended for a year.

It didn't cost that much to go to Bucknell, but I knew Dad would have been a little strapped if I went there. However, at Penn State, the tuition for an in-state student was something like a hundred dollars a semester, which meant a lot financially, because most of us in those days didn't have a lot of money. So six of us, all pals from high school, headed west across the mountains to Penn State, which was an up-and-coming school. It wasn't called "Happy Valley" back in those days, but for me, as for countless other young people before and since, it fit that description to a T.

The fraternity houses were emptying out as the wartime military and reserve training programs, which had provided a steady stream of occupants, were shutting down, and they were looking for new members. My friends from home and I decided to pledge as a group. If one particular fraternity wanted just one of us, we decided we'd say, "Take all or none." So on that basis, we all pledged Sigma Phi Epsilon.

My dad was a Phi Gamma Delta brother at Bucknell, and he said, "If you aren't going to go to Bucknell, at least take a look at the Phi Gamma house." But I joined Sig Ep. I always tried to please him, but at some point in time, you have to make your own decisions on some of these things.

A lot of the brothers were ex-GIs who were coming back to finish school. They were older, had been in combat and so forth, and my first roommate was David Hughes, a former Air Force captain and a great guy. An engineer who had another year to go to finish, he was the one who taught me what in my opinion is one of life's most important lessons: the proper way to drink.

I wanted to be like the big boys and not just have a beer, which I learned to drink pretty young. Never to excess, of course. But once in a while maybe it'd slip. You never set out to get drunk in those days. We didn't have binge drinking like they do today, which is a problem. I can't imagine setting out to get drunk. I *can* imagine having fun and getting a little drunk, but not setting out to get drunk. That makes no sense.

But anyhow, I knew I was a grown-up guy—seventeen or something—and my roommate had a bottle of bourbon. One night I said to him, "David, could I have a little of 'our' bourbon?"

He said, "Sure. Go ahead, kid."

So I took some ice and put a little bourbon in the glass. Then I reached for a bottle of ginger ale. David said, "Hold it! Stop right there. Never, ever put any sweet stuff in your drink. First of all, that's what makes you sick. Not the booze—it's the sweet stuff that makes you sick. So if you're going to get in my good bourbon, you are going to drink it either straight up, or with water or soda water, or on the rocks. But none of that sweet stuff."

So that was a good lesson, because too many kids do start off mixing it with stuff to make it taste better, and that causes you to get loaded faster than you would otherwise.

I've given that lecture to many young people in my life. If you're going to drink, drink properly. And it's true. If you don't drink properly when you're in college, it can cause problems later. You'll go out and get a job, and then your boss will want to take you out for dinner or cocktails or something, and if you don't know how to drink, and you get drunk the first time you're out with him, you've shot your career almost right away.

So my advice to young people with drinking is this: You don't have to drink. But if you do drink, drink the right way.

Bill Douglas, another veteran and Sig Ep brother, would play a major role in my life when we were both living in Buffalo. He introduced me to the woman who would become my wife. Recently he was interviewed for an article Penn State's public information department wrote about me. In it, he is quoted remembering me as a "very pink-cheeked, naïve freshman from Williamsport. As we were all just coming back from World War II, pilots and officers in the military, we thought most of the freshmen were inferior to us, but Bill transcended that. He was able to get along with everyone, which wasn't easy to do. I think he's been so successful because of that. He's a great bridger of gaps and his father was the same. They were more like buddies than they were father and son."

The fraternity was a wonderful place to live—that is, after we got through the hazing, which was pretty rough in those days.

You had to wear little beanies—they called them "dinks"—that marked you as a freshman, and you also had to carry matches to light the upperclassmen's cigarettes. One day I was walking along with one of my pledge brothers, Dick Russell, and an upperclassman came up to him and said, "You have a match?" And Russell said, "Yeah, my ass and your face." Well, this was reported back to the fraternity, and he had to carry a two-by-four, painted like a match, on his shoulder, with his name on a sign hanging around his neck, for a week. And of course, everyone harassed him after that for being such a smart aleck.

Some of the other hazing was pretty rough. For example, you'd have to climb on your hands and knees to the third floor and sip this awful-tasting stuff, then crawl back down–either swallowing it or, if you were lucky, spitting it out when nobody was looking.

I was in the last class where the paddle was used. I'll never forget, there was a collegiate heavyweight boxing champion who had gone into the service, then later come back to school. Big guy. He'd had a couple of drinks one night with some of the older brothers. Then he somehow caught sight of me and said, "Assume the position, pledge." He took the paddle, whacked me across the fanny, and threw me clear across the room.

Years later he attended a little golf tournament I sponsored up at Penn State for alumni of the boxing team. He's around eighty-five now–still playing golf, in pretty good shape–and I reminded him how he drove me across the room that night. In fact, every time I talk to him I remind him of what he did to me back then. So at least I'm getting my money's worth of laughs out of it.

My next roommate turned out to be a fellow named Bill Sipple, from Pittsburgh, whom everyone called Fritz. He had also been a soldier, serving as an Army Air Corps pilot, and was studying to be an architect. He was elected president of the fraternity, so we got the best room in the house. He refinished it, and I just supplied a little beer. I wasn't very good at the manual stuff, and he knew it. He was such a wonderful guy. After a year or so, he said, "I just have too much homework"–he didn't have time for everything that was involved with being president of the fraternity–so we decided I'd run for house president so we could keep the room. We kept that room until I graduated.

All that studying paid off for Fritz, because he was accepted in the graduate architecture program at Princeton, where he won a prestigious national award given to one student every year. He went back to Pittsburgh to establish his practice, and made his mark by designing such landmarks as Three Rivers Stadium and the Civic Arena, which, according to his obituary in the Penn State alumni magazine, "boasted the world's largest retractable roof at the time." Fritz passed away in 2007 at the age of eighty-two.

Back in my freshman year, some of the Sig Eps had decided I would be a good one to run for freshman class president. So I campaigned in all the other fraternity houses, and I lost by about ten votes, to a guy who was back from the Air Force. He was a handsome devil and had campaigned in the girls' dormitories, which I had unwisely neglected. I had the fraternity votes but the girls outnumbered them. I got a few girls' votes but not enough. So I learned a lesson from that, too. When you're trying to persuade people to see things your way, be thorough in the process!

Our routine was pretty much the same every night during the week. We'd have dinner in the fraternity house—we had a good chef. After dinner we'd go up and do our homework, and by about nine we'd be finished. Then we'd go down to the famous State College hangout, the Rathskeller—known to all then and now as the "Skeller"—which had the world's best hamburgers, made by this old chef who worked there. He had just one gold tooth in his mouth. He was an African-American, a terrific guy. Spider was his name.

And so we'd get a pitcher of beer and have one of those great hamburgers and later go home and hit the sack and go to class the next morning. It was pretty good. Not a bad life in those days. I was about seventeen, eighteen years old during my early years at Penn State, and these guys were coming back from the military. They were twenty-three and twenty-four. But the guys who worked at the Skeller were convinced I was older, and I was the one vouching for the ex-GIs, who were over twenty-one, anyhow. So that was fun, that game.

I built up my friendships and loyalties, starting with my

47

fraternity brothers, and then spread it out from there. You'd also make a lot of friends in the classes you were taking.

Freshman year, I had all the basics–math, English, chemistry–and I got "3"s in all of those. Three was the best grade you could get in those days.

Uncle Wilk wanted me to get at least a little engineering experience, so I took a mechanical drawing course. We'd sit in this drawing lab every Saturday morning from eight to twelve, and I couldn't even draw the margin around the paper straight. It was useless.

So the professor came to me at the end of the semester and said, "Are you going to continue in engineering?"

I said, "No, I'm going to liberal arts."

So he said, "Good. I'll give you a zip. It won't hurt you any but you won't get any credit for the course."

I said, "That's fine. I'll take it and run." Because you could get either a minus one or a minus two, which would penalize your overall grade average going forward.

So I went to the dean of the engineering school and told him I wanted to declare a liberal arts major. He tried to talk me into staying. He said, "Well, you play bridge. You could be an engineer."

I said, "I don't play bridge."

Then he said that if I could do this or that, I could be an engineer. But I couldn't do this or that. Finally I got a little desperate and said, "I never did see the results of the aptitude test we took during freshman week."

He said, "That's a good idea, Schreyer." So he had his secretary bring in the file. He took one look at it and said, "Your request is permitted. Granted! The last thing in the world you should be is an engineer."

So I went over to liberal arts for a couple of semesters, and then took business administration for the last two years, classes on subjects like accounting, insurance, and the forerunner of marketing. Things like that, which well prepared me to go to the Harvard Business School, which my uncle thought would be a great idea.

I remember one professor named Ralph Wherry, a professor of insurance. Insurance itself was a broad subject that we all have to know about, anyhow. But he could make it so rational and sensible, and so interesting. It was just a privilege to be in his class. I had some pretty good professors, but he stands out. He could explain all the marketing aspects, made it so you could understand all the actuarial concepts and just get saturated in the subject of insurance. Maybe I liked him so much because I always got a good grade, but he made it so I could. He was really the best.

We had a business law professor named Tanner who was a bit different. I took Business Law 1, and that was a good course—interesting basics. After finishing that I decided I'd take Business Law 2, a more advanced course. But the class was right after lunch, which is dangerous. I sat in the back of the room, and I'd fall sound asleep.

The first exam, I got a 40, which was a wake-up call. The second exam, I got an 80, which gave me a 60 average going into the final. So I went to see the professor. I said, "Professor Tanner, I just got to tell you that I really enjoyed your course. It was very enlightening and I really enjoyed it. I don't know why I got a 40 in that first exam."

He said, "Schreyer, I know all about you. I've been checking. Big fraternity man. And I know you're president of your fraternity and you're a big shot on campus and all that crap."

So I said, "Yes, I do those extra things, but I'll tell you what let's do. Just to show you how dedicated I am to business law and your class, I would like to suggest that whatever I get in the final will be my final grade. Whatever I get. If I get a 30, I flunk. I just want to show you the confidence I have in myself and in the course and you." So he said, "OK, that's a deal."

Now, I left there chuckling because I had to get at least a 65. So I studied like the devil for it. I picked out twenty cases that I thought might be the obvious ones he'd include in the exam, and ten of those twenty were in the exam. So I got 100 on the test and he had to give me an A in the course.

I had fun with that one. And I also remember that when I left his office that day, I headed outside to my parents' Chevrolet convertible, which I happened to have up there that week, since it was the end of the semester. I was walking past the Sparks Building–the liberal arts building–and spotted some girls from the Kappa Kappa Gamma sorority. One was from my hometown of Williamsport, and they said, "Hey, Bill, can you give us a ride downtown?" I said, "Sure, girls. Come on."

So the top was down and four of them jumped into the convertible. That's when I looked up and saw Professor Tanner watching out the window with his arms crossed, just shaking his head. It's the little things like that that you remember.

Athletics was also an important part of my life at Penn State. My mother didn't want me to play football, but she didn't tell me not to box, so I decided I would take a shot at going out for the boxing team. The coach was Leo Hauck. He'd been around Penn State for years, and he's still a legend out there.

Leo had a great way of telling you when you were doing something wrong, or at least something he didn't approve of. I remember I was combing my hair after a shower one day– I had hair then–and I heard him say, "You big sissy!"

I said, "I wonder who you're talking to?"

"You, Schreyer, and I say you're a big sissy!"

"What do you mean I'm a big sissy? Why do you say that?"

"Well, look at how you're combing your hair."

"Well, how would *you* do it?"

"You just take a towel, go like that," he said, making a wiping motion across the top of his head. "That's all you gotta do."

Of course, he was bald; he had a few little hairs up there, but that was it. He was pulling my leg, you see. That was Leo.

Anyhow, I went out for the boxing team, along with a guy who'd gone to high school with me who was a good boxer, a southpaw. His father had taught us both how to box. This other guy really was better than me—bigger and better.

Then there was another kid who had come back from the service. I was in the gym working out one day, and he said, "You want to spar a little bit?"

I said, "Oh, sure. That would be great." So we went at it.

He wasn't trying to hurt me, but man, when he hit you, you were hit. When we finished, I said, "God Almighty! Did the Marines teach you this?" I heard he'd been in the Marine Corps.

He said, "Oh, no, no. I boxed at Penn State before I went in the service." It turns out he was a national middle-weight boxing champion. Jackie Taghe.

So eventually Leo, the coach, said, "I like the fact that you're enjoying boxing. I'm watching you. But I think maybe you might enjoy being the manager more."

I said, "I think you're right."

So that way I got to go to all the boxing matches, and be the manager, and make a few bucks on the side to pay for incidentals.

Penn State was heading toward being a big, first-rate football school when I was there. Bob Higgins was the coach at the time. He was later replaced by Rip Engle, who hired Joe Paterno.

One year I had my dad up for the Bucknell game. In those days, Penn State and Bucknell were pretty evenly matched. That particular year, the final score was something like Penn

State 69, Bucknell 7. So my dad said, "I want to thank you, kid. It was nice of you to invite me up for this game, this week, you know?" He had a lot of fun teasing me about that over the years.

Pitt–the University of Pittsburgh–was another big rival back then, and I think I was there the last year we played Penn–the University of Pennsylvania–which shows how many years ago that was.

Pitt was a tough rival. Over the period of all those years, until the last time they played, it was almost even between the two. I think we had a slight edge, 55 to 50, or something like that, but not much more.

In those days, Beaver Stadium was near the center of campus, just east of Rec Hall, and tailgating was a tradition, though nowhere near as big as it is today. People would take sandwiches or something and eat out of the backs of their cars, and have a little something to drink. It hadn't reached the marvelous level of sophistication and extravagance of today, but people had fun doing it.

On game days, cars used to be lined up coming in from Philadelphia, from Pittsburgh, from all parts of the state, all converging on State College. It would take forever to get out of there. That's one thing that hasn't changed a bit.

I had an active social life during my years at Penn State, dating and so forth. I think it was at the end of my sophomore year that I was introduced to a little blonde named Clare by one of my fraternity brothers, who was dating her best friend. Real pretty girl. She was from the Pittsburgh area, had a good sense of humor, cute as a button. We had quite a romance for a while.

It's funny. I always, just by coincidence, dated girls who happened to be Catholic. And I brought a lot of girls home to meet the folks–*just* to meet them. My mother, who was Catholic, would say to people, "I hope he knows he's too young to get serious," which happened to be the truth. The only one she was crazy about and thought I should marry was the one I did marry–Joan. But we'll save that story for another chapter.

When I was dating Clare, I would meet her between classes, sometimes at lunchtime or mid-afternoon. We'd go down to the Corner Room, one of the great hangouts right in the center of town in the State College Hotel. It was owned by Matty Mateer, a fraternity brother who was Sig Ep's leading alumnus in town. Matty was a great guy and occasionally he'd give us Sig Eps a free sandwich or something when we went in there. They had great ham sandwiches, called "Ham à la Corner." So Clare and I would go in there and I'd say, "Would you like a sandwich?"

She'd say, "No, I don't really care for it. I'll just have coffee."

So they'd bring me my Ham à la Corner, cut into quarters, and she'd say, "Well, maybe I'll just have a quarter." I'd say, "Jeez, I offered to get you one of your own. Now you're going to take a corner of my Ham à la Corner! All right, have it."

The other specialty the Corner Room had was chocolate cake–the best chocolate cake à la mode, with vanilla ice cream. They'd bring it and Clare would start taking bites, and I'd have to order two pieces of chocolate cake!

Around the time of graduation, when I knew I was going to work in what we called the "slave" program at Merrill Lynch, with very low wages, I said to my roommate, Fritz Sipple, "I'm going to take my fraternity pin back tonight."

I'll never forget it. Clare and I had a date, and everything was fine, and I took her home. When we got there, I said, "Now, Clare, I'm going to work on Wall Street, and you're going to be a senior up here, and I want you to enjoy your senior year. Just have as much fun as you can and date whoever you want." I tried to explain why I was doing this for her sake.

And she said, "Bill, are you asking for your fraternity pin back?"

"Well, I just want to be sure that you don't feel obligated."

Then she said, "Well, Bill, you put it on, so you take it off."

My hands were shaking like a leaf getting that fraternity pin off the upper left side of her chest. Later my dad kidded me: "I bet you had as much fun taking it off as you did putting it on."

We made a date for homecoming in the fall, and it was almost like old times. But I realized it would not be fair to keep seeing her because with that "slave" program, I could hardly support myself, let alone get involved with any woman in a serious way, at least until I finished training and got into production. But that was a real romance. I was crazy about her.

Clare eventually married someone from another fraternity whom I didn't know, and had two boys, I'm told, because I did some checking years later. Her sons went to Penn State, too, so I guess it all worked out very well. You occasionally think of old friends like that.

As I mentioned earlier, during high school I worked as a board marker at the Merrill Lynch office; my dad would pay me three dollars a week. I had other odd jobs, too. A guy named Jones was the manager of the Sears-Roebuck store in Williamsport. He was the highest-paid executive in town. He made $25,000 a year, which in those days was pretty good money. In fact, one of my goals in life at an early age was to make $25,000 a year. That was big bucks!

So one Christmas holiday I said, "Dad, would you tell Mr. Jones"–because they knew each other well–"I'd love to work in the sporting goods department at Sears if there's an opening." Well, they didn't have an opening in sporting goods, but there was one in the shoe department. I took the job.

So I was there one Saturday and this old lady came in. She must have tried on fifteen pairs of shoes. "No, no. I don't think I like those," she kept saying. So at one point I was back in the storeroom looking for more shoes, and Mr. Jones walked in. He said, "How you doing, kid?"

I said, "I'm taking care of that lady out there, but I'm just having an awful tough time."

So he said, "Well, keep trying." He came back a few minutes later and I still hadn't sold the lady any shoes.

Finally I said, "Mr. Jones, if I sell her a pair of shoes successfully, would you see if you can get me in the sporting goods department?" He looked at her and he knew damn well I couldn't sell her.

I went out and I went to work on her. Christ, I tried different styles. I tried different comfort levels. I mean, I tried everything. Flattery, for example. I said, "They really look good on you, Mrs. So-and-so."

"No, this wouldn't be right. I don't think my husband would like these."

So we tried on more pairs.

I said, "Well, how do these feel on you?"

"Oh, they feel good."

I said, "Well, walk around in them a little. Just walk a little bit. Gosh, they look good on you."

She finally bought the last pair of shoes I had to show her. Then I got transferred to the sporting goods department. So persistence paid off, particularly with that little motivation there at the end of the rainbow. I just wore her down. Dad got the biggest kick out of that story.

❊

I was in ROTC at Penn State—the Reserve Officer Training Corps—in the Army Air Force. As part of that training I spent the summer of 1947 down at Langley Field in Virginia. It was pretty strict, which was probably good for me at the time.

There was one fellow, a cadet colonel by the name of Phil

Jones, who had been a master sergeant in the Army and was studying to be a Presbyterian minister. Great guy. He had a commanding voice and a good sense of humor. I'd see him walking around the place, just walking with purpose. At one point I said, "Phil, all I ever see you do is walk around with a yellow pad in your hand."

He said, "Well, that's the key. Always walk with purpose. And always carry something in your hand. Nobody will ever stop you. You can go do what you want to do—go to the PX, do anything you want to do. People will say, 'Look, he's on a mission of some kind.'"

Phil became a very good, successful minister. He did a great job. His wife, Priscilla, was a beautiful girl. She died just recently, as a matter of fact. But that's what I was doing at Langley Field. I'm glad I had that summer experience there. It was good for me and a very happy time. The war had just ended, and we had won. We celebrated VE Day and VJ Day. We all thought, "The future's going to be terrific." And it was.

I had such a great time at Penn State. It was a real growing-up experience for me, largely because of the friends I made in the fraternity house who were older—everything from a Marine Corps pilot to an Air Force bomber pilot to a Marine who fought on the ground. All of them—officers or enlisted men—were just outstanding individuals.

I think being raised the way I was—with older people, getting to know older classmates from high school, and especially with my father's influence—I was always more comfortable with older guys, and made them comfortable with me. So those bonds were pretty strong. I still keep in touch with four or five of those guys.

In the years since I left Penn State, I've watched it keep developing—not just in athletics, but also as a first-rate university. People have sometimes asked me, "What makes you so loyal to Penn State?" I think a lot of what contributed to that was the quality of people who went to Penn State when I was there, and the professors. You really don't forget it.

I'm a strong believer in loyalty. Loyalty to close friends, and loyalty to an institution that I've been part of–whether Penn State, Merrill Lynch, or the Roman Catholic Church. That feeling of loyalty is a strong feeling you can take pride in. I've always felt sorry for people who went into a business and then changed jobs every year and a half. They never found what they were looking for, or maybe they never knew what they were looking for.

Another source of pride is that Penn State kept developing –sometimes because of, and sometimes in spite of, whoever the president was. After I graduated, Milton Eisenhower, President Dwight Eisenhower's brother, was named president, and he was certainly one of our most famous presidents.

But we took a slightly different, more irreverent view back then. We called him "Milkshake Milton," because he took the bars out of the fraternity houses. Dad was so mad at him, because Dad had put up the money to build a big bar down in the basement of the Sig Ep house. They had to tear it out, and he said, "I never thought an Eisenhower would do that."

In fact, Dad wasn't all that excited about electing General Eisenhower when he ran for president. He wanted Robert Taft–a real Republican.

❋

I graduated in the spring of 1948. The ceremony was outside in the old Beaver Stadium, and I remember it was a beautiful day. The folks and various relatives came up. I was dressed in my Army uniform, and got my second lieutenant's gold bar, along with a bachelor's degree in business administration.

I'd been accepted at the Harvard Business School—but deferred for a year. They wanted me to be older, to go out and get some experience before they admitted me. At that time Merrill Lynch was just starting up their training program, so I decided to join it instead. You see, I always knew I would go with Merrill Lynch. Having grown up in the board room in Williamsport, I knew the customers, I watched the market, and I was fascinated by the whole thing.

Dad, Uncle Charlie, and Uncle Wilk all told me, "Just keep an open mind." I did keep an open mind, but I also knew what I wanted to do.

And so at the tender age of twenty, I embarked on a journey that would take me first to New York City, then to Buffalo, then to Wiesbaden, Germany, and the world beyond.

They Called It "Apprentice," We Called It "Slave"

Robert A. Magowan was a very smart man. Among other things, he married the boss's daughter, Doris Merrill, thus becoming the son-in-law of Charles E. Merrill, the founder of Merrill Lynch. So through family connections and his own very considerable skills as a businessman, he became a senior executive at Merrill Lynch at a relatively young age.

In 1948 he was thinking about hiring a few college graduates who had not gone to business school but were about to. The thinking was, "We need to get some young blood in here." They got a lot of ex-GIs who were a little bit older in the regular sales-training class—Don Regan was one of them.

After I'd gotten word from the Harvard Business School that I was accepted for September 1949 but not for 1948, I wasn't sure what to do, so I talked to my father. Then he spoke with Bob Magowan, who said, "I'm thinking about starting this new program. Have him come down for some interviews and we'll see how he does."

I was interviewed by John Rice and Harold Oliver, who were then the senior guys in the personnel department. I was offered the job and started on June 28, 1948. They called it the "apprentice program"; we called it the "slave program." The pay was $225 a month, which amounted to about $61 every two weeks after taxes were withheld. And whatever I got in my paycheck, I'd always get two weeks' worth of dimes so I could be sure to get back and forth on the subway.

There were just a few of us in the program. One was Jack Huntley, who was the son of a partner, Earl Huntley, in the Los Angeles office. And there was a fellow by the name of Horton Prudent, who was from a very wealthy family and didn't stay with the firm for too long, although I did hear from him from time to time for years afterward.

I remember checking into the St. George Hotel in Brooklyn, which was an easy commute to 70 Pine Street, the Merrill Lynch headquarters at the time. Later I moved into an apartment on East Seventy-fourth Street with Jack Huntley and one of the other fellows.

Bob Magowan, known throughout the firm by his initials, RAM, impeccably dressed, very sharp, had been a Naval commander during World War II. He was always tough, but also fair. As head of sales, he was the number three partner in the firm at the time.

In 1948, Merrill Lynch already was the largest brokerage firm in the nation—twice as large as the nearest competitor, in fact—with 98 offices in 96 cities. Its annual revenues were $26.7 million, with a net profit of $5.5 million. There were 86 partners, 2,800 employees, and an estimated 100,000 customers. The firm had a grand total of $14 million in capital.

They started me out in the research department. I was sitting in research one day, doing correspondence or writing a report on something or other, and I heard this voice say, "Schreyer!"

And I said, "Who is that?"

The guy next to me said, "That's Mr. Magowan calling. You'd better get in there."

So I went in and said, "Yes, sir?"

THEY CALLED IT "APPRENTICE"

"That was a damn good report you wrote on such and such, Schreyer."

I said, "Well, thank you very much, sir."

I turned around and started to walk out, and he said, "Hey, Schreyer."

"Yes, sir?"

"Just remember that a pat on the back is only eighteen inches above a kick in the ass."

Well, I never forgot that, and later on I told his grandson Merrill Magowan about it. When Robert Magowan died, Merrill told the story at his funeral, from the pulpit of St. Grace Cathedral in San Francisco: "The fellow who is now chairman of Merrill Lynch told this story about my grandfather." Doris Magowan was shocked and gave her grandson hell for telling that story in church. But it was a great little story, and I've had a lot of fun with it over the years.

Mr. Magowan took an active interest in us "slaves."

"What do you guys do after work?" he asked one day.

I said, "We live over on Seventy-fourth Street."

"Why don't I come over and we'll cook some dinner."

I didn't know how to cook. Jack Huntley didn't know how to cook. The third guy, he was from Texas and could cook a little. He could do a steak. So we saved up our money to buy a few steaks. Then Mr. Magowan came over and said, "How about a martini? Do you have anything to mix drinks in?"

We rustled around in our sparse kitchen, and the only thing we could come up with was a coffeepot. He whipped together my first real martini in that pot—very dry, straight up. "You've got to learn how to drink these if you come to Wall Street," he advised us.

So then we cooked the steaks, and Mr. Magowan kept saying, "You're doing this wrong, you're doing that wrong," but he did it in a fun way. He wasn't being a pain in the neck. He told us a lot about the history of his father-in-law, Charlie Merrill. We just sat there together in the kitchen, and we were quite amazed that he was just a regular guy. We had a lot of fun together, and then he left. Those are the things you don't forget.

A few years later he went out to California to run Safeway Stores, which Mr. Merrill also controlled. By that time I was on active duty in the Air Force, and Magowan wrote me a beautiful, long note, explaining why he was making the move, and that he was leaving all of his money, which he quoted at roughly a million dollars, in Merrill Lynch, which said all that needed to be said about his commitment to the firm.

❋

My roommates weren't Catholic, so I'd get up Sunday mornings and take a bus by myself from Seventy-fourth Street down to Fiftieth Street, where I'd attend Mass at St. Patrick's Cathedral. This one morning, I remember, I got on the bus and sat down next to a gentleman. The bus was filled and at one point a couple of elderly ladies got on, so we got up to let them sit.

The man and I both got off at Fiftieth Street, and he asked me, "Where are you going?"

I said, "I'm going to St. Patrick's."

He said, "Well, I am, too."

So we walked along, went into church. As we walked out after Mass, he said, "What do you do for a living, kid?"

"Well, I'm with Merrill Lynch."

"You're with Merrill Lynch? Anybody who works for Merrill Lynch and goes to St. Patrick's on Sunday—I'll buy you lunch."

He was a partner in a small firm on Wall Street. A great success story, wonderful guy. At lunch I asked him, "How come you go to church every Sunday?"

He said, "I've been very fortunate in life. I feel the very least I can do is go by once a week and say thanks."

That made quite an impression on me at that particular time, and it's a story that I like to tell to young people.

❀

Jack Huntley was from a wealthy and successful family, too, but he was pretty tight. I had a savings account at Chase Manhattan Bank and I would take ten dollars from my paycheck and put it in savings. After a period of time I got up to a couple hundred bucks.

One day Jack said to me, "Bud, how much do you have in your savings?" I told him a couple hundred bucks.

He said, "Look, I have an account at Chemical Bank, and whenever my balance falls below a thousand bucks, they give me an extra service charge. How about letting me have the two hundred dollars so I can keep my account over the limit?" I told him to go to hell. At any rate, he ended up flying his airplane into a mountain many years later. It was a tragic ending, but he'd always seemed to be heading for some sort of tragedy.

After the apartment on Seventy-fourth Street, I lived by myself for a while at the West Side YMCA, which was pretty lonely. Eventually I ran into a couple of guys from Penn State, and we decided to get an apartment together, out in Jackson Heights, Queens. It happened to be in the same building where a bunch of Pan Am stewardesses lived. So we supplied the liquid refreshment and they did the cooking; turned out to be a lot of fun.

The training program lasted two years and I rotated through all the various home office departments: research, operations and the wire room, sales and the pension funds. There was a great feeling to the firm at that time and it was great to be part of it. The war was over and everybody felt good that we had come out of it so strong. Harvard Business School slipped entirely off my radar screen. As I said, Merrill had become the leading investment brokerage firm in the country, and there was great pride in the principles and ethics that Mr. Merrill and his partners had established. So everybody was proud to be part of a winning organization like that.

I enjoyed working with the people in the wire and order department, who were dedicated and hardworking. They didn't mind working extra hours when the markets got busy—busy in a relative sense, since it was nothing compared with today. That I had built strong friendships and relationships with these people would be of great value to me after I left New York. If I needed help on something, I could call on someone I knew personally to get it. The importance of personal relationships is something that I first learned from my father, and it has been a big part of how I have conducted every aspect of my life.

I think it was my second day on the job when I met another individual who is a very important figure in the history of Merrill Lynch: Winthrop H. Smith. Charles Merrill, after correctly forecasting an impending stock market crash, withdrew most of his capital prior to 1929 and got out of the brokerage business entirely a year later. Win Smith had gone with the big "wire house," E. A. Pierce and Company. In 1939 and 1940, Win Smith was instrumental in convincing Mr. Merrill to come back into the business, merge with Pierce, and create what would become the modern Merrill Lynch. That's when Mr. Merrill dreamed up the "Wall Street to Main Street" concept that has been carried out all these years, getting more successful all the time, right up to today's "Total Merrill."

Win Smith was Mr. Merrill's number two and was basically running the firm when I met him. Anyway, that second day on the job, the head of research told me, "Miss Mae Fallon would like to see you." Mae Fallon was Mr. Smith's longtime secretary and assistant. She said, "Mr. Smith would like to see you in his office." So I went in and sat down. He asked me how my dad was doing and so forth, and gave me a nice warm welcome. He was a reserved man, but also a very warm man. Some people get respect from the people they work with, and others get affection. Win Smith was one of those rare individuals who got both.

At the end of the meeting, he said, "Schreyer, do you have any long-term goals with the firm, anything special that you have in mind?"

I didn't know what to say, and I wasn't trying to be a wise guy, but I looked around his beautiful office and said, "Gee, Mr. Smith, I kind of think I'd like to have your job someday."

He just smiled. Years later, I found out that my remark had made such an impression on him that he'd recounted it to a number of his fellow partners: "Keep your eye on this guy Schreyer. He wants our jobs already—and it's only his second day on the job!"

Another fellow I met that same summer I started was Edmund Lynch Jr., son of Charlie Merrill's original partner, who had died a number of years earlier, at a relatively young age. Eddie Jr., a senior at Yale, was in the training program with me. We worked together in the research department and got to be friendly. One weekend he invited Jack Huntley and me to sail on the yacht his sister and her husband had. We sailed from Huntington, Long Island, out to Southampton, and slept on the yacht.

During the day, when we were on the beach, a gentleman came by and said, "Ed, would you bring the boys over to the Meadows Club this evening? I'd like them to meet Mr. Merrill."

After he left, I asked, "Who was that?"

"What do you mean, you dumb bastard?" Ed responded. "You've met him, Schreyer. That was Win Smith."

"Gee," I said. "I only met him once, and he had a gray flannel suit on. I guess I didn't recognize him in his bathing suit, without his glasses."

So that night we went to a big party at the Meadows Club, one of Southhampton's swankiest private clubs. It was a formal affair; I had to rent a white jacket. We were introduced to Mr. Merrill, and I was so impressed with the man—soft-spoken, with piercing eyes, friendly, and above all else, so warm. We shook hands, and the first thing he said to me was, "How's your father feeling?"

I didn't realize at the time that Mr. Merrill was suffering from heart disease, too. I was so impressed and so pleased that he would ask about the condition of my father. We spent quite a bit of time with him that evening, and it made a big impression on a young kid from Williamsport, I can tell you that.

Though his activities with the firm were extremely limited because of his heart condition, I had the opportunity to meet Mr. Merrill maybe two or three times over the next couple of years. And he was just a very wonderful man. He had a great vision, bringing Wall Street to Main Street. The rest is history.

But that night in Southampton was quite a party. There was a band playing, and everyone was dancing.

Bob Magowan was there, and at one point he called me over. "Bill, go cut in on Doris," he said, referring to his wife. "I know she doesn't like that guy."

Which meant *he* didn't like the guy, but as her husband, it wouldn't look right for him to cut in on Doris, so he had me do it.

The next night we drove to the estate where Ed Lynch's mother lived. She was now Mrs. McDonald, married to, as I recall, the chairman of the Maryland Casualty Company. It was late at night and we were driving for what seemed like forever, and finally we arrived at this beautiful, huge estate. There, I got my first taste of how the super-rich lived.

The butler met us and took our bags. Jack Huntley and I shared a big guest suite. Of course, we had a sandwich and a bottle of beer before we went to bed.

The next morning Ed, Jack, and I were planning to drive back to the city with Ed's stepfather, Mr. McDonald, in his limousine. There was a knock on the door, early, and the butler woke us up and said, "May I draw your bath?"

Jack was sort of a character anyhow, and he looked over at me and winked. So the butler drew the bath and he brought a little cup of it to have Jack see if the temperature was about right. "A touch warmer, please," said Jack.

As we were getting dressed, he glanced out the window and said, "Take a look at this estate. My old man is a partner in this firm and we live like peasants compared to this." We had a pretty fancy breakfast, and then we drove into the city.

From the outset, Ed Lynch and I became pretty good friends. He took his work seriously, and after graduating from Yale, he came back and ended up being our oil specialist. Underneath it all, he was a well-meaning guy and I saw a very thoughtful side of him a lot of people didn't see, because he was a fun-loving, hell-raising guy in his youth.

His family had an apartment uptown, and I remember he had me stay over one night when the family wasn't there. He said, "Here's your bathroom," which was adjacent to the private bedroom I slept in. When he heard me in the shower in the morning, he put out a bath mat for me to step out on. It turned out to be a mat of rubber boobies—falsies! I laughed like hell and he got the biggest kick out of my reaction to that.

Each of the Lynch kids inherited $21 million, I think it was, when they turned twenty-one. Ed knew that I was living on my meager income, so he had my name put on the list of young men who were invited to the debutante "coming-out" parties. "They always want extra guys there," he told me. "All you have to do is rent a tuxedo."

For one of the parties he fixed me up with his sister, Signa Lynch. So I would be escorting her, and of course it was a good deal for me, because when you're making sixty bucks a week, you just wouldn't eat much that day, and you'd get to the party and there was plenty of good food and champagne. So it was a pretty fun life at that time.

I'll never forget Signa coming in one day to the office. Mr. Merrill's secretary came back and told my supervisor in the research department, "Miss Lynch would like to see Mr. Schreyer in Mr. Merrill's office." So he relayed the message, and I thought, "Oh, God!" I mean, this was Mr. Lynch of Merrill Lynch—the daughter wants to see me. That was a little different league than I was used to.

So I met her and said, "Signa, how about a cup of coffee or a Coke or something?" She said fine. I wanted to get off that executive floor. As we got to the elevator and pushed the down button, out comes Winthrop Smith and his guest, none other than Mr. McDonald, Signa's stepfather. It had been some time since I'd last seen him.

She said, "Bill's taking me downstairs for a drink." This was the middle of the day, and of course I meant a Coca-Cola or a cup of coffee. But all I could say was, "Come on, Signa, let's go."

My mother was so worried that I would get serious about Signa Lynch, partly, I think, because she would be a little embarrassed to have her or any of her family come and see where we lived, in Williamsport, Pennsylvania. I said, "Don't worry about it, Mom." I would be dancing with Signa, but there was no spark of romance at all.

When Signa announced her engagement to this other guy who was always hanging around, Dad clipped the announcement out of the paper and sent it to me with a note: "That's right, goddamn it, you blew it for all of us." We laughed about that for a long time afterward.

Years later, in the mid-1980s when I was CEO, the firm was going through a particularly tough time of restructuring and Ed Lynch, who was basically retired and living on his boat, wrote a letter to *The New York Times* blasting management. I was pretty mad at the time, but we talked later and came to an understanding. There were no hard feelings. I've never believed in holding grudges in life. They don't get you anywhere, and your energy is better spent on other things.

⊛

A most exciting moment during my time as a trainee was when we opened our famous one hundredth branch office–in Omaha, Nebraska. It was almost like a magical office; there was such a big mystique about it. The manager there was going to take one of two trainees, and it was between a fellow named Jack Wark, the son of a partner who ran the over-the-counter department, and me. He chose Jack.

I finally made it out to Omaha about a year or so ago, on a trip with Merrill Lynchers Paul Critchlow, an Omaha native and former University of Nebraska football player, and Jim Wiggins, a Penn State grad, to see Penn State play Nebraska. (That year, we lost.) We visited the Omaha office, and I told them that it was really the most disappointing thing in my whole Merrill Lynch career that I wasn't selected to work at the Merrill Lynch office there some fifty years earlier.

"But now," I said, "after having been here and finally seeing Omaha, frankly, I'm glad I went to Buffalo." They laughed like hell. Everybody got a big laugh out of that.

As much as I'd wanted to get the Omaha assignment, it actually was a break for me that I didn't, because going to Buffalo clearly would become such an important part of my life, for so many reasons.

CHAPTER 6

Buffalo Days

After two years in the "slave" program at Merrill Lynch headquarters in New York City, it was time for me to move on. I was still very young at the time, twenty-two, and there were a lot of places I could go because a number of branch offices needed people.

Win Smith and a couple of the partners told me, "If you really want to learn the business, we suggest you go up to Buffalo and train under Howard Roth." They didn't say this at the time, but since I had a reputation for being a little bit cocky—let's just say that I did not suffer from a lack of self-confidence—I think part of their reasoning was, "Roth is one of the toughest guys in the system. He'll either make or break this kid."

Buffalo appealed to me because it was two hundred miles from Williamsport—about a four-and-a-half-hour drive. With my father's heart condition, and because I was still a bachelor, I would go down about every third or fourth weekend to see the family. It was easy and accessible, not like being in the Midwest or on the West Coast.

My parents helped me move to Buffalo in the fall of 1950, and on the way, we stopped for a little vacation in the Adirondacks with John F. Wark Sr., who had a place there.

Wark, who ran the over-the-counter department in New York, was the father of Jack, my fellow trainee who got the Omaha assignment. John Wark was also a great admirer of Howard Roth. He particularly liked Howard because Howard did a lot of over-the-counter business, which you got extra sales credit for, so everybody was happy.

John, his wife, Estelle, and my parents were great friends. John and Estelle were typical New Yorkers; they knew nothing about anything that wasn't New York City. One time they were visiting the folks in Pennsylvania and Dad, being the great kidder that he was, said, "Estelle, one thing you've got to take home with you are capon eggs, that's a must." She hounded and hounded John until finally they had to break it to her: Capons don't lay eggs.

Anyway, on that trip up to Buffalo, John introduced us to some Buffalonians vacationing there, including a man who was the dean of something called the Saturn Club, a private men's club and residence. "When you come to Buffalo, please give me a call," the man told me. "You can join the Saturn Club. Because you're a bachelor, we'll put you up."

In Buffalo, Mr. Roth had made a reservation for me at the Richford Hotel, which was not exactly the Statler—not the greatest spot in the world, to say the least. So I was there about a day, and I thought, "I'll call this man I met on the way up here." He set me up as a guest at the Saturn Club, and then I joined the club and lived there until I got married, three years later.

It was the perfect place for a young man trying to establish himself and make his mark in a new city. It was a stately stone-and-brick mansion located on Delaware Avenue, in one of the city's finest neighborhoods. They had nice bedrooms, a gymnasium, a swimming pool, and a back room grill that at the time had a men-only policy. It was great for me to get home late, go down and work out and swim, go to the back grill and roll poker dice for drinks, meet a lot of great people and have

71

a lot of fun, get dinner—then go to bed and get up and go to work the next day. It was a great way of life.

The men's grill—hidden away in the back of the club—was set up in Old English style and had a sign above the fireplace: WHERE THE WOMEN CEASE FROM TROUBLING, AND THE WICKED ARE AT REST. Many a time the telephone would ring and I'd hear the head bartender say, "Gosh, he just left, Mrs. Ritling, he just left here five minutes ago. He should be home any minute." And that would be the signal you'd better get the hell out of there, and get going!

One of the members was a man by the name of Jay Cooper Lord, of the Lord Day law firm of New York City. He had plenty of money and had married a Buffalo girl. One night we were playing poker dice, and we'd gone around the table until there were two finalists left—Jay Cooper Lord and me. I couldn't afford to lose. I mean, this was a big bill this night, and it got down to the two of us in the finals.

So he rolled, I rolled. He rolled four fours in the first throw, and I rolled four fives. And then I beat him on the second roll and collected the jackpot, thank God! He said, "Well, what do you do?"

"I'm with Merrill Lynch."

"With the kind of luck you have, I should do business with you."

"That's a good idea," I said. Well, I called him a few days later and made an appointment to see him. He gave me his list of securities, and I had research do an analysis of them. He became my biggest customer for a long period of time. Old Jay Cooper Lord was quite the aristocrat. I remember him at a black-tie affair, after having had quite a bit to drink, looking at a bunch of us with mock disdain: "You're all a bunch of f—ing peasants!"

Living at the Saturn Club was terrific because I met so many Buffalonians, many of whom, like Jay Cooper Lord, became early clients of mine. One of the earliest was a man named Bill Regan, who was the distributor for Bellows Liquors. He died, unfortunately, at too young an age, and his son Ned came back out of the Navy to take over the business. Some years later, Ned was elected comptroller of the State of New York. He and I became good friends and stayed that way over the years.

Working under Howard Roth was an experience that had an enormous influence on me. First of all, he was a substantial partner in the firm, and only those with something significant to offer were made partners. There were only a few out-of-town partners at the time, in Chicago, Detroit, Dallas, Atlanta, and Howard Roth in Buffalo. He was a handsome man, and he always looked the part of a Merrill Lynch partner. He dressed impeccably and taught me the importance of "Look sharp, be sharp." Even on the weekends he wore the best-looking sports coats, so I made it a point to dress well, too.

Howard believed that you should work hard and be successful, but that you should also enjoy the better things in life. He owned beautiful sports cars—he always had Jaguars. And he loved auto racing. He'd go down to Watkins Glen or over to Monte Carlo for the races. He believed in good European vacations. He lived the good life.

In the office, though, it was no-nonsense all the way. Howard had the reputation of being a master merchandiser of securities, particularly over-the-counter securities. He set the rules, and he was very tough, but also very fair. First of all, he had an extraordinary reputation for compliance. He said, "If you ever make a trade in a client's account that you can't justify to me is in the client's best interest, you're fired. I expect you to do business, but to do it the right way. You can buy and sell—I want you to do that—but don't do any over-trading. If you don't believe it's the right thing to do, don't do it." So I watched that carefully.

And there was no such thing as a "Reg-T" violation under Howard Roth. That means money not being in the account on time to cover any securities purchases. Furthermore, there were no extensions, ever! I remember the first time I had a client whose money wasn't in on time, and I had to seek an extension to avoid a Reg-T violation. I went to Howard, and he said, "Well, why don't you have the check? Why didn't you get the money?"

I said, "Well, he was in the hospital."

"Is he dying?"

"No, but he's in the hospital."

"Go out to the hospital, collect the check."

So I went out to the hospital and collected the check. It was a lesson. One of many important lessons I learned from Howard Roth.

One day after I'd been working there for a while, he called me into his office and said, "Schreyer, you know what's wrong with you?"

I said, "Offhand, Mr. Roth, I can't think of a thing."

"You talk too goddamn much."

I protested. "How am I going to get an order if I don't talk?"

"I didn't say you shouldn't talk. You're a pretty good salesman, but you should just talk up to a point and then ask for the order. Instead of that, you just keep talking. The guy says, 'I'll think about it.' Never calls you back, would be my guess."

"Well, you're right," I conceded.

So he said, "Just make the calls short, make them to the point, ask for the order, and then go on and make another call."

The next day, I was still pretty much in my old mode, talking away on the phone, and Mr. Roth came by and put an egg timer on my desk. And every time he walked by, he turned that egg timer over.

To this day, I can't stand to visit for long on the telephone with anybody. I mean, I'll talk and once I've covered whatever it is the call is about, I'll hang up and go on and make other calls. So that was a very important lesson, because too many people do talk too long on the telephone. It wastes your time.

Howard Roth could be brutal sometimes, but you really learned from it. Employees, particularly the producers, would react to him in one of two ways. They'd either do like I did–listen and learn–or they'd just give up completely. He was a pretty good turn-off for some of them who couldn't measure up and didn't stay. But I'd go out of his office thinking, "I'll show you, you son-of-a-so-and-so," which is what he wanted. He also believed that as a successful businessperson you owed the community something, and he was active in a number of civic affairs in which he had a particular interest.

He really was a mentor, and in me he saw a kid who would respond to his kind of training, direction, and management.

The Howard Roth method worked when I was out making cold calls, which was always tough because we really had no training for it. I remember one time, at the end of a fruitless day of pounding the street, I called on a man named Isaacson, who was president of the Great Lakes Pressed Steel Company. I went in about four o'clock in the afternoon and gave him my pitch. He didn't say a word. Finally I got so nervous I said, "Well, it's nice seeing you, Mr. Isaacson. I hope to see you again sometime," and I started to leave.

He said, "Wait a minute, wait a minute, Schreyer. I've been thinking about something. I've been thinking I want to sell some Connecticut General Life Insurance stock that I own, and since you're here, I'll be glad to give you the order."

That was my first real order. It was for sixty-seven shares of Connecticut General, which I added to the market the next morning; it was executed at $76 dollars a share. Both of those pairs of numbers add up to thirteen. And my production number was 261–two times six plus one equals thirteen. Just a little more proof that thirteen is my lucky number. Remember, my mother was the thirteenth of thirteen children, and I was born on the thirteenth.

The following Friday there was a special offering of Curtis

Wright stock. So I called Mr. Isaacson and, with the proceeds of the Connecticut General sale, he bought two hundred shares. He made my week.

Then there was the time that I asked Howard Roth for a raise. Now, one didn't do that to Mr. Roth. But I went in one day and said, "Mr. Roth, I want to ask you to consider an increase in my salary."

"Oh," he said, and his lip began to curl. That was always a sign you were doing something he didn't care for.

"Yeah," I plowed on, "you know, Joan and I—we're engaged and we're going to be married—and I just feel I need some more money."

"Is that so? I'll think about it, Schreyer." And out the door I went.

He let me cool my heels for about two weeks. Then he called me in and said, "Schreyer, I've been reviewing your progress and I'll raise your salary to five hundred fifty dollars a month."

I thanked him and started to leave, and he said, "Look, Schreyer, I just want to tell you something. If anybody ever demonstrated how *not* to ask for a raise, you did."

"What do you mean?"

"Well, you came in here and told me you were going to get married and would appreciate an increase in salary. That's *your* problem. If you had told me you were working your tail off and thought you deserved an increase, that's one thing, but I don't care if you've got ten kids and they're all starving. If it doesn't justify, it doesn't justify!"

So I said, "Well, I guess that's a very good point. You're right. But let me ask you this. If I'd asked for it the right way, would I have gotten a bigger raise?"

"Not a goddamn nickel more," he thundered.

So once again, out the door I went, this time feeling much better after I had asked him that question.

❋

Slowly but steadily I built my business in Buffalo. It was a wonderful time in my life. Even after my initial assignment there, I would return to Buffalo twice during my Merrill Lynch career—once in 1957, after completing my two years of active duty in the Air Force, and again in 1965, when I succeeded Howard Roth as the office manager.

I received my first taste of management in 1957, when, back from the Air Force, I was made the office sales manager by Mr. Roth. It didn't involve any extra pay, but he did find a way to compensate me by giving me three of the biggest accounts in the office, who had been his clients.

In 1962 we experienced a steep market decline. I remember I was acting office manager at the time, as Mr. Roth was vacationing in the South of France. He called in one day, and I was looking for some serious guidance. I briefed him on the situation and said, "What do you think?"

"How would I know? I haven't lived through one like this since 1929," he told me. "You figure it out."

It was classic Howard Roth. But we did figure it out, and while he was gone, we got through it all right. The accounts were handled well and we calmed the clients. Everyone conducted themselves as you would expect at Merrill Lynch.

I do remember one time things got a little rough, though. It was an incident involving Ed Polokoff, one of our big producers and a great friend. One day a client of his came in burning mad. He said Polokoff had been delinquent in getting his orders executed, and he figured we owed him $30,000. He was so upset with Polokoff that he came to see me, the sales manager. He opened his coat to show me that he had a gun, and he said he was going to have to threaten Polokoff if we didn't give him his money back, give him what he thought he deserved.

Well, I acted like any red-blooded American would under the circumstances. I stood up as tall as I could behind the desk and said, "I'll have a check drawn for you for thirty thousand dollars in five minutes. Sit down and relax, Mr. Jones"—or whatever his name was. I think Polokoff was more than a little bit worried about those orders.

That incident ended well, but we had others over the years in Merrill Lynch offices that did not end so well. As I mentioned early on, when I was CEO during the stock market crash of 1987, a customer came into one of our Miami offices and shot and killed the manager over his losses. It just goes to show a truism on Wall Street: People can lose control of their emotions when their money is at stake.

Unfortunately, that wasn't the only incident involving the shooting of an office manager. A few years later, a disgruntled employee shot and killed one of our managers in Boston. The employee was African-American and felt he'd been discriminated against by the manager.

But fortunately, those kinds of incidents are the exception. You're much more likely to see Merrill Lynch people working in their local communities to promote harmony and understanding. Ed Polokoff was like that, and he was quite a character. I always tried to catch up to him, or even beat him, in the amount of business I did, but could never quite manage it. In 1965, when I had just come back to run the Buffalo office, no sooner was I in the door than he asked me to serve as the Community Division chairman for that year's Annual Jewish Appeal. This was the part of the appeal that worked on the Catholics and other Christians in the community to kick in some financial support in the ecumenical spirit. I said, "Sure, I'll do everything I can to help."

Well, we raised a decent amount of money, and at their annual dinner they presented me with a beautiful watercolor painting of a scene in Jerusalem by an accomplished Jewish artist.

I was asked to say a few words, so I stepped up to the

podium. "Ladies and gentlemen," I began. "As a former goy, I just want to thank you for this beautiful Bar Mitzvah gift."

The crowd went wild, and I got a prolonged ovation. I was almost an honorary Jew after that, and we got all the business in Buffalo from the Jewish community. I kidded Polokoff–"It's how you've gotten to be such a big producer so fast!" We had so many great times together, he and I and guys like Joe Steinmetz and Irving Endlich, who were brokers, and customers like Grace and Hoppy de la Plante–it was just a great office.

Polokoff, Steinmetz, and Endlich were the three top brokers in the office–I was fourth and could never quite catch those three. Joe Steinmetz was an ex-Marine, and I learned a lot from him even though he irritated the hell out of me. I'd go into the office on a Monday morning when I was just starting out, and it would take me all week, maybe, to get an order.

Joe would be doing great business; he'd take all his order tickets and put them on a conveyer belt that ran right past my desk. He'd say, "Hey, Bill, look at this, all the tickets up there."

"You son of a bitch," I'd mutter under my breath.

"Keep working, kid. Keep working."

He'd tell a story on himself about when he and his wife went down to the Caribbean Islands. His wife was a real athlete. She'd run down the beach and leap into the water. Joe would very slowly tiptoe down and stick his toe in to see how cold it was.

One day this native watching him said, "Hmm, she da man, you da woman." The big ex-Marine loved to tell that story on himself.

Another of my close male friends in Buffalo was Adrian Dedecker, D.D. for short, one of the great insurance salesmen of all time. He and I were charter members of the POETS Society, which met for lunch every Friday at the Buffalo Club, which was right up the street from my office. We didn't sit around reading Emily Dickinson, though. You see, POETS stood for "PISS ON EVERYTHING, TOMORROW'S SATURDAY."

This group was all clients, and by the time we were having drinks, one of them would say, "Hey, Bill, what do you like today?"

"Well, I like XYZ stock."

"OK, get me a couple hundred shares."

So I'd go over to the bar to call in the order, and the other guys would say, "As long as you're going, get us some, too." So that was my order bench on Fridays. Anyone who says you can't mix business with pleasure didn't know the Buffalo Club back in those days.

In 1962, with Howard Roth's blessing, I decided to formally enter management, which meant going back for training in New York City. Mr. Roth was back from his vacation in France, and about three weeks before I was supposed to leave, he started looking over the office production figures. He said, "Schreyer, I'm really concerned. What am I going to tell Mike McCarthy? I have to tell him your production has slipped." (McCarthy was the managing partner at the time.)

I said, "Mr. Roth, I've reassigned half of these accounts."

"You're not leaving for another three weeks. Let's get that production up."

So he kept the pressure on right until the day I walked out the door. And then, of course, he wished me well.

He took great pride when I went into management training, and then led the Trenton office, and finally, when I returned to Buffalo to succeed him in 1965. He had a lovely office overlooking Delaware Avenue. Before I arrived, he told me, "I'll be out of my office by noon."

When I got there–this was on a Saturday–he had moved into a little office next door, which had been my old office. He was all set up, everything was in place; he was very meticulous, very fastidious.

I was a new member of the Buffalo Club, and he was a member there, too. He said, "I'll buy you lunch at the Buffalo Club."

"Good," I said. "Let me unpack my bag."

"Take your time."

So I unpacked my bag in his old office. This didn't take long—just a briefcase full of stuff—and we went up and had a martini and lunch. It was his way of welcoming me back to Buffalo. He called my attention to a couple of things he thought I ought to know about, then I was on my own.

I felt great about succeeding him. We had a lot of good friends there in Buffalo, and we were one of the top offices, ranked about twentieth in the system. I'd gone back there with the attitude that that's where I would be for the rest of my career. You might continue to move up, but you don't dwell on those things. I've always told young people, whatever management job you get, go in there with the mental attitude that you're in there forever.

I started Monday morning and didn't miss a beat. My style was entirely different from Howard Roth's; that didn't make it right or wrong, but it was entirely different. I know he winced many times at some of the things I did. But to his credit, he never interfered, said a word, made a suggestion, or was a problem in any way, shape, or form. In fact, we had a lot of fun together in the years I was there.

He'd come into the office every day to manage his own affairs. By the time I left there, he'd ended up being closer friends with all the guys in the office than he was when he was running the place. I heard that he took half the office out to celebrate on the day in 1978 that I was named president of Merrill Lynch, Pierce, Fenner & Smith.

I was truly saddened when he died, at the age of ninety, on December 6, 1986. He had retired on January 1, 1974, after thirty-two years with the firm.

We expanded the Buffalo office by about 50 percent over the four years I was manager. The whole experience was a successful one for me. And I had great fun competing with the other financial institutions in town for the choice pieces of business.

One of them was the Seneca Nation's tribal account, which involved managing a considerable amount of money.

Marine Midland Bank was in the same building we were, and I got to be close friends with its chairman, Claude Shuchter. We played golf during the golfing season, always had lunch together on Saturday, and did things with our wives on the weekends, most every weekend we weren't traveling.

This one particular Friday afternoon, when I spoke to Claude, he said, "I'll see you tomorrow."

I said, "Well, Claude, I'm going to be tied up tomorrow."

"Where are you going to be?"

Even though we were very close, I said, "Well, it's confidential—a client matter."

"Okay, see you tomorrow night, then."

Marine Midland, his bank, was competing with Bache and Merrill for the Seneca Nation account. It was the first time that the Federal Bureau of Indian Affairs was permitting an outsider to manage part of that money.

So Claude didn't know it, but I climbed into my little Ford Mustang and went down with our institutional account representatives to make a pitch to the tribal elders. We were the last to make our presentation.

That night as we socialized, Claude asked me again, "Where the hell were you today?"

I said, "Well, you'll probably read about it one of these days."

A few mornings later, one of the directors of the bank, a neighbor of mine, was out walking the dog and passed by the house. I was still in my bathrobe having a cup of coffee, and when he saw me in the window, he started doing a little Indian dance. Then he gave me the victory sign. It had been in the morning paper: "Merrill Lynch Wins the Seneca Account."

A couple of minutes later Claude called me. "Now I know where you were, you son of a bitch."

And I said, "Yeah, well, I wasn't going to go down there and compete with you head-on." It was that sort of good-natured competition. Of course, I've noticed over the years that competition is particularly good-natured when you win.

It tickles me that today, forty-plus years later, two of my protégés at Merrill Lynch, Paul Critchlow and Brian Henderson, are still calling on the Indian tribes to win business for the firm. Many of the tribes are now operating billion-dollar casino businesses, and are looking to issue bonds and obtain other sophisticated financial services.

I've told Paul and Brian that they've got a great tradition and foundation to work from, so the important thing is that they just not screw it up.

I have so many great memories of the Buffalo days, of all the friends we made. People like Stubby Miller, who lives out in Oregon now but still keeps in touch. He's very loyal, checks in twice a year. His parents were close friends of ours. His father was the greatest salesman I ever met. I forget what the hell he sold, but he sold a lot of it! Stubby's son is now in the investment business and is going to be coming by to pay me a visit. It's wonderful to have the kinds of friendships that stay vital and alive down through the generations. That's the kind of place Buffalo was, and it's why it was so hard to leave.

Of course, my greatest Buffalo memories of all are about the two women who happen to be the loves of my life.

CHAPTER 7

Joan and DrueAnne

The only person I knew in Buffalo when I arrived there in 1950 was a Penn Stater, my fraternity brother Bill Douglas, who was working for Lincoln Electric Company. Bill had been a captain in the Marine Air Corps. He was a handsome guy, looked a little bit like the movie actor Van Heflin, and he had married a Miss Penn State, a beautiful girl named Joyce Hutchins.

I called Bill when I got to Buffalo, and he took me out to dinner. He had a baby girl at the time. He said, "You just got here and you don't know anyone. Would you like a blind date?"

I said, "I'm not big on blind dates. I'll make my own mistakes."

He said, "Well, there's this girl I know from my sales calls who's a knockout. If I were single, I surely would like to take her out."

I said, "Tell you what I'll do. I'll call her and tell her you suggested I call, and then I'll make the date rather than you setting up a blind date."

Her name was Joan Legg. I called her on a Thursday night for a date the next night, Friday.

"Are you busy tomorrow night? Would you care to go out to dinner?"

She was very pleasant on the phone but said, "I'm terribly

sorry. I'm busy." Whether she was or wasn't, she was not about to accept a date on one day's notice. That's the way it was in those days.

So I said, "Tell you what let's do. Let's make a tentative date for a week from tomorrow. I'll come by where you're working earlier in the week and introduce myself to you, and if you don't like what you see or I don't like what I see, we both have the option to cancel. Nothing to lose."

She said, "All right." Later she told me that she had said to her friends, "I just have to see what this conceited guy is all about."

Now, I had the advantage in this arrangement. I let her sweat on Monday, and I didn't show up until Tuesday afternoon. I walked into the office where she was working and whispered to someone, "Which one is Joan Legg?"

She pointed over, and I took one look and said, "Wow!" I quickly went to the men's room around the corner and combed my hair. Then I sauntered over and introduced myself.

"Hi, I'm Bill Schreyer."

"Nice to meet you, Bill."

"I'll take a chance and move ahead with this if you will. I'd love to have a date Friday night."

She looked up and nodded her head and said, "Fine." She still had to find out what this character was all about.

So we went out for dinner and dancing at a good spot in Buffalo. Then we met some other friends at another spot, and got home pretty late. When I was dropping her off, I said, "You know, we've been together so long tonight, it's really like two dates. I think you ought to kiss me good night." So I gave her a quick smacker good night, and we made a date for the next night. Thus began a courtship and engagement that would last for the next two years.

When we started dating, Joan was pinned to a guy from Niagara Falls who was going to school out in Michigan somewhere. When I found out about that, I said, "I can't have

STILL BULLISH ON AMERICA

you pinned, it wouldn't be fair to this guy. Why don't you just wrap up the pin in a box and I'll mail it back for you." So she wrote him a nice note and they broke up. Being proper, she mailed the pin back herself. I met the guy years later, and I think she made the right decision.

Joan was a native of Buffalo. Her grandfather, her father's father, was a leading undertaker in town. He had embalmed President William McKinley when he was assassinated there in 1901. He was a wonderful man.

Her grandmother never had a good day in her life. We would always say, "Oh, she's so weavy." But after Joan and I were engaged, and I was out making cold calls, I would stop by Grandma's house just to say hello if I was anywhere in the neighborhood. She would say, "Have you had anything to eat? Would you like a cup of coffee?" She made the world's greatest scrambled eggs, with a lot of cream in them. So she made me scrambled eggs and toast whenever I dropped in there. That's about all she ever did. I mean, she couldn't really cook.

The other side of the family were the MacDonalds. They were Scottish, and had immigrated to Canada. Joan's mother's father, Mr. Mac, was a great guy. He was very successful in the building business.

Ida was her grandmother on her mother's side. She was nicknamed "Little Hitler." She was about four foot ten, and a tough, very strong-minded woman. Her sister lived with her at the time, and they had a farm out in the country where they raised animals. They would go out and bring home good chops and meat, stuff like that.

With Ida, I was always being told, "Don't say this and don't say that." I think everyone was concerned about bringing a Catholic into the family, but we never had a problem with that. The first time I was over there for dinner, I sort of flirted with Ida a little bit. On the way out I thanked her for dinner and everything, gave her a big kiss good-bye, and then a very, very small—not disrespectful or anything—pat on the fanny.

86

And she loved it. She giggled and said, "Oh, Billy." Once she started calling me Billy, I knew I was home free. So there was never, ever any problem.

Joan's father, William B. Legg, was with the Buffalo Savings Bank. He was in the real estate area, in mortgages. He had a good job. Or as good as any jobs were in those days.

Joan's mother was Gladys. We called her "Happy Bottom." I liked her a lot. She loved driving my cars fast. She had a nice figure and she was a good dancer. God, could she dance. I'd go out to their house every Sunday, and she'd have made the best roast leg of lamb I've ever had. I salivate just thinking about it. Joan and her mother were very close, and she ended up living in a retirement area not far from us in Princeton, until she died in her mid-seventies. We got along very well.

Of all the girls I took home to meet my folks, Joan was the only one my mother ever liked. My dad liked all of them. My mother liked Joan. She was very conservative and mature, I guess you'd say, handled herself very well, and she was an instant success.

One night when we were home visiting in Williamsport, Joan was sleeping in the middle bedroom, and my dad and I were sharing the guest bedroom with two twin beds. Dad was closest to the hallway and the light, and I was over by the window.

At about three o'clock in the morning, I woke up when I heard some noise. Then I saw Joan come into the bedroom. She walked past my father and came over to me, gave me a shake, and signaled me to follow her. Didn't say a word. "Well," I thought, "geez, maybe I'm luckier than I think I am. What's going on here?"

So I followed her back to her bedroom and said, "What did you have in mind?" She pointed underneath the bed, as if somebody was under there or something. So I got down on my knees and looked.

I said, "There's nobody here."

87

She said, "Thank God," got back into bed, and fell sound asleep.

The next morning, I got down to the breakfast table before Joan came down and told my dad about what had happened. When she came down, she started to bend over to give Dad a little kiss on the cheek, and he said, "Don't touch me, you spook!"

"What are you talking about?" she asked. So I related what had happened, and she said, "Oh, I guess I never did tell you that I travel–walk in my sleep once in a while." We've had a lot of fun kidding her about that over the years.

⁕

During our courtship we had what I call our two-year religious war. Joan was Episcopalian and I was Roman Catholic. She became a better Episcopalian because I was trying to convert her to Catholicism, and I became a better, stauncher Catholic because she was trying to wean me away a little bit from that.

I was a regular communicant of St. Michael's Catholic Church in downtown Buffalo. The priest there was a Jesuit, Father Jim Redmond (the same priest I'd spoken with after my father died), who had converted more people to Catholicism than just about anybody. He worked on Joan and they became good friends, but no cigar as far as conversion was concerned.

At one point Father Redmond was hosting a bishop who ran a big diocese down in South America. He was a Jesuit from central casting, a handsome man with gray hair, just a very imposing figure. After Mass one Sunday I was visiting with this bishop, looking for support for my position with Joan.

He said, "Listen, are you really in love with this girl? Do you want to marry her?"

I said, "Yeah, I do."

"Let me give you a little advice: Never maintain your position in matters of no importance."

I could have died. "What?!" I said.

"Well, don't worry about meat on Friday," he told me. "The Church will probably change that rule in due course, anyway. You stick to the big principles, but don't get hung up on all the technical rules of the Church."

So that's where I got the phrase "Don't sweat the small stuff," which became known many years later as one of the "Sayings of Chairman Bill." (Of course, the minute you get older, you start sweating the small stuff more and more. When you get to be eighty, little stuff annoys the hell out of you!)

In any event, those wise words of advice ended our religious war, and Joan and I got engaged. My parents came up for the engagement party, but Dad died just before we were to be married. We postponed the wedding for a time, and finally were married on October 17, 1953.

At the time, if it was a mixed marriage, you couldn't get married in a Catholic church in the Buffalo diocese because some previous bachelors from the Saturn Club who had gotten married in mixed marriages had gotten a little loaded in anticipation of the festivities, so the bishop just said, "No more mixed marriages in the church."

Joan said, "I don't want to be married in the rectory," which was the alternative the church was offering, but a guy named Eddie Walsh solved our problem. He said, "My wife's non-Catholic, too, so we were married in a little church in Canada." So we went over there and they didn't ask any questions. In fact, I think the old priest had had a couple of pops before he got there for our nuptials. He didn't even require that Joan sign the agreement to raise our kids Catholic.

After we were married there, we stopped off at Joan's church and had the marriage blessed by the Episcopal minister, who happened to be a guy I played squash with a couple of times a week at the Saturn Club.

Then our Merrill Lynch friend Eddie Polokoff offered, "Hey, there's a temple right nearby. We can go and get the rabbi to wrap this thing up, and you can be sure you're fully married in a totally ecumenical fashion." We laughed, but decided two faiths were enough. We had the reception at the Saturn Club and then went off on our honeymoon to Sea Island, Georgia.

When we returned, we moved into a beautiful old home owned by the Simons, who owned Simon Industries, which included a brewery in Buffalo called Simon Pure. Old Mr. Simon had this beautiful house—it looked like a castle almost—right there on Delaware Avenue, about four blocks up from the Saturn Club and the cathedral. They had a wing that his daughter and son-in-law, who were friends of ours, used to live in. We took over that apartment. It was all fixed up for us, and it just had everything. Well, almost everything.

I will never forget what happened that first Monday night in our new home. I picked Joan up from work and we went back to our newlywed apartment. I was fixing myself an old-fashioned. I drank old-fashioneds then with Canadian Club, ice, and a little fruit. Joan was out in the kitchen, and she said, "Bill, would you put up this tea towel rack for me?"

"Oh sure," I said.

I wasn't very mechanical, but I went out to the kitchen and, cripes, it took forty-five minutes to get the damn thing up. And then it wasn't really quite straight. By the time I sat back down, the ice had melted, my drink was watery. I took a sip. It wasn't as good as it should have been.

Joan put two tea towels on the rack and it immediately fell to the floor. She broke up laughing. I said, "That's the last goddamn thing I'm going to ever do around the house."

She said, "You're just like your father."

I said, "Like your father, too."

So that's worked to my benefit all these fifty-five years and still counting. I've never been handy around the house, able to fix things. Joan used to say, "You'll come around." But actually, I haven't. I've gotten away with it all these years.

In fact, my aversion to housework became so well known that my good friend Charlie Sanders likes to kid me about it by telling a story he swears is true. The way he tells it, early in our marriage, Joan came to me with a piece of paper on which she had written down a list of chores that needed to be done around the house. I put down my newspaper, looked over the list that Joan had handed me, and pulled out my pen. Across that list I wrote in big capital letters, "APPROVED," and handed it back to her. That is a true story, except for one minor detail: It happened to my Uncle Wilk, not me. That man was certainly a positive influence on me in more ways than one!

That first decade of married life in Buffalo, including the two years we spent in Germany while I was on active duty in the Air Force, was a wonderful time. We had a great life with a lot of great friends.

It was one day in 1962, shortly before we left Buffalo for New York City, where I was to start management training, when I got my first indication that our life was about to change in a very important way.

It was a Saturday morning, wintertime, and I was in the office. The markets were closed, of course, but a lot of us worked on Saturday mornings in those days. I was Howard Roth's sales manager at the time and I made it in every Saturday morning.

So this particular Saturday morning, Joan walked in, which was quite unusual. Howard Roth ran a very tight ship. Wives and girlfriends just didn't drop by the office–that was sort of an unwritten rule.

So I asked her, "What are you doing here?"

She said, "Sit down."

I said, "OK, what's on your mind, kid?"

"You know that the so-and-so's are having a baby," she said, referring to a couple we knew. "We've been married nine years, and I think it's time we adopted." Then she got up and walked out.

My mouth dropped open. Clearly, Joan had concluded that we would be unable to have children, but until then, it was something that had just never come up.

After she left I said to myself, "Now, what the hell do you suppose that was all about?" I was an only child. It was not a big issue with me as to whether we had a child or not. I was busy working, we were enjoying life, I was perfectly happy.

On the way home I stopped by the Saturn Club to have a little pop in the back room with my men friends. I got home and Joan wasn't there. I waited, and finally she came home and I said, "Now, what the hell is this all about?"

She went into it, and I said, "I tell you what let's do. I'll make a deal with you. Let's each think about this seriously for six months. We won't even discuss it. Six months from now we'll talk about it again, and if you're really serious about wanting to proceed, we'll go ahead and do it." I figured that would take care of it. She would forget about it and it would go away.

Six months, one hour, two minutes, and thirteen seconds later, she brought it up again. I said, "Well, by God, if you think this is what we ought to do, we'll do it. How do we go about this?"

Joan had done her research, and she said, "The Cradle Society in Chicago is considered one of the best agencies. But the problem is, they had a bad experience in Buffalo, so Buffalo is not in their territory."

I said, "Let's check somewhere else, then." She checked on a couple of places in New York, but they had a lot of rules and policies we just didn't like.

It was about that time that I was transferred to New York

City for the management training. Later we'd move to Princeton, New Jersey, after I took over the Trenton office. The Cradle Society covered both those locations, so thus began what I called the longest pregnancy in history. It lasted about twenty-one months.

We put in our application, a lady from the agency made a couple of house visits, and we were approved. The call finally came just before we were moving back to Buffalo. I said, "God, if we tell them we're going back to Buffalo, we'll lose twenty-one months." So we went through the process and told them later.

Our daughter was born on October 9, 1964, and about six weeks later we went out to Chicago to pick her up. We were with our vice president in Chicago, Russell Stern, a dear old friend, and his wife. That was one of the most exciting moments in our lives.

We arrived at the office of the lawyer for the Cradle Society and filled out a lot of forms. Then Stern said, "Schreyer, if we go right next door, there's a place to get some sandwiches and we can bring some lunch back for the wives." So we went next door to a neighborhood bar and restaurant, and while I was ordering food, I announced to the entire establishment, "Hi, I'm about to become a new father." I bought everybody at the bar a drink, including me—a good stiff martini—to celebrate this incredible new experience of becoming a father.

After we returned to the lawyer's office, they put Joan and me in a little room and then brought in the baby. She had a lot of dark hair. They'd put a little bow in it and combed it just the way Joan happened to have her hair fixed that day, with little bangs down over the forehead.

Then they left us alone with the child for about twenty minutes, to see if the chemistry was right. And obviously the chemistry was dazzling. Something just grabbed me, right then and there. Something miraculous happened, and it hit me again: I was about to become a father.

Next, we went down to the court to go through the legal proceedings. Afterward, we went back to the Sterns' house for champagne, then flew back to Newark, New Jersey, where our friends who owned the house we were renting met us at the airport with a limousine and a big bottle of pink champagne.

We named the little girl DrueAnne, after our great friend Gene Cartwright's wife. She quickly became an important part of our lives. Boy, I really got into that fatherhood routine in a hurry. Women are born mothers, but men become fathers, I think. At least that's my philosophy.

But I'm getting ahead of myself. First I want to tell you about the two wonderful years we spent in Wiesbaden, Germany, courtesy of the U.S. Air Force.

CHAPTER 8

Lieutenant Schreyer
Reports for Duty

❁

By the early months of 1955, I was doing well enough as a Merrill Lynch account executive that Joan and I were able to escape the Buffalo winter and take a beautiful two-week vacation down to Nassau in the Bahamas. Upon our return I was stunned by what was waiting in the mail: orders from the U.S. Air Force to report for active duty on March 7, 1955.

To say I wasn't expecting this would be the understatement of the century. Through the ROTC program, I had graduated from Penn State commissioned as a second lieutenant. But I hadn't had to do a thing after that. Korea came and went, and I never got called. Now, though, the Air Force had gone through their records and called in about a hundred lieutenants from ROTC who had never served the two-year required tour of duty.

I was starting to really roll at Merrill Lynch and thought to myself, "My God, my whole career is being interrupted. Who needs this?!" I told Joan, "Heck, I'm a little bit overweight and the war is over–there's no vital requirement. Maybe if I talk to them, I won't have to serve the tour."

They no longer used the old Army uniforms I'd worn at

Penn State, so I went to the Army Navy store and bought a new uniform in Air Force blue–only one, because I figured that's all I would need after I talked my way out of serving.

I went over to see the ROTC officers at the University of Buffalo, and they said, "Oh, no, we're only fussy about weight if you're a pilot. You're not a pilot; you'll be a financial officer." They told me I would be stationed in Germany, either in Wiesbaden or at a base in Spangdahlem near the French border.

So I called Joan and said, "Hey, we're going to Germany." She was excited about it, actually, because we had no children at the time and it would be a new experience.

This old sergeant at the university, a great guy, said, "Are you going to take your wife?"

I said, "Well, sure I'm going to take my wife."

"My God, son," he said. "That's like taking a ham sandwich to a banquet."

I didn't tell Joan that story until after she came over to Germany. I didn't want her worrying about it over the few months between my arrival and hers.

Merrill Lynch had a policy that you could return to your job–in the office from whence you came–after your military obligation was completed. When I told Howard Roth I'd been called up, he said, "It ought to be a damn good experience for you." So off I went to Camp Kilmer, New Jersey, to await my orders, and there I learned a very important lesson about when to pull rank–and when not to.

Probably about 98 percent of the officers who were called up would fly to their posts–in my case, Germany. Every day you'd look at the bulletin board for your specific orders, and my name didn't appear and didn't appear. I think I arrived on a Monday, and by Friday morning there were still no orders to fly out.

Joan was coming down for the weekend to Bronxville, in Westchester County, to visit with my aunt and uncle. It was a two-hour drive from Camp Kilmer and I wanted to go see her. So I went in to have a talk with the chief warrant officer.

"What's up with me?" I asked.

"I don't know," he said.

"Look, I want to go spend the weekend with my wife."

"I wish you wouldn't. I'd prefer you to stay on base, because your orders could come any day."

"But I could be back here in two hours."

"No, I still prefer that you stick around."

"Listen. I haven't been back in the Air Force long, but I remember enough from my ROTC training to know that a second lieutenant still outranks a warrant officer. I'm going to New York."

"Yes, sir," he grumbled.

Big mistake. I got back from the weekend and still had to cool my heels for a couple of days. Then my orders came. No airplane for me. I was assigned to travel with the troops aboard the USNS *Upshire,* commonly and not-so-affectionately known soon afterward as the USNS "Upchuck."

Ten days on the high seas of the North Atlantic in March is not exactly a pleasure cruise, I can tell you that! So that warrant officer took care of me very nicely. He let me know who outranked whom. He didn't get mad—he got even.

We sailed out of New York Harbor on a Thursday, and the next day, Friday, I remember dining in the mess with a Catholic Air Force chaplain. In those days, the Church still prohibited meat on Fridays, but I noticed that the chaplain, a very senior officer, a colonel, was chomping away on a piece of rare roast beef. I knew that Catholics received a military dispensation to eat whatever was being served, but it still bothered me.

"Father Brennan," I said, "I still feel kind of funny having meat on a Friday."

He said, "Lieutenant, let me give you a little advice: Don't be holier than the Church."

I thought about that and finally said, "Pass the roast beef!" Tasted pretty good.

The seas were very rough, and everyone got sick. I held out until about the third day, and then I got sick, too. And then you get over it. You weren't in command of anything aboard the ship; you weren't given a job or anything. You were just being transported over. The rest of the trip went pretty smoothly.

When we arrived in Bremerhaven, Germany, on the North Sea, and prepared to disembark, I reported up on the main deck to the officer in charge of handing out the orders: "Schreyer here."

"Schreyer? I don't have that name here. I can't seem to find it. Oh, here it is. You're going to be the train commander to take all the troops from Bremerhaven down to Frankfurt. You're in charge of the whole thing. You'll be the only officer aboard."

Now, I had never in my life commanded a group of people in the Air Force. I had been in the military all of about three weeks, much of that time spent throwing up on the high seas.

It got worse. "Now, you're going to have to sign here, Lieutenant." Turns out I had to sign a receipt saying that I would be financially responsible for everything on the train— from the locomotive to the last knife, fork, and spoon—that was found to be missing when they made a count upon our arrival in Frankfurt.

"God almighty," I thought to myself. "How did I get into this mess? That's what you get for fooling around with warrant officers." We laid over in Bremerhaven that night, and I sure didn't sleep very well.

My luck changed, though, when we boarded the train the next day. I got to my compartment and looked over into the compartment next to me. There were four master sergeants sitting there. I looked them over and there was one, the oldest, who looked like the kindest and most understanding of the group.

"Sergeant, could I see you for a moment?" I said to him.

I told him of my stupidity, that I'd only been in the military a couple of weeks, and threw myself upon his mercy. He was from Georgia someplace. He said, "Lieutenant, I'll be happy to help."

I said, "You move in here with me. Give your pals a little more room."

And he said, "You just relax, have a good night's sleep, and leave everything to me."

So I had a good night's sleep and, as it was starting to get light, I heard him getting up. I said, "Do you want me to do something?"

"No, I'll get the troops fed first. Then you and I will have breakfast afterward."

I peeked out and saw all these soldiers walking through to the chow car, with the master sergeant and his buddies all looking after them. Finally he came back and said, "Come on, let's have breakfast." We sat at a window looking out at the German countryside and had a pretty good breakfast.

At one point, he said, "Lieutenant, when we get to Frankfurt, all of the men will disperse, they're gone. So I'm going to stop the train in North Frankfurt, before we get to the main station, and you'll see what we're going to do."

We stopped at the station in North Frankfurt, and they got all the troops out onto the platform. Then the sergeants went through all the cars looking for forks, knives, things that could be stuck under the seats or thrown around. They accounted for just about everything. Then they put the troops back on the train.

We got into the main station in Frankfurt and the troops did disappear. When I signed off on the receipt, it cost me about $1.75–a couple of forks were missing, or something like that. So that was a pretty good deal, and I learned something about working with people. That master sergeant was a great guy. He went off somewhere, and I never saw him again.

A friend reading this manuscript suggested that this train story essentially reveals the formula for my future success as a CEO: Size up the situation, be smart enough to know what you don't know, figure out who might be able to help you and make them your friend, enlist the people you've made as friends to help you, then reward them with privileges and recognition. Maybe that is the formula, but I can tell you that was the farthest thing from my mind at the time.

I arrived at Wiesbaden, which was the headquarters of the Air Force in Europe, and found it an absolutely beautiful place. I remember checking into the American Arms Hotel, the bachelor officers' quarters, which was a modern, beautiful facility, and that was when I started to feel better. I said, "God, I've got to stay here," rather than be reassigned to Spangdahlen, which was not as nice.

I had been assigned to the deputy chief of staff, controller, which was the financial office for the European operations. I was classified as an accounting officer. Why? Well, I had listed my title as "account executive" in the reservist survey, so in typical military fashion, they assumed I was an accountant, which I did not know the first damn thing about.

So I went up to the head office, where the general was, and there were two bird colonels and one lieutenant colonel who was the executive officer of the controller group, reporting to the major general. Higgins was his name. I said, "Colonel Higgins, I really feel I could be a big help here in the head office. Here's my background, I could really do a good job. I know most positions here are for captains, majors, and above, but I'd really like to take a crack at it. I'm an excellent accountant."

He said, "Well, I'll give you a shot. Go down and see Colonel Cortega in accounting. If you can convince him to give you a job here, we'll see what happens."

Colonel Cortega looked like a tank commander from the World War. I mean, he was a tough son of a gun. I made my pitch. I said, "If I had been on active duty since I got my commission in 1948, I think I'd be a captain by now, maybe even a major."

Later on he told my wife that he got such a kick out of my sales pitch; he wanted to see if I could do anything. There was a slot open in the expense sector, and I got in there working for a Captain Mayberry, who was the closest thing to Captain Queeg I've ever met in my life.

As soon as I got in there, I knew I was in trouble. I said to myself, "Gee, I've got to work this thing out somehow." The general had an officer working for him as his personal assistant, a Captain Mellow, who was rotating back to the States. There already was a replacement in the pipeline, but they didn't know who or what yet.

I took the captain out for a couple of beers, told him about Merrill Lynch, and that I could be very helpful. Maybe, if he could introduce me to the general, I could provide some useful service. "In fact, I'd love to have your job," I told him.

I'll be damned if the general didn't call me. Major General Thomas R. Rampy. He was a Scotsman and he drove an old 1938 Chrysler; bought his tires from a used-car place. Very nice man, but very conservative.

He said, "Lieutenant, I understand you're with Merrill Lynch, and you're over here serving a tour. I've got two thousand dollars to invest. Can you make me some money?"

"Yes, sir." I bought him three hundred shares of a Canadian oil company that was supposed to have good speculative potential, for $7 a share. Merrill Petroleum—no relation to Merrill Lynch. It had fluctuated between $6 and $8 over the previous two years, and I hoped I could keep him living on hope until I got out of the Air Force, or at least not lose him any money.

So I'll be darned if Pacific Petroleum didn't take Merrill Petroleum over for $20 a share three weeks after we bought it. The general tripled his money, and guess who took

Captain Mellow's place? Lieutenant Schreyer was now the administrative officer for the general of the controller group, working directly with all the other senior officers.

Soon word spread around the base—I helped spread it, of course—and before long I was handling accounts for a lot of the officers through our Geneva, Switzerland, office, which was the only office we had in Europe at the time. There were a lot of full colonels stationed at headquarters, and they all made pretty good money. This made the relationships with all of the other officers very nice, and I was eventually doing more business while on active duty in the Air Force than I had done as a trainee just starting out in Buffalo. The only problem was I wasn't being paid for it.

They had military phones on the base, and initially I didn't feel right about charging the calls to the military, so I would call Joan, and she would then call down and place the orders with the Geneva office. When I told the general this, he said, "That holds up the orders! Why don't you just call direct? It's no big deal."

One of the officers I did business with was James R. Dale, a Virginia boy who was a dashing, handsome lieutenant colonel. He was a pilot in military intelligence. He didn't tell me much, even though I tried to pull it out of him. Dale had a great sense of humor, and among the women he dated was the American movie star Ava Gardner, who still to this day is considered one of the sexiest women who ever lived. Not bad.

I remember he went over to see her once in Spain, and she had left her car out at the airport for him to drive into town. On the way in, he met this young woman who was pushing a baby carriage. He made a date with her and never did go in to see Ava, just took the car back and left it at the airport where he had picked it up. I'll tell you, he was more damn fun.

The first trip I took outside Germany was with Dale, who

was flying his plane to the South of France and invited me along. We were at the Martinez Hotel in Cannes and I remember the date, April 22, 1955, because it was Joan's birthday. Dale and I were having some wine, and I called her at her parents' home, where she was living temporarily, to wish her a happy birthday. This did not make for a great, happy birthday for her. She's thinking, "Imagine that. I'm home in Kenmore, New York, and he's celebrating my birthday drinking wine on the French Riviera."

I said, "I like this Air Force life." And Joan came over about three months later. We lived in a housing development they had built for the headquarters of the Air Force, and they were really very nice apartments. We were on the top floor, the third floor, and living there was very pleasant. We did all our shopping in the commissary. I'll never forget, often I'd drive home and Joan would ask me to pick up something on the way. We had this German lady who was the housekeeper. She'd clean the house and help with other chores, and every time she'd see me pull up, she'd run down those two flights of stairs and carry the groceries up. Now, I was a young lieutenant. I'd say, "Hildegard, you don't have to do that. I'll do that."

"No, no, no. You good to me, I good to you." That's about all she could speak of English. And she was good. She worked really hard.

Naturally, I belonged to the Officers' Club. And then there was a civilian club for the civilians who worked for the Air Force. That was a great club. We had dollar steak nights and twenty-five-cent martinis. You know, it was pretty hard to beat that. So our friends were fellow Air Force officers or civilians from different parts of the United States who had come to work there. We met a number of very good German people, too.

While World War II had been over for ten years, I wondered what the German attitude toward Americans would be when I went over there. Let me put it this way, they didn't turn their backs and walk away. They were very friendly. There was no bitterness that I could see, particularly in Wiesbaden, which had been the headquarters of the German Air Force, too. And thanks to the military being headquartered there, it was a prosperous city–great restaurants and great stores.

Mainz, which was not more than fifteen miles away from Wiesbaden, had been 95 percent ruined in the war. So the attitude of the people at Mainz was not nearly as friendly as that of the people who lived in Wiesbaden and hadn't been touched. Overall, I felt that most Germans we met were very friendly. They weren't too happy with Adolf Hitler and his regime, either. They had lost the war, and that didn't make them think more highly of the damage that was done to Germany. Some people looked at us as rescuers, some looked at it as, "That's just the way life is and we'll make the best of it."

There was a gambling place in Wiesbaden we went to, and it was a classic, beautiful place. The law of Germany then was that if you were a citizen of Wiesbaden, for example, you could gamble in any other city, such as Frankfurt, but you couldn't gamble in your own town. They didn't want people losing their money, going out every night and gambling. If you were that dedicated to it, you could drive over to Frankfurt, but that would discourage a lot of people from going as often as they would if it were available right there in Wiesbaden.

We also went to the beer gardens, traveled up the Rhine to the wine country, went to Munich for Oktoberfest. You could go off in a hundred different directions and be in entirely different environments.

My Uncle Charles Schreyer came over for a visit one time with my Aunt Marie. He was the conservative chairman of the board of the West Branch Bank and Trust Company and a deacon in the Lutheran Church. But I'll tell you this, he loved *Playboy* magazine and he always found good-looking women very alluring, but he was above reproach. He just enjoyed looking at those beautiful *frauleins*. So I took him to the Oktoberfest beer garden and we had a great time singing the old German songs. He was about sixty at the time and he was enjoying every bit of it.

My military job as the administrative officer was to work together with Colonel Higgins, the executive officer, to coordinate the flow of information to General Rampy from all the various directorates: accounting, finance, management analysis, and so on. There were half a dozen different functions like that that supported the operation of the controller's function overseas. It was a pleasant job. It wasn't like trying to open up new accounts in Buffalo, New York.

The general had a staff meeting once a week, usually on Tuesday mornings. There was a two-star general, full-bird colonels, one lieutenant colonel, and me, Second Lieutenant– soon-to-be First Lieutenant–Schreyer. I enjoyed being with those older men, who had seen the war and were career Air Force guys who'd stayed on after the war. It was a stimulating experience for a twenty-five-year-old kid.

Even as I was growing up, I always gravitated toward people who were older. Particularly when I got to college. I've always felt that way in anything I've ever done. I just enjoyed being with someone a little older, because you can learn so much from them.

They had a nice farewell party for me when it was my time to come back home. They kidded me about being a lieutenant. I said, "Listen, I don't know what everybody is giving me a hard time for–I'm the only guy who's been promoted around here in the last couple of years. I went from second lieutenant to first lieutenant, and you guys are still lieutenant colonels, colonels, and a general."

One of the lifelong friends I made during this period was Walter Longanecker. He was a captain and worked down the hall from me as director of the budget department. Joan and I got to be great friends with him and his wife, Ginny, who we later asked to be Drue's godmother.

Anyway, Walt and I would be walking along, and I walked faster than him. He'd say, "Lieutenant, watch your rank. You should never walk ahead of a senior officer." After that, I did it deliberately just to piss him off. He loved it.

Walt retired as a major general and he's still a great friend at age eighty-six now. Ginny died some years ago, and in fact, we recently fixed Walt up with a friend of ours down at the beach, a widow. She calls him "Major" because she thought that was his first name. We're going to try to fix them up again and see what happens.

Our time overseas was set against the backdrop of the Cold War, which was of course centered in Europe. Joan and I traveled to Hungary in 1956, right before their attempted revolution against the Soviet Union. We would go into a restaurant, and when they found out we were Americans, they treated us like heroes, even though we hadn't done anything, we just happened to be there. Later, in Vienna, we heard that the Russians had rolled their tanks into the streets of Budapest and squelched the revolution. It was an election year in the U.S., and President Eisenhower, who was running for (and would win) reelection, did not get us involved in the events in Hungary. It was his judgment to make at that time, but there was a lot of conversation and second-guessing about that afterward.

I also remember going to Berlin over the Easter holiday. We went up with another Air Force couple on the train. We stopped at the border zone and the East German police came in and woke us up. They were firm but they weren't nasty, and they wanted our identification and all of that stuff. So we all got out of bed and did what we had to do. It wasn't that big of a deal in hindsight.

West Berlin was a terrific city. It was interesting to see how well it was doing. And we were able to go into East Berlin, too; we thought that we might not be able to. I had top-secret clearance because of being involved with the general, and I was a little nervous about going into East Berlin. We weren't told not to by our own people, but they warned us that if we decided to go, "Be careful."

At any rate, it was absolutely like going from heaven to hell. That's an exaggeration because I have not been to either of these two places—yet. But West Berlin was booming. People were positive, smiles on their faces, they were doing well. When you crossed over into East Berlin, it was very heavy. People seemed sad and there was no life there whatsoever. So it was really like night and day. The people weren't having much fun, whereas in West Berlin, they were having fun and the bars and restaurants were doing well and there was a very happy mood. It made a lasting impression on me to see the difference between a free Germany and a Communist-controlled apparatus. Thirty years later, President Reagan made that stirring and historic speech—"Mr. Gorbachev, tear down this Wall"—and soon the Wall did come down. So I feel fortunate that we were able to spend some time there, because we were witnessing history.

Though I didn't get paid for the business I was doing for Merrill Lynch while in Germany, they did let me know it was appreciated. Win Smith Sr., the managing partner at the time, wrote me a note saying he had heard about what I was doing, and if I could get to Paris on such and such a date, he would be there with his wife and stepson and would like to see me.

So I went to General Rampy and said, "Sir, here's the situation."

He said, "Well, sure, that'd be fine. As a matter of fact, I think our airplane has to go over there around that time anyhow, to pick up some stuff."

To make a long story short, I flew over to Paris on the general's airplane and had lunch and a nice visit with Win Smith. I got quite a kick out of it. Here was Lieutenant Schreyer being flown in style by a couple of captains.

I told Mr. Smith about my experiences in Germany, and I told him why we should open offices in Europe. In fact, I followed up with a letter saying we should open in Frankfurt, certainly, and in Wiesbaden near the military base. I got a letter back from Mike McCarthy, who was number two at the time, and he said, "Bill, we appreciate everything you're doing for the firm over there, but why don't you just relax and enjoy your tour of duty, and let us run the firm."

General Rampy was going to retire from the Air Force, and wanted to know if he could meet the head of our firm, so I helped him get an interview with Win Smith. He really wasn't the right guy for Merrill, and I knew that. He was more of an accounting or finance guy, rather than someone who would be successful in investment banking or brokerage, but still, I liked him and was glad to help him get an interview.

At the time, I was planning my own departure from active duty, and under Air Force rules, I could return to the U.S. in December 1956 or February 1957. So I told the general, "If you send me back in February, that's fine. But if I go back in December and get back on the Merrill Lynch payroll, I'll automatically be paid the regular annual bonus employees get, which would mean a lot to me."

The general mentioned this to Win Smith at their meeting. "You know, that Lieutenant Schreyer is a very creative young man."

"Yeah, very creative," said Win Smith.

They kidded me about that for years, maneuvering to get back in time to pick up the annual bonus. With all the business

I'd been doing for Merrill Lynch over there, though, I wasn't loaded with guilt for doing that.

❀

For Joan and me, going to Germany was the best thing that could have happened to us. Two of the best years of our lives were spent over there. It was our first taste of the international life, and my first exposure to the potential of international business.

In 1955 I got the first Ford Thunderbird, which was a great car—soft-top convertible, black with red interior. It was shipped over to Germany after I got there. It had a powerful engine and the Germans loved that. They revered great automobiles and just wanted to look under the hood.

The first trip I took with Joan, we drove that T-bird down to Spain, to Barcelona. I was told by the Air Force people that if we came on any gypsies, to keep right on going—fast. Don't stop for them. So at one point, we were headed along and I looked up and saw a whole horse-drawn caravan of gypsies stopped up ahead. So I gunned it. I went through there like a bat out of hell and kept right on going. I was going a hundred miles an hour. I was a pretty good driver in those days.

At the very least, I'd been told, the gypsies would rob you. That's probably all that would have happened, although they'd been known to hurt people or even kill them. *That* wasn't in my schedule.

We got to Barcelona and stayed at this nice hotel, which didn't cost anything in those days. I said, "Joan, while you get fixed up, I'll go down to the bar and have a drink." I went down and sat next to some American who spoke perfect Spanish. In fact, I think he was with Pan American Airways. And after my second drink, all my Spanish came back to me.

I'd had four years of Spanish—two in high school and two

in college–and I thought, "Now is the time to use it." So I'm starting to *hablar español* like I was a native. Everybody in the restaurant thought that was terrific. We had a lot of fun there that night.

We stayed in Barcelona for a day or so and then we went over to Majorca, which was a beautiful, unspoiled, gorgeous place. We went back and stayed another night in Barcelona, then we got in that good old Thunderbird and shot all the way through to Wiesbaden, and I went back to work the next day. It was a great way of life. Thinking about it now, I may re-up!

I had paid $3,600 for the Thunderbird, and sold it to an Air Force major for, I think, $4,000. So that worked out pretty well. Then I bought a Mercedes 190-SL, the first of the SL series. Since I was heading back at that point, I had it shipped to me in the U.S. It was a beautiful, elegant car, but a little bit underpowered. I'd get a little embarrassed going up a hill with a Volkswagen passing me. Later on I upgraded to a Porsche, which had a little more oomph.

All during my time overseas I was thinking about the potential for Merrill Lynch. I'd explore with people–"Would you like to see Merrill Lynch in Europe, in Germany, in Frankfurt?" And the answer was always yes. The banks were really starting to grow and become powerful, both in corporate and investment banking work and with individual investors who wanted access to U.S. securities.

You could just smell the potential there. So I've always been a strong proponent of international activities on the part of Merrill Lynch, and pushed the firm in that direction when I was CEO.

I really think that living internationally is a broadening experience for young people in their twenties, or even earlier now. Not just travel, not just speaking the language, but getting involved in another society and seeing what the potential is. That's why so many years later, when Joan and I endowed the Schreyer Honors College at Penn State, we made scholarships for international study a big part of it.

So, as 1956 began winding down, Lieutenant Schreyer was ready to return to civilian life and resume his Merrill Lynch career. As it turned out, it would prove to be a rocky reentry, as my love of the international life got me on the wrong side of my old mentor, Howard Roth, which was not a place you ever wanted to be.

CHAPTER 9

Putting Down Roots

As I was leaving the Air Force and preparing to rejoin Merrill Lynch, I almost got myself into a little career crisis. I say "little" now, but at the time, it seemed anything but.

I'd gotten to know Andy McKee, the manager of the Geneva, Switzerland, office, and one day he said, "Bill, why don't you come to Geneva? You have experience in the foreign office, and you can cover Germany."

I was taken with the international life, and I thought that was a great idea.

I told him that if the firm thought it was a good idea, I'd be happy to do it, and Joan would, too.

Well, as fate goes, Andy was in New York at that time, walking the third floor of the 70 Pine Street headquarters to go see Win Smith or Mike McCarthy, and he ran into—you got it—Howard Roth. He said, "Howard, Bill Schreyer is doing such a great job, I was just going to see Win Smith about having him come to the Geneva office when he finishes his tour of duty."

"Oh, you are, huh?"

Now, Andy was just the manager of a little foreign office. Howard Roth was the powerful partner in a big office. He stormed directly to Smith and said, "McKee is coming in to see you. He's going to ask Bill Schreyer to come to Geneva. The firm's policy is very clear: You shall return to the office from whence you left."

He was pissed off. He wrote me a blistering letter about my arrogance—who did I think I was? He really let me have it. He told the boys in the office that Schreyer had become impossible. Of course, half of them were friends of mine, and they all understood that you don't cross Howard Roth.

I remember driving back to Buffalo, and I said, "Joan, I've got to tell you. I don't know what's going to happen over the next few months, but if I see that my career has been stopped at Merrill, well, we're going to have to think of something else."

Anyhow, I got back to the office, and I was suitably contrite, and I put my nose to the grindstone. Mr. Roth was a little distant for a while, but three or four months later, he asked me to be his unofficial sales manager. This gave me my first opportunity to really get involved on the leadership side, in management. It was a job without extra pay, but the way he compensated me was by turning over three of the biggest accounts in the office, who had been clients of his.

So the relationship got back on track, and it was absolutely the best thing that could have happened to me. Going back to Buffalo was the right decision, and I continued to get tremendous experience working with Roth. Our relationship remained a strong one right up until I succeeded him as office manager, which he couldn't have been happier about.

I was fortunate to have mentors in my life—people like my father, and Howard Roth. If you're open to it, you can learn an awful lot from people like that. But there are always times when you need to assert your independence, to be your own person. When the opportunity arose in 1962 to go into management training, it was one of those times for me.

Howard supported my desire to go into management

training. It was in his interest to have me stay in Buffalo, but clearly it was in my interest to go into training. I wanted his blessing, and the fact that he gave it to me is another reason I revere him. I was accepted into the program after a number of tough interviews. In June of 1962, Joan and I headed to New York City. The program involved acting as manager in various offices. For me, it was Garden City, Long Island, and the old Church Street office in Brooklyn, which had one of the toughest client bases in the world—all speculative, alley-trading types. *Day trading* is the term in use today.

This was right after the market crash that had occurred in 1962, provoked when President Kennedy threatened the steel industry with price controls, and the clients weren't doing all that well. I remember the first day I was there in Brooklyn, sitting in for the manager who had become ill—probably, as I think back on it now, from too much stress. I was handling customer complaints, and one customer came in after another. Finally this little old lady came in complaining about the value of the stocks in her account.

"Ma'am," I said, "you need to take a long-term view," but before I could go any further, she cut me off.

"Mr. Schreyer, I don't think you understand us too well here in Flatbush. Anything over fifteen minutes is long term."

At around three in the afternoon the office would empty out; that's when everyone would get on the bus to go to the track for some serious betting. As I said, that was a speculative-minded crowd we had in that office. I've often thought that we should have kept that office open to act as a training shop for future managers. It was there that I first met Eddie Goldberg—he was a young man clerking at the time. He came to work for me when I took over the Metropolitan Region and did a great job. And later he ended up running operations and technology for the entire firm during and after the years I was CEO.

The management training program could last anywhere

from three to eighteen months. You acted as a trouble shooter, visiting different offices. I was visiting the Boston office when I got called back for a permanent assignment. My first job as a manager was going to be in Trenton, New Jersey. I came back and told Joan we were headed to Trenton, and her first reaction was, "What did you do wrong?" We were living downtown in a nice apartment house at 11 Fifth Avenue, and we kind of liked New York. Trenton at that time didn't sound like the most wonderful assignment in the world.

Trenton—then and today—was a pretty tough town to live in. The two most desirable suburbs seemed to be Yardley, Pennsylvania, across the river in Bucks County, and Princeton, New Jersey, which was not really a suburb, but a small town in its own right. We chose Princeton because we fell in love with the place instantly. It was about a twenty-five-minute commute to the office.

We really couldn't afford to buy anything—Princeton was expensive then, just as it is now—so we rented a beautiful house from an executive of the Laidlaw brokerage firm, who lived out in the country on a farm and had bought this house in town for future use. We figured we'd rent for a period of time until we found a house we liked and could afford.

Joan arrived, and it didn't take more than a week for her to get the house in order, get all settled in. At that time we were in the process of adopting Drue. I'll never forget coming home one night, and as soon as I walked in that back door from the garage, I could tell there was a certain tension in the air. So I poured myself a little cocktail—it was Friday night, after all—poured Joan one, too. I figured I might as well get things out into the open. I said, "Well, it's pretty obvious that you're feeling sorry for yourself. What's the problem?"

That did it. She unloaded on me, "We've been here for over a week, I've settled the house, we don't know anybody, I don't know how I can get to know anybody, I've got nothing to do."

I said, "Well, why don't we have a little cocktail party?"
She said, "We don't know anybody."

"Simple," I said. "We can invite the garbageman, the postman, the man we buy liquor from downtown. We can have all the vendors here and have a hell of a time."

She gave me such a dirty look and said, "You so-and-so." But she had to laugh, and soon afterward we joined the Springdale Country Club and got involved in various social activities in Princeton. We thoroughly loved it, as we would for many years to come, right up to today. We didn't know it then, but we were putting down roots in a place that would be our home—except for a few years back in Buffalo—for nearly the next fifty years.

The Trenton office had about thirteen or fourteen brokers in it. The manager I succeeded was a fellow named Jack Loughlin. He was a very aggressive guy, a great salesman, but he didn't worry too much about Reg-T violations, extensions, errors. My instructions were to tighten up on the compliance while making sure that the sales continued to increase—in the right way.

John J. Loughlin was one of Merrill Lynch's classic Irishmen. I remember he had invited us over to his house for cocktails one Saturday when, just by coincidence, that afternoon Penn State had beaten Notre Dame. He opened the door and I said, "Well, Jack, Penn State sure kicked the shit out of Holy Mother Church today, didn't we?"

He laughed and said, "You're bad, Bill. You're bad."

I laughed, too, and told him, "You've got to feel good about that."

Jack loved Sea Island, Georgia. Years later, when I had moved up in management, I saw him after Mass one day and he said, "I understand the office next to Sea Island has opened up. I've got to have that office."

I knew that we had just tentatively selected someone for that post, but I said, "Let's see what we can do, Jack." He got that office. He did a good job down there and then he retired.

Right after I got to Trenton, we moved from an old building downtown to a beautiful new office out on State Street. This was the first office that I had all on my own as a manager. In short order I met all of the financial advisors—"account executives," we called them then.

Like so many other times in my life, I was well served by following my father's advice. He once said to me, "If you're ever lucky enough to get your first management assignment, for the first six months, don't do anything. Don't go shifting people around. Get to know the people well, and make your own judgments in a very thorough way. Then do whatever you think you need to do."

Often I've seen a new manager who thinks he's got to change everything right away. It's funny how the guy you succeeded wasn't as good as he ought to have been, or as good as you are. But I followed my dad's advice, and it worked pretty well.

The top producer in Trenton was a guy named Alex Rubin. I went around to meet him as he was unpacking his boxes in the new office. He gave me sort of a limp handshake and said, "New manager, huh. I've seen managers come, and I've seen managers go."

For weeks he'd come in, say "Good morning," and keep on walking. Some days I didn't even get a "Good morning." Then, one particular Tuesday night, I was working a little late. Alex stuck his head in the door and said, "Hey, boss, you working tonight?"

When he said, "Hey, boss," I knew I was home free.

I said, "Yeah, I plan to stay to do a little work."

"Do you want to have a little supper across the street when you're done?"

"Sure, I'll call Joan and let her know."

"That would be great," he said.

I called Joan and said, "Mission accomplished!"

Alex and I became great friends. He was always a guy you could count on. He was never, ever a problem. A great producer and a good man.

I'm not sure exactly what broke the ice with him. Maybe it was the fact that my management style was so different from Jack Loughlin's. Jack was tough and controlling; wanted his people to sell this, buy that, do it his way. I let Alex run his own book his own way, because he was so successful.

I ran the Trenton office for two years—from 1963 to 1965. At home, I was learning how to be a father to our new infant daughter, Drue. There were some things about that experience that I just never could get used to. The first morning after the day we brought her home, I went into the little room where she was being taken care of, to try to act like a helpful father. I took one look at what was going on and my eyes filled with water. Not out of joy—but from the changing-of-the-diaper routine. I fled down the front stairs, gasping for breath, and ran outside. That was about the closest I ever came to that experience—except for one other time, which I remember vividly to this day. It was the time that Ed Moriarty came over and saved me.

That day, Joan and the lady who was the godmother and nurse to Drue were heading downtown in Princeton to do a little shopping. Joan said, "Bill, the baby's just been changed. Everything is fine, don't worry about a thing." Right about then, Ed, one of my colleagues at Merrill Lynch who lived nearby, pulled up and came in for a visit. A little while later, we poured ourselves a drink. Then, of course, the baby started to cry, and I said, "Ed, what do we do now?"

"Aw, come on, nothing to it," he said. So we went upstairs, and I watched him change the baby. He was my hero. After he had a bunch of kids himself, several years later, his wife, Ginny, told me that was the first time he had ever changed a baby. Never told me that, the bastard. It was a different age in those days, a different age. And thank God for that! With Joan and me, the philosophy of "You run the house and I'll run the office" has always worked out successfully.

Ed Moriarty succeeded me as the manager in Trenton. For a while, we were great friends. He was one of the best and most effective office managers I've ever known. He had patience and persistence, and he treated all employees equally, whether it be the margin clerk or the biggest producer. He ran the "SD" office—our biggest—the flagship office in lower Manhattan.

Then he ran the municipal bond department, did that very well. When I became president of the company, I asked him to consider running the Capital Markets division, and of course he accepted. That's where he started to have problems. The investment bankers just didn't have confidence in him. He didn't seem to enjoy their company, either. Let's face it, a lot of people don't like investment bankers when you get right down to it.

One of the toughest things I ever had to do was tell him I was going to have to take him out of that job. He couldn't believe it. He said, "What am I going to tell my son?"

I said, "Gee, just tell him that you have a new position, that's all." But it really bothered him, and until the day he died, he avoided me. I felt bad about that—we had been close friends—but I had to do what I felt was right for the organization.

Another great Merrill Lynch friend during those years was Eddie Weizer, who ran the Newark office. His was the bigger office, so we'd compete a little bit, but it was all in good fun. He and his wife became great friends of Joan and mine; they loved to drink, raise a little hell and have fun. They were loyal supporters of mine as I rose in the Merrill Lynch hierarchy.

In 1965 I got the word that Howard Roth was planning to step down as manager, and that based on my successful performance in Trenton, I would be offered the opportunity to succeed him as the manager in Buffalo. It wasn't something I'd been actively pursuing, but of course we leapt at the chance. It was a much bigger office, and we had so many great friends and family to return to in Buffalo.

I have always believed that when you get an assignment, your vision should be sort of like the headlights on a car: Put on the low beams and drive. But once in a while, flash the high beams on and see what's out there up ahead. Then put the low beams back on and get back to work, get back to concentrating on driving the car.

And so we returned once again to Buffalo, where we spent another four happy and satisfying years, until I flicked on the high beams, and duty and destiny called me back to headquarters in New York City.

Leaving Buffalo for a second time was really tough, but back in Princeton again, we reconnected with a group of friends who have enriched our lives for close to four decades now. People like Mike and Liz Fernandez, whom we've known for twenty-five years. They're traveling friends, both Canadians. Mike worked for Carter-Wallace and we met them through the Sanderses. Liz is an author—she writes racy, provocative books—and they're just fun to be with.

Charlie and Daphne Townsend are also great friends. Charlie used to be with Morgan Stanley, and he and Daphne married after each had lost their first spouse. Louise Bristol and her daughter, Sarah Ritchie, are part of our crowd. Louise is a great tennis player and was one of our sponsors for getting into the Bay Head Yacht Club. Ed and Lady Ramsdell are also great friends from the Jersey Shore; we bought the land for our beach house from them. Jim and Nancye Fitzpatrick are also a great couple to be with. Jim's very much an intellectual, a money manager, and he serves on the external advisory board of the Schreyer Honors College.

Part of the gang that always comes over on Christmas Eve are Jim and Ann Love, who've been old friends for years.

Jim was a Broadway producer and they're both fascinating people we love to spend time with, and we're close with their kids, too. Janet Gaston is an unforgettable Princeton character. We rented their house when we came here for the first time. Janet was a former Powers model; she had been picked at one time as one of the most beautiful women in the world. She loves to party and she's very funny. She lives down in Florida now, but keeps in touch with us all the time.

No accounting of our Princeton friends would be complete without Bill and Butz Noonan. Another buddy from Merrill Lynch's management training program, Bill saved me from being sent to Waco, Texas. I was up in Boston one day on business and Bill was at the home office. The Waco vacancy came up, and they tapped him. He never forgave me because—the way he told it, anyway—if I had been in New York that day, they would have sent me and not him. He kidded me about that until the day he died.

Of course, Texas didn't work out so badly for Bill because he eventually became director of the entire region. Bill was a superb after-dinner speaker—very funny and captivating. He was not a joke teller, but a story teller. He could do funny dialects and that sort of thing. It's a great skill to have when you're in a sales-oriented business.

When Drue was going to school down in Texas, Bill and Butz were like a second family to her, and when her daughter, Kelly, was born, they were like another set of grandparents. Drue spoke touchingly of those days at Bill's funeral. The Noonans moved to Princeton in the 1980s, and they also kept a home near us in Indian Wells, California. Butz remains a close friend.

I've always said that after the age of fifty, it's all a matter of maintenance, and as we've gotten older, it's no surprise that a number of our friends happen to be maintenance specialists, otherwise known as doctors. People like Dr. John Shelmet and Dr. Michael Ruddy, whom we first met courtesy of this or that ailment, and who since have become personal friends. Another distinguished physician is Dr. Kenny Goldblatt, Joan's personal doctor for over twenty years, who, with his wife, Ellen, have also become great friends. A son, Aaron, and a daughter, Ariel, both attended the Schreyer Honors College. I'm happy that all concerned seem to be very pleased with the results.

CHAPTER 10

Moving Up the Ladder

❈

It was the late summer of 1968. I was sitting in my office in Buffalo, which was decorated with elegant furniture we had purchased—well within the allowable budget, I might add—from a major client. I looked out onto a beautiful view of Lake Erie, but I might as well have been sitting on top of the world.

I had achieved one of my career dreams, which was succeeding my old boss and mentor, Howard Roth, as office manager. I loved Buffalo. I had married a Buffalo girl, belonged to all the right Buffalo clubs, had a circle of wonderful friends, and business was going well. I enjoyed life there immensely.

Then the phone rang. It was John Fitzgerald, assistant to Donald T. Regan, the man who, at the age forty-nine, had just been named president of the company. Before that, John had been assistant to Don's predecessor, Mike McCarthy. In those days we were still organized as a partnership structure, with a minimum of bureaucracy, and the branch office managers still reported directly to the president. Of course, someone actually had to do the work, and that fell to John Fitzgerald.

Being anyone's assistant – particularly if that person is heading a large firm like Merrill Lynch–is a difficult job, to say the least, but John Fitzgerald did it in such a smooth and effective way. You never realized the power he had in that position because he never held it in your face. He did a superb job of dealing with all the various managers' problems, or their personal egos, or whatever came up whenever it was necessary. When I was manager in Buffalo, I didn't call Mike McCarthy, I called John Fitzgerald. We had a lot of assistants to the chairmen and presidents over the years, but nobody ever did it better than John.

He got to the point quickly in his phone call. "This is what we're in the process of doing," he said. "Don wants to regionalize the management structure, and we'd like you to come to New York City as a regional liaison officer."

"Let me think about it," I said. The memory of my father's words kept ringing in my ears: *If New York leaves me alone, I'll leave them alone.*

A few days later Don Regan called. I said, "Don, here I am sitting in my office looking out at a beautiful view. I've got a great office going. Good lifestyle. A lot of friends."

He listened to all that, then simply said, "I'd appreciate it if you'd do it."

It wasn't quite that he expected me to do it. Unlike many things that would follow, if I truly didn't want to do it and felt I couldn't, he would have respected that. I said, "Well, I'll think about it over the weekend and I'll call you."

As I thought it over, another factor was weighing on my mind. About a year earlier, I had found out I had a heart problem. I was starting to get chest pains, and I discovered that one of my two major arteries was going, very slowly. My doctor in Buffalo sent me down to Boston, where a cardiologist he had the highest respect for did the exam. The exam showed that the artery was shutting very slowly—a process that probably had begun when I was a kid. But there had been no heart attack or heart muscle damage because a collateral system was supplying enough oxygen.

They put me on beta blockers, which were just coming

out then. From 1967 to 1984, I never had a problem, never took a nitroglycerin pill. It didn't affect me at all. Just took one simple pill a day, and that was it.

My records were kept very confidential, and I was happy that nobody at the firm knew about this condition. It had no effect on my work, so there was no reason for anyone to know. The fact is, if people think you've got some problem, you're dead from the standpoint of moving ahead. As I was considering the move to New York, my own doctor advised me not to go. "The pressure could kill you," he said. It's been a pleasure to prove him wrong these last forty years.

After all of those considerations—my health, our great life in Buffalo, my father's aversion to the home office—I concluded that there were a lot of reasons why I shouldn't go. But then you start thinking about the other side of it—about shooting for the stars. You say to yourself, "God, if I don't, I'll never know where it might have ended." I mean, if you don't take a shot at it, you might never get another one. Then you'll second-guess yourself for the rest of your life.

So I said yes to the New York job.

Looking back on it all these years later, I realize there was one step I overlooked. I should have checked the definition of the word *liaison* before I agreed to the job. It must be Greek for "no real authority."

So, from my beautiful and spacious office in Buffalo I found myself relocated into cramped quarters at our headquarters at 70 Pine Street, where I had started out twenty years earlier as a trainee. John Fitzgerald said, "Oh, we have to get you an office," and they gave me one of the smallest offices I'd ever seen. I think we had orange crates for desks for a couple of weeks.

They had organized the liaison officers by region. I had the Northeast, which included Buffalo. Since we had no real line authority, it took a bit of missionary work to be effective in this role. If you called the manager of a smaller office, you got a lot of respect and attention. If you called, let's say, the manager in Philadelphia or Boston, you got patience at best, but they let you know you were not the boss. So it took handling people in a slightly different way—it took the power of persuasion—to get the job done.

The next step in Regan's regionalization plan was to reorganize by function, so that there were sales directors, who were responsible for bringing in the business, and service directors, who were responsible for processing it once it was in the door. I was on the sales side. Don had very cleverly brought in powerful partners from the branch system to make this work, people like John Orr, the head of the Chicago office, Dick Kent, head of the Detroit office, and David Harris out of Atlanta. John Orr was made executive vice president of sales. Harris reported to him as a group VP, and, as a regional sales director, I reported to Harris.

Because of how heavily concentrated the Northeast was, I strongly recommended that they carve out a new region—to be called the Metropolitan Region—which would include the New York City offices, Brooklyn, Long Island, up to Stamford, Connecticut. We had many customers in this area but the offices had a lot of problems. They were overloaded, we had opened too many of them, they had very little to do with one another, and they didn't receive much direction from above. They were really competing with one another instead of working together.

My bosses listened to my reasoning and said, "OK, if we do this, do you want to be regional director?"

I said, "I'll take it. I think it'll be a great job." I saw it as an opportunity to make an impact. They expected Philadelphia and Boston to perform well, but if we could straighten out the problems in the Metropolitan Region, improve compliance and things like that, it would be an opportunity to prove myself and rise above the rest of the crowd.

I also negotiated with them. I said, "Where do you have Puerto Rico?"

"Probably out of Georgia," they said.

"Hell, what do they know about Puerto Ricans in Georgia? I think that ought to be part of the Metropolitan Region." So they laughed and gave it to me. It was a great place to focus some management attention around February, when I was tired of the New York City slush and subways, and wanted some sun.

I became the regional vice president of the newly created Metropolitan Region, with full line authority, in 1972. Less than a year earlier, on July 27, 1971, Merrill Lynch had become the first major Wall Street firm to become a public company and list its shares on the New York Stock Exchange. I recall the first meeting I hosted for all of the region's managers, at one of the big hotels in Midtown. It was a typical New York crowd—about 40 percent Jewish, 40 percent Irish Catholic, the rest a mix of everything else. To break the ice, I recalled the humor used by my Uncle Wilk so many years earlier.

"By the way, I just want to clear the air," I said. "I want you to know that I have nothing against any race, creed, or color." I hesitated for a moment, then continued. "I just happen to prefer German Catholics. And if I find one more in this firm, that'll make two of us." That got a good laugh, and disarmed them all a little bit.

We set about addressing the problems in the region. We consolidated offices probably by a third, improved the quality of the managers, and got people working together. Eddie Goldberg, whom I had met when he was a young man just starting out in the Brooklyn Church Street office, came with me as operations manager, and Dan Tully ran the Stamford office—which was the best office in the region.

By virtue of my position, I was elected to the board of directors of Merrill Lynch, Pierce, Fenner & Smith, the legal entity that was our broker-dealer, in April of 1972. So I had begun my climb into the ranks of senior management. Soon I would find out the unexpected turns that this climb would take.

A year or so earlier, around the time we went public,

we had acquired C. J. Devine, which was a dealer in U.S. government bonds. Mike McCarthy had made that decision and he told me years later he thought it was one of the best acquisitions we ever made. We didn't pay them anything for it, just gave them the ability to obtain a lot of stock in Merrill Lynch. This made all of the original Devine partners wealthy men as time went on.

Acquiring C. J. Devine was an extremely important move for the firm in our evolution into the global markets power-house we would become. You see, prior to that, we used to take virtually no positions with our own capital. We were largely an agency business, buying from one party and selling to another. But if you're going to be a government bond dealer, dealing with large institutions, then you've got to be able to stand up and take large positions, committing your own capital. You have to learn to hedge, manage risk, anticipate market moves, and all that sort of thing. This was the first step in becoming a major capital markets firm.

One day in 1973 I was called into Don Regan's office. George Shinn, president at the time of Merrill Lynch & Co., Inc., the holding company, was there, along with Ned Ball, who was president of Merrill Lynch, Pierce, Fenner & Smith, and Bud Dunn, one of the old-timers from C. J. Devine who was getting ready to retire. I wondered what the devil I was being called in for.

Don got right to the point. He said they wanted me to become chairman of Merrill Lynch Government Securities, Inc., which by law needed to be a separate subsidiary from Merrill Lynch, Pierce, Fenner & Smith. I said, "God, I don't know the first thing about government bonds."

"We know that," he said—a little too quickly, I thought. "But you do know something about leading and managing people, and that's why we want you to do it."

I was flabbergasted. How do you say no to the chairman and two presidents? You don't. As we walked out of the office,

I said to Ned Ball, "Is this the right thing to do?"

He said, "The right thing is to put you in the right position."

I went home that night and told Joan the good news about the promotion. And apparently I must have been anxious and done a lot of talking in my sleep that night, because the next morning she said, "You did a lot of tossing and turning last night."

"Is that right?

"And by the way, who's this Fannie Mae?"

I laughed and said, "Well, at least I wasn't talking about Freddie Mac. There's nothing wrong with old Bill."

It was the start of an exciting time for me. I had always wanted to be chairman and CEO of something, and here I was chairman of this subsidiary dealing in government bonds. Don Regan had warned me going in, "You've got a tough group there." They were a hard-boiled bunch–scrappy, argumentative, typical bond traders with a dealer mentality. You've got to be when you spend the day fighting over a few basis points in the price of a bond. Their attitude was like my dad's about the home office: "We'll leave headquarters alone if they leave us alone." But my marching orders were to get them more integrated with the rest of the firm.

Once again I found humor a good weapon to use to disarm them. My first day there, I walked into the trading room and stood by the tape machine. One of the tougher characters, Maurice Winsky, a T-bill trader, came over to say hello and size me up.

"Top of the morning," I said. "Now, tell me something–do I have this right? As I get it with bonds, if the yields go up, that means the prices go down?"

He rolled his eyes and said, "Oh my God, what have they sent us?" Of course, he knew I was kidding, and he and his associates turned out to be a great bunch of guys. There was Bob Meyerhoff, head of sales, George Grimm–"Grim

George," I called him—who ran the long bonds, Roger Shay, and Dennis Shea, who remains a great friend to this day.

What characters they were. We'd have an executive committee meeting every Monday afternoon in my office, where they'd sit around and get into fierce debates with one another. At one point, I just wheeled my chair away from the conference table back to my desk and started doing some work.

Finally one of them noticed I had left. "What are you doing?" he asked.

"You guys don't listen to me, anyway. You sound like the Marx Brothers over there." They just laughed. But they were very talented and very competitive.

Early on they tested me a little bit. We had position limits, meaning there was a strict limit to the amount of money you could commit to any single T-bill position or trade—one billion dollars at the time.

So one day the boys came in to see me and said, "Now, tomorrow, this bill is going to come out and, if we can buy them right, we think we should go big. This looks like a slam dunk."

"We have a limit of a billion, don't we?" I said.

"Yeah, we do. We should go for..." And he held up two fingers.

"Two billion?!" That seemed like real money to me.

"You'll have to get permission from Don Regan to do it. You have to go right to Regan, that's the way he wants it."

"Well, fine."

As they walked out the door, I said, "Let me ask you something. Do you really, really think we should do this?"

"Absolutely." Then they left.

I called Don. "Don, I'll tell you the truth. I don't know whether these bastards are setting me up to lose money or testing me. I wouldn't know a Treasury bill if I tripped over the damn thing. I'm a stock and long-term-bond guy."

"They want to go for two billion? Two? Well, it's your call, kid."

I'll never forget that. *Your call, kid.*

I said, "I've only known them for a couple of weeks, but they seem like they're serious about their business. So I'd like to request to go for two billion."

"You got it," he said.

Next I called the guys and said, "You got it." And they ended up hitting a home run. We made a ton of money on that.

Luck and timing count for a lot in life. I ran government securities during a time of declining interest rates. Bond prices kept going up, and the stock market was in the doldrums. We made more money than the broker-dealer, Merrill Lynch, Pierce, Fenner & Smith, one of those years. I kidded Roger Birk, who was president of MLPF&S at the time, "Hell, Roger, we made more money than you did."

Treasury securities were in demand, and I thought we should be selling them to banks and financial institutions internationally. Roger Shay and I took a three-week trip around the world, calling on the central banks in Europe, Saudi Arabia, and Japan, urging them to buy from us directly. It was my first taste of international business travel. I used my head, and had flowers delivered every Friday to my wife and daughter, so they knew I was thinking of them.

Our last stop was South Korea. On the way out to the airport I saw this American couple with a group of Korean kids who had been adopted by Americans. I called Joan and said, "I don't think I can pull this off, but how about me bringing one back?"

She said, "You can bring one back—go ahead. But you're waiting for the airplane. I doubt if you can do it that fast."

Of course, I was half-kidding and half-serious, but they were really precious kids. Beautiful kids.

Eddie Ryan took over government securities after I left. He was a good friend of Don Regan's from Philadelphia, and also served for a while as chief financial officer of the company. Poor Eddie Ryan. He got in there when the market was going the other way, with interest rates going up, and it was impossible to be highly profitable at that particular time. He said to me, "You sure have a great sense of timing, Schreyer."

Yeah. Luck plays a big role.

I led Merrill Lynch Government Securities from 1973 to 1976, and I learned a lot during those years—among other things, the importance of controls and limits, of having a reasonably disciplined trading strategy, and of maintaining good relationships with institutions like the Federal Reserve Board.

From experience on that side of the business, you understand a lot more about what's going on in the market. You learn the risk side—like when we'd bid for a large issue of notes or bonds at auction, get our allotment, and know we were at risk until we moved it out. That's when you have to hedge your position with derivatives and other kinds of securities. We had a few kinds of derivatives back then, but nothing like what exists today. These were lessons that would come in handy for me as the institutional and capital markets businesses began playing a bigger and bigger role in the evolving Merrill Lynch.

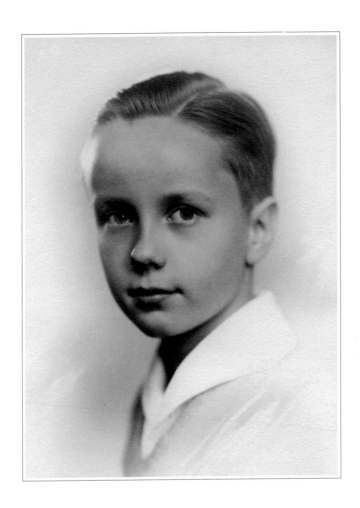

William A. Schreyer, 1940s

(*Left and Right*) Dad and me, taken in the Thirties and Forties. (*Below*) Dad, second from left, and his associates in the Merrill Lynch office, where I spent many happy hours as a boy.

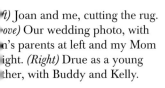

(*Left*) Joan and me, cutting the rug. (*Above*) Our wedding photo, with Joan's parents at left and my Mom at right. (*Right*) Drue as a young mother, with Buddy and Kelly.

(Above) Saturday in the Oval Office,
with President Reagan, who had just
delivered his weekly radio address,
Don Regan and Dan Tully. *(Right)*
Joan and me with "The Gipper."

(Above Left) Back in the Oval Office, this time with "41," President George H.W. Bush, Joan, and *(Below Left)* Joe and Sue Paterno. *(Above)* An audience with His Holiness, Pope John Paul II.

(Above) Joan and me at my 80th birthday brunch in Princeton with members of the Morris clan, Janelle and Mac are at center. *(Above Right)* Ruth Rempe and the Nittany Lion. *(Below Right)* Cruising with Charlie and Ann Sanders.

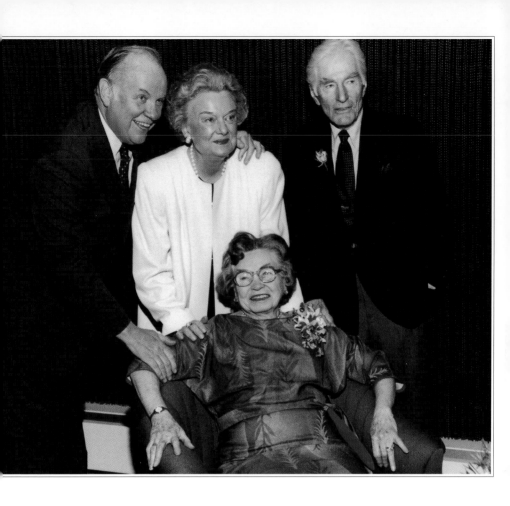

(Above Left) Joan and me with dear Buffalo
friends Claude and Tix Shuchter. *(Below Left)*
Buffalo buddies Bob and Ann Adam. *(Above)*
With Aunt Helen and my favorite uncle, Wilk.

(Above) The Fraziers, Kelly, Charlie, Drue
and Rod. *(Above Right)* Traveling in France
with the Fraziers and Bob and Sandy
Poole. *(Below Right)* "Good Scouts" Kelly
and Charlie with their proud grandparents.

"Still crazy after all these years!"

"Get It Together, Kid":
The Formation of Capital Markets

⊛

Merrill Lynch had become a public company in the summer of 1971. By 1976, five years later, we were organized as a holding company, Merrill Lynch & Co., Inc., with several operating subsidiaries. Don Regan was chairman and CEO of Merrill Lynch & Co., Inc., and he also maintained the chairmanship of what was by far the largest operating subsidiary, our broker-dealer, Merrill Lynch, Pierce, Fenner & Smith—MLPF&S for short.

Within the senior management structure, Roger Birk was president of MLPF&S, and George Shinn was president of the holding company. Both Roger and I, in my role running government securities, reported to Shinn.

George Shinn never did get along with Don Regan, so before long he quit and went to First Boston to become their CEO. Roger Birk was named president of the holding company, and Tom Cassady took over Roger's job as president of MLPF&S. I reported to Tom in the next role I undertook after government securities, as did Alan Shure, EVP of operations, and Ross Kenzie, EVP of all sales. Kenzie would become my major rival for leadership of the company.

In 1976 Regan asked me to become executive vice president of Capital Markets. At the time that consisted of a few but not all of our institutional businesses–investment banking, corporate finance, and the municipal bond area, but that was about it. When he gave me the job, Regan said, "Look, we've never gotten our capital markets act together. Get it together, kid, and run it as it should be done." I didn't particularly like being called "kid," but I saw that this would be an important next step for me. If I did it right, there would be an opportunity to make a difference that would really be noticed.

Capital Markets was structured as part of MLPF&S, and it was apparent right from the start that the thing was not organized properly. While I was supposed to be running Capital Markets, I didn't even have line authority over important parts of the business such as institutional sales.

As I thought about it, it became clear that if we were going to successfully target the institutional client, then I should have the weapons to do that. This would mean an organization that combined government securities, institutional sales, research, trading, investment banking, and the institutional aspects of our real estate business and of Merrill Lynch International. In short, it would involve a major change in the way we were organized, and in any large organization, whenever you start talking about major structural change, turf battles come to the fore. Too, there are always strong arguments to maintain the status quo.

I started working on an approach, getting a few close associates involved in the process. We came up with what I thought was a genius master plan–one that would pull together all of our institutional businesses into a single group. In essence, this plan would split Merrill Lynch into two companies under the holding company umbrella, one serving the institutional markets, and one serving the retail–or individual investor–markets. I knew it would be controversial, but I thought we would have a chance of succeeding if I could get my friend Harry Anderson to support it. Harry was vice chairman of the board, a longtime member of executive management, and he had a close relationship with Don Regan.

I had lunch with Harry one Friday to present my reasoning behind the idea and let him know in advance what was coming, before I circulated the plan to everybody concerned. Harry showed a lot of interest, saw exciting possibilities, and said he'd talk to Don Regan about it. What I had failed to calculate was that Harry himself wasn't sure where he'd fit into the whole picture. He did talk to Regan, but not in the way I had hoped.

Regan was very open and very fair in how he handled it. He said, "We'll have a meeting. In fact, we'll do it out of the building." Roger Birk chaired it, and we met at the Downtown Association, a dining club located near Wall Street, for a breakfast session that I will never forget. I felt I was in the middle of a Polish firing squad. That's when everyone stands in a circle facing inward, then shoots.

Literally only one person supported the plan, Tom Christie, who, with his background in investment banking, saw the wisdom of what I was proposing. Everybody else was opposed to it because it would have taken something away from somebody. In fairness, there were legitimate questions, too.

Don Regan was decisive. He said, "We're not going to do it." He later told me that it was the right idea, but its time had not yet come. And he warned me: When you do do it, be very, very careful that you don't allow an "us versus them" mentality to develop, with the two sides of the company losing a sense of cooperation and coordination. It was a wise admonition on his part.

So we weren't going to create a separate capital markets entity—at least not yet. But my problem remained. Here's how I stated it in a history of the company, *A Legacy of Leadership*, that was published in 1985:

Merrill Lynch had all the key ingredients for institutional service in place—an institutional sales force, research, a trading desk that could effectively handle large blocks of stock. But as we were then set up, each of these functions reported to a different individual in a different part of the organization.

We focused on our product rather than on our client. We tended not to look at the institution as a whole—and so recognized neither its manifold and often interrelated needs, nor the total profit potential we could recognize from filling them. It seemed quite clear to me that we could improve our aggregate performance with a more coordinated approach.

So my dilemma was this: If I couldn't change the structure of the company, how was I going to "get it together, kid," and accomplish a more coordinated capital markets organization? My solution lay in, for want of a better term, the volunteer confederacy I was somehow persuasive enough to bring about. It had started with a weekly Capital Markets Group breakfast I'd begun even before I put forward my ill-fated master plan. Everyone who ran one of the institutional businesses—about two dozen in all—would get together once a week, whether they reported to me or not (and most of them didn't).

We met every Tuesday morning in the old executive dining room, starting at eight o'clock and wrapping things up by nine or nine-fifteen. I had a breakfast buffet put out, and we'd go around the room and everyone would give a report on what was going on in their areas. Suddenly people were discovering ways they could work together and support one another. While it was not the formal structure I had sought, it did serve over time as a way to bring some cohesiveness to our institutional efforts.

These efforts got an exponential boost in April 1978, when Merrill Lynch acquired White, Weld & Company. White Weld was a midsized securities company chaired by a Wall Street blue blood by the name of Paul Hallingby Jr. It had about five hundred securities salesmen, but its real crown jewel was its investment banking operation. It was also starved for capital and struggling for survival.

Since I was heading the Capital Markets Group, it was my job to lead the integration of White Weld into Merrill Lynch along with Ross Kenzie, who was the head of all sales at that time. If my memory serves me, we were closing the deal on a Friday night and we were discussing what to name the merged business. Hallingby was standing there and he said, "I wish there was some way we could get White Weld on there." I suggested the name Merrill Lynch White Weld Capital Markets Group, and it was all done in about eight seconds. It had big psychological value for the White Weld people, so it made sense to keep the name, just as it made sense to drop it a short time after. It was too long a name, anyhow.

The merger with Merrill Lynch took most of the White Weld people by surprise, and we lost a lot of them. I worked hard at making sure we kept the right people–people like Steve Hammerman, who later became our general counsel and vice chairman, and Jerry Kenney, a smart research analyst who ran Capital Markets for us for a while and became our chief strategist.

In contrast, when Ross Kenzie went off to run White Weld's branch offices, it was like MacArthur coming ashore, or General Patton charging across Europe. We did not retain the best producers White Weld had. They didn't want to work for Merrill Lynch in the first place, and they certainly didn't want to work for a General MacArthur, someone who ruled by fear and intimidation. My style was 180 degrees opposite his.

While Ross was somewhat younger than me, our careers had followed similar paths. I first met him when I was in management training and went to Boston, and I heard he was a big producer, a hotshot. I went to the Trenton office, and he went into management training. They sent him to the Akron office–Akron and Trenton were about the same size. We sort of competed in terms of offices. I went to Buffalo, he went to Cleveland. When I went to government securities, he took my place in the Metropolitan Region.

Kenzie was a West Point graduate. He and Don Regan had certain similarities, but Ross did not have Don's quick wit or sense of humor. It was a heavier kind of atmosphere with him. When he was head of sales, he'd put out big, thick books about all of his accomplishments. I'd put out a little report, two pages or something, and whenever I got his book, I'd throw it in the wastebasket. I was doing my job in capital markets, and I didn't want to even be annoyed by whatever it was he was doing. He could be very caring of people, but he could also be too tough on them.

After Regan picked me in 1978 to succeed the retiring Tom Cassady as president of MLPF&S, I happened to be back in Buffalo one day for a golf outing and to see old friends, and I ran into two guys I knew who were on the board of the Buffalo Savings Bank, where Joan's father used to be an employee many years earlier. They said they were looking for a new president, and I said, "Geez, I got a guy who would be just great for you. His name is Ross Kenzie. I know the Buffalo Savings Bank, and I know what he's very good at. Matter of fact, he's just as big a bastard as you two guys are, so I think you'd get along very well!"

When the trustees at the bank were checking out Ross's references, they called Don Regan. I heard this later from one of the guys up there. They asked, "Why did you pick Schreyer over Kenzie?"

Don simply said, "I wanted an Omar Bradley, not a General Patton. I needed someone who could lead and bring people together." He told the press that one reason I got the MLPF&S presidency was the successful integration of White Weld into the Capital Markets Group with a minimum of disturbance.

Regan had begun to rely on me for a lot of details on the capital markets side. One day he received a call from Pete Peterson, who was running Lehman Brothers at the time. Peterson had been commerce secretary for President Nixon and had quite a healthy opinion of himself. I don't mean to suggest he was pompous, but if you ever do look that word up in the dictionary, you'll find his picture right next to it.

Anyway, Peterson called Regan one day about something or other, and Regan didn't feel like dealing with it. He said, "Schreyer, call him back." So I went out and returned the call, but Peterson wouldn't talk to me. Great men talk only to great men, of course.

A short time later Regan said, "Did you get ahold of Peterson?" I shook my head, and he thought I meant I hadn't called him. He chewed me out in front of everybody.

So now I'm mad. I went out and called Peterson again and he still wasn't available to talk to me. I said, "Well, if somebody wants to talk to me for Mr. Peterson, tell him Mr. Regan is not going to talk and I'll talk to the next guy, and that's it."

The second-in-command at Lehman was Lew Glucksman, one of the legendary Wall Street traders. So Glucksman called and started giving me hell for something we had done, something they were upset about. I had never met the man, and he really let me have it. He was known for his colorful four-letter words.

Finally I said, "Are you through?"

He said, "Yes, that's it."

I said, "Go f– yourself."

He hung up and later I was told he said to somebody, "That guy Schreyer's all right. He speaks my language."

(Later, in the 1980s, Peterson and Glucksman had a famous falling-out that led to Lehman's being sold to American Express. It was another Wall Street merger that just didn't work. Lehman was spun off again less than a decade later and did pretty well for a while as an independent company–big in fixed-income trading–until it fell victim to the credit crisis in 2008.)

✸

I learned of my next assignment just a few months after the White Weld acquisition. It was July 1978. We were getting ready for the fall planning and budgeting, and I was working on a bunch of drafts with my guys up at the Essex House, where Merrill Lynch had a corporate apartment. With the White Weld investment banking heft behind us, I was going to hit them hard again with my plan to create a formal, separate Capital Markets Group.

While we were up there, I got a phone call from Tom Cassady asking me to come downtown, about one-thirty or so. It sounded routine, no big deal. Our headquarters were now at One Liberty Plaza–the old U.S. Steel Building, just to the east of the World Trade Center complex and its twin towers. I got there, and Regan told me I was going to take Tom's place as president of what was by far the largest operating subsidary of the company. He said, "You can't tell anybody except your wife," and that it was going to be presented to the board the following Monday.

Obviously I was excited about it. Going back uptown, I knew I couldn't tell my colleagues about it, so I just said, "On reflection, maybe we ought to soft-pedal this proposal to split into the Capital Markets Group. Maybe it's too early to take another run at this. Let's just say that it makes some sense to consider doing this."

When they found out the following week, after the announcement was made, I said, "Now you know why I told you to soft-pedal it." In my tried-and-true fashion, I kept things the way they were for a while, not making a lot of changes right away, until I got the feel of things. And, of course, eventually we did create a separate Capital Markets Group, because it was the right thing to do.

I was fifty years old at the time. Roger Birk was two years younger, and Regan was nine years older. I went around to shake hands after my appointment was announced, and old Ross Kenzie just said, "Well, I'm really shocked. I can't believe you got this job and I didn't. I don't think it's going to work, Willie."

I said, "Ross, I'll tell you what. Let's give it a shot for six months, and after that we'll both know whether it's going to work out or not. I'll do my best to work with you."

But he knew he had gone about as far up in the company as he was going to go. After that six-month period, I called him up to the Essex House to tell him why we were going to take him out of his job as EVP for sales. He said, "Do you think you're going to fire me?"

"I'm not firing you from the firm, but I'm taking you out of this job."

"I'll be damned," he said. "I'm not surprised you did it, but I'm surprised Regan and Birk let you get away with it."

I assured him that both men were 100 percent behind the decision, and said, "You haven't heard a word I said all morning about what the problems and concerns are." And he hadn't. He wasn't listening.

We finished, and he said, "You cut the pie like a war. You won and I lost. That's it, I can accept that."

I said, "Do you want to take the rest of the day off, go home and tell your wife?"

"No, I'm a big boy."

I guess he called his wife and said very bluntly, "Bill Schreyer fired me today, I'll see you at dinner." That's the kind of guy he was.

He did end up running the bank in Buffalo, and having a very good, successful life. I saw him a few times after he retired, and I enjoyed catching up with him. It was never anything personal.

Looking back on that period of my career, I can say that

the most satisfying part was the leadership role I was able to play in the formation of our great Capital Markets franchise. I remember that early on in that process, I had a conversation with John Whitehead, who at the time served as a co-head of Goldman Sachs. (Later he became an undersecretary of state in the Reagan administration. And after 2001, he stepped back into public life to lead the authority that was created to rebuild the World Trade Center site after it was destroyed in the 9/11 terrorist attack.)

Anyway, one day he and I were at the New York Stock Exchange for some reason, and we shared a car uptown. John has always had a very clever, good, direct way of asking you a question.

He said, "From what I understand, what I'm seeing and hearing, I know you're really trying to build up your investment banking side, growing it and being more competitive."

"That's right, John," I said, waiting for what would come next from the great Goldman Sachs.

"Why don't you be satisfied with being the world's largest co-manager of deals? We'll supply the merchandise, and you'll distribute it."

"Gee, John, that wouldn't be any fun."

Years later, after I retired and he invited me to join AEA Investors, I reminded him of that conversation.

"Aren't you glad you didn't listen to me?" he said.

"I sure as hell am, John. I sure as hell am."

Merrill Lynch reported in its 2006 annual report that the capital markets businesses accounted for over $5.7 billion in pretax profits—more than twice that of the private client and asset management businesses combined.

My goal at the time was to create an investment bank that would eventually rival Goldman Sachs and Morgan Stanley, and it is especially satisfying to me that that's exactly what we did.

CHAPTER 12

Regan, Reagan, and the Hunts

❋

I had become chief executive officer of Merrill Lynch, Pierce, Fenner & Smith in January 1980, reporting to Roger Birk, who was president and chief operating officer of the holding company, Merrill Lynch & Co., Inc. Roger, in turn, reported to Don Regan.

As CEO of the holding company, Regan maintained ultimate authority. He made it clear that he wanted me to run the subsidiary, MLPF&S, without him being so much involved anymore. Of course, I went right ahead and did just that, but I soon learned there were limits to Don's willingness to cede control.

We began every year with a big managers' meeting where we set out our strategy and performance objectives and gave everyone their marching orders. It was a tradition that the company follows to this day. This particular year, 1980, we were having the meeting in Palm Springs, California. We had all our top people out there a day early to rehearse our presentations, and it went very well. I thought, "God, this is going to be a dynamite meeting!"

Later in the day I made a call back to the office. My assistant, Ruth Rempe, told me that Roger Birk was on his way out to California, but he had left me one message: "If you call in, whatever you do, do not talk to Don Regan."

I said, "Well, that's ridiculous. Of course I'll talk to him. I want to let him know how great things are going. I know he'll be very pleased."

So I had Ruth switch me over to Regan's office. Betty Lehrman, his longtime, faithful, great secretary, said softly, "I don't think you want to talk to Mr. Regan."

I said, "Betty, what are you talking about? Put me through."

So she did.

"Regan," he said curtly.

"Don, I just want to tell you what a great rehearsal session we had out here, and how great things are going. This is going to be one of the great managers' meetings of all times."

Silence.

"Don," I said, "are you there?"

"Yep, and frankly, I don't give a damn." Then he really unloaded on me. "What the hell do you think you're doing, you and your Gang of Four. You're trying to bypass me, cut me out of the loop, put me in isolation. And I just want you to know that I resent it."

"Don, what are you talking about? Are you kidding?"

"I'm absolutely not kidding."

Later I found out that Dakin Ferris, one of our senior executives who was running the company's real estate operation, had been standing out in Don's anteroom waiting to see him. When he heard Don going after me over the phone, he quietly went back to his office, closed up his briefcase, and went home. People just did not want to deal with Don Regan when he was in that kind of mood.

When Roger arrived in California I told him I had spoken with Don, and he said, "Geez, I wish you hadn't. He was mad at me for letting you get away with this."

"Get away with what?"

"Having this meeting without inviting him."

So that's how I learned there was a distinct limit to Don's willingness to give up control.

We had a consultant named Marty Cohen, a psychiatrist who did a lot of motivational work with our regional directors. I remember I had a confidential session with him around the time of this incident and asked about Regan. "What's wrong with this guy?"

"Well," he said, "it's not unusual. Guys start thinking about their career transitions, about retirement or whatever, and they get paranoid. They think subordinates are trying to run around or over them, push them out of the way. If a man has a reasonable ego at all, they all get that way."

Don Regan could be truly tough on you if he thought you'd made a mistake. But it was never personal, and he didn't hold a grudge. You'd see him ten minutes later and it'd be, "How ya doing, kid?" He called me "kid" his entire life.

John Whitehead from Goldman Sachs didn't get along with Don at all. He once asked me, "How could you work for a guy like that?"

Well, my view is you can work for anyone if you understand them. All I ever wanted to do was excel, and Don always motivated me to do better. For me, he was an inspirational guy, because if you could please Don Regan, you could please anybody. He didn't pass out compliments very lightly; he was tough, but fair–like Howard Roth–though more dynamic in many ways. And he always did his homework. If you submitted a plan or budget for the next year, his presentation book was always marked up, and he really grilled you about it.

I knew Don Regan almost from the first day I joined the firm. I was twenty, and he was twenty-nine at the time. The leaders of the firm back then, Charlie Merrill, Win Smith, and Mike McCarthy, recognized that they needed some younger blood. The average age of the managers was running into the sixties, and of account executives, into the fifties. So they brought in a sales promotion team, consisting of the best younger men who were doing well as producers, to go around

the country and determine what was needed in the future–
recruiting and getting the best people possible.

They were all good men, but Don Regan was clearly the
star of this group. He had been a lieutenant colonel in the
Marine Corps, led men in combat in the South Pacific, and he
was tough-minded. He was ambitious in the right sense of the
word, and when he finished the sales promotion job, they sent
him to manage the Philadelphia office. He was the guy who
all of the younger people in the firm particularly looked up to.

Don also had some qualities that weren't so admirable.
You could have a perfectly good, one-on-one conversation
with him, but if a third person was in the room, the dynamic
was entirely different. More often than not there was no
real conversation, because Don would be performing for that
other person.

He left Merrill Lynch in 1980 to become Ronald Reagan's
first treasury secretary, and in that job he helped engineer a
historic tax cut that was credited with creating much of the
economic prosperity of that time. Then, during Reagan's
second term, he switched jobs with James Baker and became
White House chief of staff. One night at a cocktail party, they
put their heads together and decided they ought to swap jobs.
The next day, I guess Baker mentioned it to Reagan, who said,
"Whatever you want to do is OK with me."

Don saw himself more as a chief of staff than as a cabinet
secretary–particularly with a man like Ronald Reagan, who
was a big-picture guy all the way. So he got in there and he was
very efficient. He ran the White House with an iron hand,
which I would think you'd have to do to have a well-functioning
White House. But it wasn't too long before he started to clash
with Nancy Reagan, and that was his downfall. Nobody got
between Ron and Nancy Reagan. It was the most dangerous
place anyone could ever be in Washington at that time.

It turned out that after Reagan nearly had been assassinated early in his presidency, Nancy feared for his life and

began consulting her Hollywood astrologer about his every movement. She would be sent a copy of the president's schedule for the following week, and she would change this or that–"No, this is a bad day," and so on. She'd change the whole thing around, and it drove Don nuts.

Finally he went in and told the president, "Look, either I'm going to be your chief of staff, or you can let Nancy be the chief of staff." And that was the beginning of the end for Don. He and the president had a good relationship, but the words "number two" were never in Don's mind. His job was to run the White House, and he was going to run the White House. The president was not good at that sort of thing, and Donny was very good at it. He was in fact the guy President Reagan needed. But even beyond his problems with Nancy Reagan, he upset too many people, and I guess Reagan got tired of defending him.

He was forced to resign in the middle of the Iran-Contra scandal. The Nancy camp accused him of basically usurping presidential power inappropriately–in essence, acting like a prime minister when in fact he was never elected to do that. He got his revenge when he wrote his memoirs and exposed the existence of the White House astrologer. That made big headlines at the time.

During his White House service, probably in 1985, Don invited Dan Tully and me to come down and visit him in Washington, and it was just like meeting up with an old friend. We were in the Oval Office. Reagan had just given his radio broadcast to the nation, which he did every Saturday at noon, and we had a nice visit with Don and the president.

Reagan loved jokes, and he said, "I've got a new joke." The top of his desk was totally clean, but he opened the center drawer, and it was a mess just like everyone else's. He said, "I don't know where I put that joke." He rummaged around and finally found it. Then he read it to us and we all laughed.

Unfortunately, I don't remember it. It was good, but not that good, obviously not that memorable.

After Don left the White House, Merrill Lynch was going through a particularly tough patch in the late 1980s, and *Fortune* magazine published a highly negative article. In it was a surprise for all of us: Don Regan was quoted saying some unkind things about current management–and I was CEO at the time! This put a strain on our relationship for a while, but remembering what my father had taught me so many years ago, I determined to handle the situation with humor.

I'd go around the country and people would ask my reaction to what Don Regan had said. "Let me put it this way," I responded. "Will Rogers was famous for saying that he never met a man he didn't like. Obviously, Will Rogers never met Don Regan."

Eventually all of that blew over and Don and I resumed our friendship, which we maintained until he died. My philosophy at this stage of my life is to put unpleasant things out of my mind as fast as I can. And the *Fortune* episode taught me something else, too. Around that time Charles Brown, the CEO of AT&T, was visiting me in my office. I tossed him the magazine and said something like, "Look at the crap they're writing about us." He read it and threw it back on the coffee table. "Don't let that get to you," he said. "If I had a dollar for every similar thing that was written about me over the years, I'd be even richer than I am today." That's good advice for any young person to remember who aspires to leadership in corporate or public life. Develop a thick skin when it comes to the press. Remember you're never as bad–or as good–as the press says you are.

By giving me a succession of leadership opportunities, in government securities, capital markets, and eventually MLPF&S, Don Regan advanced my career. I had a chance to prove myself once again during the infamous Hunt Silver Crisis.

❋

While not well remembered today, the Hunt Silver Crisis was a major, market-moving event at the time. From mid-February 1980, when the crisis began, until late March, when it ended, the Dow Jones Industrial Average lost nearly 17 percent of its value. To put that into perspective, the Dow lost only about 13 percent when Iraq invaded Kuwait in 1990, and a little over 14 percent after the terrorist attacks of 9/11.

The Hunts were billionaires—one of the wealthiest families in America—with vast holdings in real estate, oil, and other investments, which they managed from their base in Texas. They had come in to see Don about financing some of their silver transactions, and of course we and a whole lot of other firms jumped at the chance to do business and develop a relationship with the Hunts.

To make a long story short, what they tried to do was corner the silver market, trading in silver futures on margin—that is, with money they borrowed from us and others. The Federal Reserve got wind of their scheme and began cutting off their credit. Then things started to get dicey. They owed us quite a bit of money, and it wasn't at all clear they would be able to pay us back.

When we realized we had a problem, everyone was mobilized. I had just become CEO of MLPF&S, and Regan said, "You wanted the job, now you take care of this. I know you'll handle it well."

When it all first started, Herbert Hunt called and said, "I need to come to New York to see you. Can you come meet me at the Drake Hotel?"

We went to the Drake Hotel, and they were all non-drinkers. They had nice Cokes and that was it. I was there along with one of our executive vice presidents, Bob Rittereiser. The Bache people were also there, and a few other of the major players. Hunt and his people got right to the point. "The facts are we can't meet our margin calls. How are we going to handle this?"

I remember Rittereiser, who was never at a loss for words, was stuttering and silent. I just leaned back on the couch and said to myself, "Billy Boy, it's going to be a long night." The rest of our people, the Merrill Lynch crisis management team, were holed up at the Essex House. Eventually we went back there, and we called Bill Rogers over from where he lived nearby. Bill was one of our directors, a principal in the law firm of Rogers and Wells, and had been attorney general under President Eisenhower and secretary of state under President Nixon.

We stayed up until about four in the morning talking about what to do, and then decided to get some sleep. I was sharing one of the bedrooms with Ed Moriarty. From previously rooming with him, I knew that he was a very heavy snorer, so just before he went to sleep, I said, "Ed, how are you going to put your boy through college if we all go down the chute with this thing?"

He said, "You son of a bitch," but my plan worked. I kept him awake worrying so I could get to sleep before he started snoring.

The next morning we were still trying to figure out what to do, and we called an early meeting in our boardroom. Two or three of the major participants wanted to just cut the Hunts off, stop them completely from trading silver. Bill Rogers leaped in and he was quite eloquent about it: "That would be the worst thing we could do. If we just cut them off, we'll precipitate a disaster, and it will be on our hands." So we didn't do it.

A day or so later I was in my office and the phone rang. It was Regan calling from Boca Raton; he was down there for a Federal Reserve meeting, where he was giving a speech.

I picked up the phone. "How ya doing, Don?"

"Shut up and listen. The Hunts are down here but nobody knows it. Volcker has filled me in," he said, referring to Federal

Reserve Chairman Paul Volcker. "They're trying to solve their problem with Engelhardt Industries, where they owe the most money." If Engelhardt had been forced into insolvency because of its exposure to the Hunts, that would have really caused the market to collapse. But this part of the crisis was averted when the Hunts sold them some valuable property rights at a discount.

Next it was our turn. I got a call from Herbert Hunt.

"Where've you been, Herbert?" I said. "We've been trying to find you."

"I'm down here in Boca. We just worked out a little solution with Engelhardt, and you're next on the list. Could you come down to Dallas?"

"When, today?"

"No, no rush. You can come tomorrow or the next day."

So a team of us went down to Dallas—Rittereiser, Bill Rogers, a fellow named Bob Arnold, who was the company treasurer, and me. We negotiated all day with the Hunts. We were trying to get them to agree to a cross-collateralization agreement, and just to show we were serious, we started selling off their stocks and everything we had in their regular accounts to cover their margin calls.

Old Bunker Hunt said, "My, my, you sold out? Do you realize you caused a big capital gains problem?"

At one point he mentioned that he owned the Kansas City Chiefs football team. "I think I sold that, too," I told him.

Finally we reached an agreement, and Bunker Hunt took us to lunch at the Petroleum Club. He was a hell of a pleasant guy. We ended up getting plenty of collateral, and we didn't have a problem anymore. Back at the hotel we celebrated our success. It had been a very dry couple of days and Bill Rogers said, "I think you all deserve a good drink. I'll make you a martini." Bill personally made a Beefeaters martini, and it tasted very, very good.

Meanwhile, Bob Arnold went by to pick up the signed

document from Bunker; at at this point, Herbert had already signed it. Bunker came out on his porch, apparently in an old, moth-eaten bathrobe that he must have had for years, and said, "My, my, you guys are certainly jumpy." But he signed it, no problem. He was just saying, "God, you guys get so excited about these little things."

The Hunt Silver Crisis became my personal measuring stick for all the crises that followed. If it was a ten, then the mortgage-backed securities loss I talked about in the first chapter was an eleven, and the stock market crash of 1987? I'd have to call that a thirteen—my lucky number!

Had we not been able to negotiate an agreement with the Hunts, it would have been a tremendous loss for Merrill Lynch. I don't think we would have been forced into a net capital problem, but it would have been a heavy loss and of course a major embarrassment as well.

We all had a stake in emerging from this crisis with our reputations intact—no one more so than Don Regan. The 1980 presidential election was in full swing and his candidate—Ronald Reagan—was running strongly against the weak incumbent, Jimmy Carter. I knew from Bill Rogers that if Reagan was elected, Don was almost certain to go to Washington as secretary of the treasury in Reagan's cabinet.

It was right after Election Day that the call came. We were in one of our infamous budget sessions, planning for the upcoming year. Don always made a really big thing about budget presentations. He liked to break people's hearts and challenge them. We were just starting our presentation when Don got a message and left the room. He was gone a long time, twenty minutes or so, and when he came back in he was just bouncing, walking on air.

I could read him and sense what had happened. I turned and whispered to one of the executive vice presidents sitting next to me, "This is going to be a cakewalk. Don just got a call from the president-elect, who asked him to be treasury secretary." We made our presentation, Don had a few cream-puff questions, and we ended around twelve-thirty.

"Why don't you and Roger join me for lunch," he said.

He told us about his phone call, how Reagan had joked about the similarity of their names–"Regan and Reagan, that's something we'll have to straighten out." At that moment he was flying high.

"Roger," he said, "you'll become chairman and continue as president, and we'll play it out. Bill, you'll probably become president of the company, but we'll do it in steps."

Roger Birk was a couple of years younger than me, and I think Don assumed that I would retire before Roger and that someone else would be named president and ultimately Roger's successor as CEO. That was his intent, anyway, though he didn't come right out and say it. It was never his intention or desire that I would ultimately be the CEO. He thought I was good as a chief operating officer, that I had certain leadership and marketing skills, but I believe that he didn't think I was tough-minded enough to make the hard decisions on things he considered primary.

The truth is, for all of his reputation as a tough guy, Don never actually fired anybody. There's a long record of people who worked for him and didn't perform up to par, despite a whole lot of coaching and counseling.

Every CEO is faced with difficult decisions, and the longer you're in the job, the more you have to make. Regan and I served longer than most, and after I did become CEO, I certainly confronted more than my fair share of major and difficult management decisions as we steered Merrill Lynch through the eighties and nineties.

CHAPTER 13

Taking the Reins as CEO (with a Brief "Bypass")

Don Regan left for Washington in January 1981, and Roger Birk succeeded him as chairman and chief executive officer of the holding company, Merrill Lynch & Co., Inc., retaining the title of president as well. I became chairman and CEO of the main operating subsidiary, Merrill Lynch, Pierce, Fenner & Smith, and a year later, in January 1982, Roger and the board of directors made me president of Merrill Lynch & Co.

So Roger was number one and I was number two in the company, and this partnership worked for a while. We reported record earnings in 1982. Roger was extremely well-organized and focused as a business executive. When you met with him, he would always have his own little list of things he wanted you to do. I remember when he first put in a system called "management by objective." All of the senior executives had to establish specific performance objectives and write them down, and periodically do a written assessment of the progress they were making. The people who reported to them had to do likewise, and so on down the line. Those of us who came up in sales never quite got used to this more operational, detailed way of doing things.

I think Roger had really liked being chief administrative officer of a company, or chief operating officer. He liked being the number two man as opposed to the number one man. He really didn't enjoy the external aspects of being number one, and it showed. He was always second-guessing decisions that we had made.

We'd make a decision as a team, and then I'd walk back to my office at the other end of the hall from his. We had a private phone line between us, and no sooner did I get back to my office than, "ding-dong," the phone would ring.

I'd pick up the receiver. "Roger?"

"Yeah," he said. "You know that thing we just discussed? Well, let's hold off on that a little bit. Maybe we ought to rethink it."

I'd try to discuss it with him, remind him why we had decided whatever it was we'd decided, and he'd say, "Bill, you just don't understand all the problems." This would go on time and time again, and it sort of drove me nuts. Roger was just a worrier. He could find a doomsday scenario anywhere he looked.

Nothing illustrates that better than my encounter with the elevator man one day as I was leaving work.

"How was your day, Mr. Schreyer?" he asked.

"Terrific," I said. "I had just a terrific day."

"That's funny," he said. "I just took down Mr. Birk, and he said he had a terrible day. Nothing went right."

I just chuckled to myself. You see, Roger and I had been in the same meetings all day.

I'll never forget the lunch we had in December 1982. It was the Christmas season, and I wanted to go out and have a little fun. I said, "Come on, Roger. I'll take you up to the 21 Club and we'll have a drink and a nice Christmas lunch."

He started in as soon as we got there and sat down. "Next year's going to be tough, Willie. Geez, it's going to be tough."

Not exactly my idea of a festive, relaxing Christmas lunch.

155

"Jesus Christ," I said, "we're just coming off a great year!"

"Yeah, but I see all kinds of problems. This Baldwin United thing could really be a problem," he said, referring to the sponsor of some annuities we had sold that was in financial trouble.

"You might be right, Roger, but it all could wait until January 2, couldn't it?"

We both laughed, and proceeded to needle each other in a good-natured way about a bunch of different things, but Roger was serious about what a terrible year 1983 was going to be. For some reason, which I don't think even he himself was able to explain, he didn't think he was going to make it to age sixty. So at some point along the way, he made up his mind he wanted to retire early. I did nothing to discourage this course of action. In fact, I brought it to a head.

Our partnership just was not working. I do not blame Roger entirely for this—I'm sure I was as much at fault as he was. But placing blame wasn't the issue. Things had reached a point where I knew something had to happen, or the firm was just not going to get the leadership it needed. Roger and I were sort of checkmating each other—never in a personal, vitriolic way at all, but we were just not making the right things happen. He was smart as a whip, but he was much more risk-averse than I was. He was also the one who wanted to do a merger deal with Travelers Insurance. I worked hard behind the scenes to make sure that never happened because I did not believe it would take Merrill Lynch in the direction we needed to go.

Finally, on Memorial Day weekend 1983, I went to his home down in Rumson, New Jersey, to have a frank discussion of the problems as I saw them. He had just returned from a trip, and I said, "I'll take the helicopter down because we need to have a chat."

After a few pleasantries I got to the point. "It's just not working. One of us has to go. If you're the one who's going to stay, you have to make a five-year commitment, and really do the job, and pick someone you think you can work better with to get things done."

It was a gamble I was prepared to play out. I had already made up my mind that had he decided he wanted to stay, I would be gone. I was totally prepared to do something different in life—I had had some informal overtures from a competitor firm—and besides, there are a lot of worse things than retiring as the president of Merrill Lynch.

Roger's foot started to tap and he got pretty intense. He reacted calmly, though, without showing any anger or frustration.

"Do you really think so?" he said.

"I think so, Roger. I think that you should tell the board you'll step aside, that you've always wanted to have early retirement. This is my view, so you may want to get some others. You know, Steve Hammerman is an unbiased person. You should have a conversation and he'll tell you want he thinks, which is probably that for the good of the organization, you should step aside."

I wasn't sure what his reaction was going to be. But he knew there was a problem and he knew he was miserable, and Steve reinforced the idea of early retirement. We had a few more discussions, and at the June meeting, he told the board, and they accepted that he would stay on until the following year, when he was fifty-five.

The irony is that after he retired and realized he was not ill and wasn't going to die, he wanted to get back to doing something. So he became number two at Fannie Mae—one of the government-sponsored mortgage agencies—and did a terrific job as its chief operating officer. He's a broad person, and I have nothing but the highest regard for him. We maintain a friendship right up to this day. We don't see each other that much, but when we do talk, it's like we've never not known each other.

The fact that I had done the right thing by Roger and by

Merrill Lynch was driven home to me at his retirement dinner at the Links Club, when at one point his daughter came up to me and whispered into my ear, "Thank you for saving my father's life." She knew he was miserable, that he hated the job, and that it just wasn't healthy for anyone to be in this kind of situation.

Roger's decision to retire in one year was announced in July 1983. I remember the look on the faces of all the executive vice presidents as they left the boardroom–particularly Bob Rittereiser's glum look. He knew that something funny had just happened in his life. I think his desire was to keep Roger in until it was too late for me or somebody other than him to take over. He thought he was Birk's favorite, but the truth is that Roger had had reservations about Rittereiser for some time, without Bob's knowing it.

Bob believed that technology was going to be the be-all and end-all of the business. He was a great champion of a joint venture with IBM that we eventually scrapped because it wasn't going anywhere. He didn't think the retail system had a good future as a business. Instead, he believed that technology and operations would function as the bottom-line profit sector for the business, with the other sectors simply being customers of that sector. It was the tail wagging the dog.

He left the firm after I chose Dan Tully over him to be my president in 1985. On the day he told me he was leaving, I asked him where he was going.

"To be CEO of E. F. Hutton," he said.

"Bob, I'm not surprised you're leaving. I think it's the right decision for you. I'm only surprised where you're going, because I could see you going to a hundred different places, but I can't picture you going to a retail firm."

"Well, I think I can make a difference," he said. His timing could not have been worse.

He was there scarcely a year when Hutton became embroiled in a check-kiting scandal. The way they were managing their internal finances—moving money from bank to bank to capitalize on the interest float—was illegal. By the time the stock market crash of 1987 came around, Hutton was too weak to survive. They had to put themselves on the block, and one of the first calls Rittereiser made was to Dan and me.

We put a team together and looked at it pretty closely, and very quickly discovered that they had reserved nothing for future legal and regulatory exposure, which could cost them millions or even billions. So we secretly decided not to buy Hutton, but pretended we were interested in order to bid the price up for the ultimate buyer.

That buyer was American Express. Their brokerage operation was being run by a young hotshot named Peter Cohen. He was pictured on the cover of the business magazines in his suspenders, waving a big cigar, and was hailed as the new Wall Street wunderkind, outfoxing and outmaneuvering slow, dumb old Merrill Lynch.

We just waited for the chickens to come home to roost, and come home they did. The merger went very badly, they lost a lot of their best producers—many to us—and American Express was indeed faced with mounting legal and regulatory costs. Finally they unloaded the entire operation to Sandy Weill, who was on his way to creating the Citigroup financial juggernaut. Sometimes it's best to have the last laugh.

But I digress. Effective July 1, 1984, I was elected chief executive officer of Merrill Lynch by our board of directors. The top job—the job I had told old Win Smith that I wanted thirty-six years earlier—was finally mine. I was sitting on top of the world. Little did I know how radically this world was about to change.

It was later that summer, and I was out in Chicago, playing doubles tennis with a couple of very good clients who also happened to be very good tennis players. Marty Riesen, the former world doubles champion, and I were a team. Our opponents were no dummies, because they kept hitting the ball to me whenever they could. I was working harder than I'd planned on, and I started to get a few chest pains. I had been taking heart medication for a partially blocked artery for something like twenty years and never had a problem, so I just thought to myself that I was working too hard. But later that afternoon I stopped playing with Marty and just had an ordinary match with a couple of regular guys, which wasn't that tough. The pain got worse, and I recognized something was wrong.

I made an appointment at Massachusetts General Hospital, in Boston, and asked my good friend from Princeton, Dr. Charles Sanders, to come along, never letting him know that I thought there'd been a change in my heart condition. I had suggested that maybe it would be smart to have a stress test, without making a big deal out of it, and since Charlie used to run Mass General, he was able to set me up with the unit that did the stress test. As the test got under way, it didn't take me long to theorize that it was starting out pretty well. But old Charles was back there with the technician. He didn't say a word, but he knew what was going on.

After the test was over, I went to see my cardiologist, Dr. Roman DeSanctis. He knew my whole history, and when I came into his office he said, "How you doing, Bill?"

"Terrific."

"How you feeling?

"Great."

"Come on, Bill, you know there's a change."

"Yeah..."

He looked over my charts and the test results and said, "You'll have to have a bypass."

"Oh, God," I replied. "I'm in this job three weeks and there's so many things I've got to get done. How soon?"

"Well, it's not an emergency. I think at the outset you could wait a little bit, but no longer than six months. We'll monitor it very carefully, but if you wake up during the night or get any new pains, you call me right away and come right up. In the meantime, I'll talk to you once a week."

I carefully planned to have the surgery November 1, which is All Saints' Day. I thought that would be good luck. But then they postponed it until November 2, which is All Souls' Day, which I didn't think was all that good. But then I remembered that November 2 was my dad's birthday—plus, 11 plus 2 equals 13, my lucky number, which was another good omen.

From July to October, no one knew about this except Charlie Sanders, who shared the news with his wife, Ann, who kept it very quiet. I didn't even tell Joan. I didn't want to have her say, every time I grunted or groaned, "Are you all right?" Besides, there was a lot I wanted to accomplish over that four-month period. For one thing, there were some significant personnel decisions to be made. One of the most important was putting Jerry Kenney in as head of Capital Markets. He had come from White Weld and was bright as holy hell. I interviewed a lot of people from outside the organization—Jerry had recommended some of them—and there were a lot of outstanding candidates. In the end I decided to go with him, reasoning that "he's here, he's a sound part of the firm. Maybe it's a little early in his career, but we'll go with him." Jerry has had a terrific career at Merrill Lynch in a succession of roles.

In October there was a party at "21." Joe Paterno and a lot of other Penn Staters were there, plus the Texas crowd, including Charlie and Ann Sanders. Everyone was doing some jitterbugging, and at one point I cut in on Ann and said, "Ann, now we're going to dance slowly here. I've got a little chest pain."

"Oh my God," she said.

"Just relax. We'll dance slowly and the pain will go away."

The next day I thought I'd better tell Joanie. At first she was furious with me for not telling her sooner, but she understood. And as she'd always done in every crucial event in her life, she couldn't have been stronger or handled it better.

Then I said to myself, "OK, it's time to start systematically talking to other people," beginning with Roger Birk, who was still chairman of the board, and the other directors. In typical Roger fashion—he had a very dry, subtle sense of humor—he listened to my news and then said, "Goddamn it, don't you die on me, you son of a bitch."

I told him, "I'm going to try not to, because that would sure mess up my plan." The fact of the matter is that Dr. DeSanctis had given me a great deal of confidence. He told me that the bypass was a very doable thing, and that I could plan to live for many, many years, doing what I wanted with my life and working as hard as I wanted to work.

After telling Roger, I visited with each director individually, flying out to Texas to see Bryan Smith and to Chicago to see Professor Jim Lorie. They all wished me good luck and gave me total support.

Then I met with the executive vice presidents and laid out the things I wanted each of them to accomplish while I was gone. Dan Tully, who was head of marketing at the time, discussed how we would have to disclose my surgery to the shareholders as a material event.

"Let's see here, Bill," he told me. "We've worked up these drafts. The first one says, 'We are pleased to report that Mr. William Schreyer has undergone successful triple-bypass surgery at Mass General Hospital, is doing well and is expected to be back in the office in a few weeks.' Now, on the other hand, if it doesn't work out well…"

I quickly cut him off. "Let's skip that one. You can write it any goddamn way you want to, and everybody moves up one." So we had a good laugh about that.

The surgery went smoothly, without a hitch, on November 2, 1984. It was performed by Mort Buckley, the same surgeon who operated on Henry Kissinger. He was a very skillful surgeon but cold as hell, with all the charm and personality of a striped viper. I went back to see him about six months later. He looked at me and said, "You're getting fat."

I told him, "So are you, Doctor." And he was. Now the poor guy is on dialysis. Oh, what a miserable life.

Charlie Sanders was in the operating room for the whole procedure, and was able to report to Joan and Drue that things had gone well. His presence was very much appreciated by me—Charlie is a true friend—but it also gave him a joke that he has been able to use at my expense ever since. He'll say to people, "I can tell you with absolute certainty that Bill Schreyer has a heart, because I've seen it with my own eyes. It's small, black, and cold, but he does have a heart!"

Saturday, the day after the operation, I was still in intensive care in my early stages of recovery. It was a game day for Penn State, and to my great surprise and pleasure, a TV set was wheeled into my room that afternoon. The doctors had decided that as long as I didn't get too excited, I could watch the game.

Roman DeSanctis remembered it this way in a letter he later wrote me:

You had had a breathing tube in your windpipe overnight. You had been heavily sedated, and had tubes and lines coming out of everywhere—and I mean everywhere! When we finally got the tube out in the morning and I asked if we could do anything for you, you said, "Get me a television." We did, and then you proceeded to watch the Penn State-Notre Dame game. I'd never seen anything like it. Fortunately, Penn State won, or you may never have gotten through the operation!

Roman's recollection was right about every detail except one: Our opponent was Boston College, not Notre Dame. As you'd expect in Massachusetts, the nurses were all Boston College fans, so I made five-dollar bets with all of them on the outcome of the game. Then I started to have second thoughts about whether this was the smartest move. After all, if Penn State did beat BC and their star quarterback, Doug Flutie, and I was to have an emergency, well, maybe the nurses would just let me die right there in intensive care. Penn State did win the game, and for me, lying there in recovery after open-heart surgery, it was maybe the best game ever.

Notre Dame was actually the next game in that 1984 season, and they beat us badly—44 to 7. That's what I love about my world-renowned cardiologist, Dr. Roman DeSanctis —his attention to detail!

I knew I'd be out of the office for about six weeks, and I planned to recuperate for part of the time at Eldorado Country Club in Palm Desert, California. I called one of our retired partners out there, Jack DuLong, who had been the longtime resident vice president in that area, and asked him to rent me a house. I just told him I needed a place where I could have some confidential meetings, and didn't want anyone to know about it. So he handled it for me, no questions asked.

I went out to California around Thanksgiving and stayed for three weeks. The recovery program was walk, walk, and more walk. I'd get up in the morning and walk over to get the papers, then spend some time on the telephone—there was a three-hour time difference with New York. Then I'd either walk or take a nap in the afternoon, or swim in the little pool at the house.

One particular day, Joanie finally got tired of playing nursey, because there really wasn't anything to do, and she was getting a little bored. She said, "Some of the ladies have invited me to play tennis."

"Great," I said. "Go ahead. You want to leave me alone? Unattended? Fine."

So after she was gone about half an hour, I said, "To hell with her," and put on my bathing suit and went over to the main pool. There were three very attractive young gals sitting there. They kept glancing over at the scar on my chest, and down my leg. I finally got their attention while they were looking at me. I pointed to the scar and said, "Bayonet. Iwo Jima." They laughed a little, but I don't think they had ever heard of Iwo Jima. I might have gotten a bigger reaction if I had said Vietnam. So I invited them over to sit down and talk. Three beautiful girls. Then I saw Joanie walking by, headed back to the house, and called to her, "Hey, come on over and meet some of my new pals."

So it all worked out very well. Here I am laughing and reminiscing about it a quarter-century later. I got right back on schedule, and before I knew it, I was off to Japan. The young Merrill Lynch guys there said, "We can't keep up with this old bird." We'd start off with an early breakfast, which the Japanese didn't do that frequently. Then we'd have a full day of meetings and client calls, late dinners, and then go out to the Ginza bars and listen to the girls sing American songs. It was a great test, but I handled it beautifully. I think it helped my recuperation, to tell you the truth, because I was back in action and doing my thing, and it was fun.

My heart was strong again, and that was a very good thing. I would need a strong heart–and stomach–in the days ahead, as Merrill Lynch faced some of the most challenging and difficult years in its history.

CHAPTER 14

Picking the Team and Setting Our Course

As 1985 dawned and I prepared to resume my CEO duties on a full-time basis, it was becoming increasingly clear to me that we needed to make some very basic structural changes at the company. In situations where big change is required, I have found that there are things you know and therefore can act upon immediately; then there are things you might have a hunch about but don't really know, so you need more information and reflection before you can act.

The thing I knew for certain was that our costs were too high. The thing I had a hunch about was that two of our businesses—real estate and insurance—were not the right ones for us to be in. On top of this, I knew it would soon be time to select my number two—the person who would become president and chief operating officer of the company and my potential successor.

The immediate problem I was confronted with was that expenses were out of control and depressing our profits. Most of our revenues were coming from our two main business sectors—first, our traditional "retail" system of branch offices, which provided products and advice to individuals and small businesses, and second, our capital markets or "institutional" business, including trading and investment banking, which provided a range of financial services to big corporations, institutions, and governments.

Cost-cutting is never an easy or pleasant exercise in a large corporation. It requires you to eliminate certain activities, downsize departments, let people go. We had just organized the company into a two-sector structure—Consumer Markets and Capital Markets—and I needed the two to work together in some degree of harmony. That was more difficult than it might seem. An account executive sitting in Omaha didn't really understand what an investment banker did or why he was paid so much. And the enmity between bankers and traders on Wall Street was legendary—they were always vying with each other for supremacy. A major cost-cutting exercise threatened to aggravate these natural differences and even tear the place apart. I'd be refereeing contests all the time as they'd be arguing about who, what, where, and how.

My solution to this particular problem was to adopt an approach that in modern political parlance would be called "triangulation." I would bring in a third party to do the dirty work and draw all the fire; the two sides of the company would be shooting at it instead of at each other. I decided to retain the management consulting firm McKinsey and Co., because of the reputation they had for doing this sort of thing.

They came in and did a very thorough, detailed job. And the beauty of it was that instead of the capital markets side fighting the retail side, they joined each other in opposition to what they considered the common enemy, which was McKinsey. McKinsey took all the blame for causing the pain and teeing up the stuff we needed to make decisions on. They were at it about six months and they did a fine job. It wasn't hard to make the decisions they recommended, and they all played out pretty well.

The McKinsey partner who led this effort was a fellow

named Carter Bales. He knew I was going to pick a new president, and he let me know he was very interested in the job himself. This didn't surprise me, because through his work with us, he had gotten to know the firm so well. Carter was respected, if not well liked, and he was never my choice for president. But we were able to use the McKinsey process to get a difficult job done and unite the firm–the two sides marching arm in arm into the sunset. Maybe I'm exaggerating a little bit, but not much.

The McKinsey process got under way even before I left to have the bypass. After I was back on the job for about a month, I started sizing up what had happened when I was gone. Jerry Kenney was relatively new in his job as head of Capital Markets and appeared to be doing fine. I got good advice and good performance on a lot of things from people like Herb Allison, who was treasurer, and Arthur Zeikel, who ran the asset management business. I had great confidence in Arthur and his vision for that business. Steve Hammerman, the general counsel, did a superb job as sort of an informal advisor and troubleshooter.

The two guys I counted on most heavily to run the company were Bob Rittereiser and Dan Tully. Tully was doing everything I hoped he would do, but Bob had his own agenda.

It was January 1985, and I knew that by the annual shareholders' meeting that spring, I wanted to make a decision on who would be president, to coincide with Roger's retirement and my becoming chairman. I had preliminary meetings at the Essex House with all of the contenders.

Bob, who headed the financial, operations, and technology functions, was never a guy who took criticism very easily. I laid out the fact that I really didn't want a crown prince or prime minister. I said, "What you really have to do, Bob, is either do it the way I'd like to have it done, or determine what you want to do with your life somewhere else." He left there knowing that his chances of becoming president weren't very good.

Then Dan came in and I gave him a balanced report on what his business strengths were and what had disappointed me. He handled the meeting so well, but quite honestly, I don't think he was sure where he stood when he left there.

I had known Dan for a good many years, growing up in the branch office system. He had spent most of his career in Stamford, Connecticut, which was part of the Metropolitan Region, which I had headed. Having gotten to know all of our managers, I can easily say that Dan was a natural leader. So I got to know and respect him early on. He was always enthusiastic—there wasn't any problem, he felt, that couldn't be solved. And he had a great, self-deprecating sense of humor as well, which I appreciated. By early 1985, I had pretty much made up my mind that Dan was going to be my guy.

I had him come down to the house in Princeton; he didn't know why. We sat out on the terrace by the pool, and we had a long conversation about the direction of the firm and what we were going to do. At last I said, "Dan, unless you have some final objection, I think I'm going to recommend that you be president and chief operating officer."

He said, "You son of a bitch, you just had to work me over one more time, didn't you?" We both laughed and had a drink. Then he went home to tell his wife, Grace.

I had to test him a little bit, just to find out how badly he wanted the job and make one final check to confirm he was the right guy. It was a good, honest discussion, and I could tell that Dan and I had the right chemistry to be able to work together. As our partnership developed, it got to the point where he could tell by looking at me and I could tell by looking at him exactly what the other was thinking. If there was a debate going on around the table, he could just tell by my body language that I'd heard enough of this bullshit, it was time to go on to something else.

Our goals were the same, but our styles were a little different. Dan reacted quickly. Sometimes he'd react to something and then afterward think it through and come back and say, "Well, we'll moderate it a little bit." It was fun seeing Dan grow and learn, which we all had to do. Every one of us had a learning experience.

He was a hands-on guy—exactly what you wanted in a chief operating officer—and sometimes he'd get his Irish up, and there would be a little bit of a confrontation with someone. But he tempered that beautifully as time went on—didn't lose his steadfastness or determination, but just mellowed a little bit. He was not a Ross Perot type—a dictator who ruled by fear.

Dan had a great sense of humility, at least in terms of what the prospect of becoming CEO meant to him. He viewed each chairman and CEO as just part of a continuum of the history of an institution that was greater than any one individual. Even when he had record results, he was always careful to note that in ten, twenty, or one hundred years, each revenue and profit figure would have multiple zeroes behind it. In other words, don't get too full of yourself.

Nothing was more important to Dan than integrity—doing the right business in the right way—and the reputation of the firm. He spent a good bit of time re-codifying and then reinforcing the principles that had made Merrill Lynch such a special company.

I know there were probably times when Dan would have done something differently than I, but he knew how I wanted it done. We'd have some discussions privately once a decision was made, just to see if we were on the same page. But once the decision was made, he'd walk out and never second-guess it. As in any large organization, there was always somebody who was going to try to get between the two of us, but we never let it happen. We'd seen things like that happen in years gone by, and we were very sensitive to it.

With a new president and our executive team in place, it was time to set our course. Merrill Lynch was still operating under the broad strategy that had been established by Don Regan. His plan was to have a three-legged stool: the securities business, the insurance business, and the real estate business. He had a dream of the company being a financial supermarket—or at least department store—meeting all the needs of the individual investor. And—as the theory went, anyway—this diversity would help insulate our earnings from the volatility of the stock market. We wouldn't be tied so directly to the ups and downs of the Dow Jones Industrial Average.

An executive named Dakin Ferris had been appointed to run the real estate and insurance business, which would be built through acquisition. Don Regan had brought him in from Atlanta, where he had run one of our larger offices. He and I had been in the same training class, and we were sort of competitive, too.

I ended up getting the job that accounted for about 90 percent of our revenues, and Dakin was in charge of growing real estate and insurance. Just to give you a little flavor of the Regan management style, one day he, Dakin, and I were together, and he laid out his five-year plan.

"Ferris, right now you've got ten percent of the business, and Schreyer, you've got ninety percent," he said.

"That's right," we agreed.

"Your goal, Ferris, is to make sure, five years from now, you're at fifty percent. And your goal, Schreyer, is to be sure he never makes it." Dakin was pretty good at reading the tea leaves after I became CEO. We had made him a vice chairman in advance of his retirement, which happened shortly after I took over.

Later I learned of a story he liked to tell his friends. "I went in to say good-bye to Bill Schreyer," he'd say, "and told him, 'Bill, if I can ever be helpful, give you any advice, or be constructive in any way, please don't hesitate to let me know.'

"And Schreyer said to me, 'Dakin, as a matter of fact, I

want you to be my sexual advisor. In other words, whenever I want your f–ing opinion, I'll ask for it!'"

So Dakin had a sense of humor, telling that story on himself, and he was dead on about my views on his businesses. I never did care for the real estate idea. There was absolutely nothing in common between a Merrill Lynch account executive–or as they're now called, financial advisor–and the real estate agent who's going to sell a house. Real estate agents had completely different backgrounds and training–in fact, many were housewives who sold houses part-time. To me it lowered the prestige of the Merrill Lynch financial advisor.

We had built a chain of real estate brokerages by trying to buy the best residential real estate firms across the country. The first one was in Dallas. We had even bought a relocation management company–the kind of business that would go into a General Motors and help its executives relocate when they were moved around the country. We also acquired a small insurance company based in Seattle, the Family Life Insurance Co.

I felt that all of this had just overextended the company. It took time, resources, and management attention away from what we should have been focused on, which was being a world-class wealth management and investment banking powerhouse with a true international presence.

In fact, the supposed synergies between residential real estate and our branch office system just weren't there. One of the ideas was that our financial advisors would refer our clients to the real estate company. But that would only happen if they were paid for the referrals, and in most states, in order to get paid, they had to be licensed as real estate brokers. It just wasn't worth their effort.

The idea behind the relocation management company was to open doors for us in corporate executive suites–but this was a miscalculation, too. A CEO looking to do a major stock issue or a big merger or acquisition was not exactly inclined to turn to the same company the human resources department was using to relocate old Joe down the hall to Peoria. In practice, it was a detriment to us getting the prestige business.

After Dakin retired, we put David Komansky in charge of the real estate business. Dave was a kid out of the Bronx who never finished college but had made a name for himself as a broker, then in management on Long Island and in the Midwest. He had quite a reputation as a "people person."

In late 1985 or early 1986, I asked Komansky to conduct a strategic review of the real estate business, to take a good look at it and decide whether it made sense for us to stay in it.

Finally the day came when Komansky was supposed to make his report to our management committee. I think I had accelerated the timetable on him. Anyway, we had other business to conduct in the morning; he was going to present his report in the afternoon. As we were breaking for lunch, about to go our separate ways, I said to him, "Dave, I'm really looking forward to your report this afternoon. I can't wait to hear what you think we should do with this piece of crap."

David may have been planning to give a balanced report— the pros and cons, that sort of thing—but that afternoon he came pretty quickly to the point and recommended that we sell the business. I considered it a great display of wisdom and common sense on his part. In 1986 we proceeded to spin off the business, first as a limited partnership called Fine Homes International, and eventually Prudential bought the whole thing. It was a much better fit for them.

I was beginning to put my own strategic stamp on the company, and with the guidance of Tom Patrick, a brilliant investment banker out of Chicago who had done a stint as a senior executive of an insurance company, we also restructured our insurance business, though this came a bit later, after I had brought him in as our chief financial officer.

The problem with this business was that the way we were

running it, we were assuming too much risk on our own balance sheet. Also, the ROE of this business—return on equity—was well below what shareholders expected of a top-tier global investment bank. Patrick restructured the business to reduce our risk and put the emphasis on insurance products that were closely tied to the investment markets—such as variable life and variable annuities. Today insurance is just another profitable product that Merrill Lynch can offer its clients. It is not, however, one of the three pillars of our business as Don Regan had envisioned.

I made sure to keep our board of directors closely involved as we made our strategic and operational decisions. The board is a CEO's only boss; it is critical to his or her success. I could give you three different takes on boards. One is to take them as a necessary evil—tell them as little as possible, only what they absolutely have to know. A second take is at the other extreme, which is to try to make them part of your management team. The risk with that is they get into micromanaging every single decision, large or small. Most people who are experienced in being on boards don't want to do that, but it can be a temptation.

The third take is, I believe, the right one: Have a good working relationship and indeed a friendship, but not too personal, not too close. And whatever you do, keep them well-informed on the important things and don't ever let them be surprised by anything.

On our board we had the extremes, too. First of all, Bill Rogers, a great statesman and great advisor. He was a big-picture guy and gave me good advice, even before I became CEO, on such things as dealing with Don Regan: "Don't be too concerned and don't feel he's intimidating you when he gives you an order. That's just his style." And of course he always shared the experiences he had as attorney general for President Eisenhower and secretary of state for President Nixon.

The other extreme was a guy from Texas named Bryan

Smith. He was a micromanager at heart. He wanted to know every little detail. I liked old Bryan; he was colorful and outspoken, almost combative. But he'd take it just up to a point, then he'd fall back. He did a lot of good because he'd make you look at things you otherwise wouldn't have looked at because you didn't think they were important.

I've worked with some amazing board members. Here are a few who stand out:

Lou Wilson. Congressional Medal of Honor recipient and commandant of the Marine Corps. Lou was a giant of a man—physically and spiritually—with a good sense of humor and ability to understand people. We went to his funeral in 2005, and I don't think there was ever a Marine more admired or respected by his peers and all who knew him.

Jim Lorie. A professor at the University of Chicago who was an expert on the behavior of the stock market. Another big-picture guy. He never said, "I want you to do this, I urge you to do that." He'd just throw out an idea or concept and say, "This is something you might think about." He was very smart and valuable.

Jill Conway—the longest-serving director we've ever had. She was still president of Smith College when Don Regan brought her on the board, and later moved on to the faculty of MIT. She brought a vision of the workplace—of careers for women on Wall Street and at Merrill Lynch—and of socially responsible behavior. She was very supportive of management and had a good, quiet sense of humor. I always enjoyed working with Jill. She wrote a best-selling memoir about growing up under very severe conditions on a sheep farm in Australia.

Bob Hanson, the chairman of John Deere. Bob was a very practical guy. Nothing mysterious about him. He called the shots as he saw them. A good businessman—people liked and respected him. Unfortunately, he had a stroke after he retired—right on the golf course—and is doing all right but has been

175

pretty much wheelchair-bound since then. You hate to see a guy with such vigor and vitality suffer from something like that.

Charlie Sanders. Probably my best friend on the board. Ran Mass General Hospital, Bristol Myers, Glaxo Pharmaceuticals down in Raleigh. Ran unsuccessfully for the Democratic Senate nomination in North Carolina. He's such a good friend that I've even forgiven him for the fact that he's a Democrat! He's a rare doctor. I mean, doctors normally aren't great businessmen, but he's a very good businessman as well as a good athlete and a loyal, good friend. He's just an outstanding guy.

Bob Luciano. Chairman of Schering Plough. I served on his board, too. He's an outstanding gentleman, a guy with great integrity who knows business inside out. He's got a good sense of humor, loves cars, and loves to play the game of golf. Why, I can't imagine, but he does. He's become a good friend, too.

Bill Bourke of Reynolds Metals. Another colorful guy. Always outspoken, never mean spirited, just outspoken and direct. Called the shots as he saw them and he didn't worry about anybody's feelings. Let the devil take the hindmost. One night we had a little gathering at a restaurant, a half-dozen of the outside directors. Dan Tully had a little drink or two, and started to pick on Lou Wilson. Now, nobody ever got mad at Lou Wilson, but something he said made Dan mad. Bill Bourke was at the table.

Our directors' meetings were continuing the next morning, and on the way to breakfast, Dan said, "I'd better apologize to Lou."

I said, "Yeah, you probably should, but don't worry too much about it. He's seen the guys have a drink before when he was a comrade in the Marine Corps."

We got to breakfast, and before Tully could say anything, Bourke said, "I want to thank Dan Tully for providing us with so much entertainment last night." It broke up the crowd. That's the kind of guy he was. Salty and down to earth.

Earl Harbison was one of the directors who joined our

board later in my tenure as CEO. He was one of the candidates recommended by an executive search firm, and when I interviewed him, it didn't take long for me to say, "This is our kind of guy."

He had a great background; he was with a first-class company—Monsanto Chemical out of St. Louis. He started out in the CIA. I'd always kid him about being a spy and he'd just chuckle. I'd try to cross-examine him but I couldn't get a damn thing out of him about CIA activities. He had a marvelous sense of humor. He took his work very seriously, but he didn't take himself too seriously—unlike some directors who take themselves way too seriously.

He was, I think, one of our most thoughtful directors. He had a great vision and understood why we wanted to globalize and become a worldwide capital markets firm instead of being just a domestic brokerage firm. He shared that global vision. I think that came from early on in his CIA days, and then he did the same thing with Monsanto, which had become a global company itself.

Earl and his wife, Suzanne, have become very good friends of ours. We don't see a lot of each other, but we stay in touch by telephone. He invites us down to Florida every year for a visit at the lovely home he has outside of Jacksonville, and we both belong to the Skibo Castle Club. We've just become good friends, and of course, he's a good, conservative Republican as I am. In fact, we recently had fun talking over the thought of either Hillary or Obama becoming president of the United States! We're enjoying all the fun that goes with that.

So, as we closed out 1986, my first full year as CEO, I felt we had charted our course and were picking up steam. We had the right management team in place and a strong, supportive board of directors. We had fine-tuned our business strategy, the Reagan Revolution was taking hold economically, and the markets were taking off. I was feeling as hale and healthy as I ever had in my life.

There was a lot to celebrate in the New Year, 1987. On January 2, the Penn State Nittany Lions defeated the Miami Hurricanes at the Fiesta Bowl in Tempe, Arizona, to win the national championship. What a great game. Penn State stopped a late drive into the red zone by the great Miami quarterback Vinnie Testaverde, to win the game 14 to 10. The Nittany Lions were led by a talented quarterback named John Shaffer–an outstanding young man who later came to work for Merrill Lynch.

So at least as far as I was concerned, the year started out on a roll. What I did not know was that the two biggest crises of my entire business career were right around the corner: the mortgage-backed trading loss of April 1987, and just a few months later, the October 1987 stock market crash that would put Merrill Lynch and my leadership to an extreme test.

CHAPTER 15

Getting the Last Laugh

As well as we weathered the mortgage-backed trading loss and subsequent stock market crash, the fates were not particularly kind in the years that followed 1987, to Wall Street in general or Merrill Lynch in particular.

Though the Dow Jones Industrial Average regained its 1987 losses in fairly short order, individual investors remained on the sidelines, and the financial markets were plagued with a whole host of other problems. After years of over-lending for dubious commercial real estate projects, the savings and loan industry was beginning to implode and would eventually require a multibillion-dollar government bail-out.

Not unrelated was the collapse of the high-yield bond market—so-called junk bonds. Led by Drexel Burnham Lambert and its mastermind, Michael Milken, junk bonds were used to fuel a wave of corporate takeover activity in the 1980s, and as prices of this asset class started to spiral downward, Merrill Lynch was not immune to the damage.

As proud as I was of our performance during and after the events of October 1987, there was no way in hell I could be satisfied two years later with the financial results we were producing. The facts were indisputable. Between 1985 and 1989, while our competitors produced an average return on equity of 15 percent, ours lagged at 11 percent. Some of that had to do with the fact that we were making investments for the future growth of our business, but the fact of the matter was that our stock price was chronically underperforming, and as CEO, I knew I had to do something about it.

Tom Patrick, a senior Merrill Lynch investment banker who would help us restructure the company, was one of the most vocal critics of the way things were going. Every time I'd talk to him, he would challenge this or that, or ask why we weren't doing it some other way. Finally I got tired of his armchair quarterbacking and called his bluff. "If you've got so many bright ideas," I told him, "why don't you come to New York and be our chief financial officer?" To my surprise and pleasure, he accepted the offer.

I wanted Tom to replace Courtney F. Jones, whom we had recruited as CFO a few years earlier from General Motors, where he had been treasurer. Courtney was a brilliant financial executive. One of the reasons I hired him was that I wanted him to modernize all of our financial reporting systems and procedures, and he did that admirably. But Courtney was a difficult guy to work with; it was his way or no way at all. He treated people badly and was hard to get along with.

Tom Patrick rubbed a lot of people the wrong way, too, but he was tough as nails and had earned his credibility in the highly competitive corporate finance business. He was co-inventor of a zero-coupon, convertible bond that we trademarked as "LYONs," short for liquid-yield option notes. There were tax advantages for companies to raise capital using these securities, and we sold a lot of them. That's one thing that gets respect on Wall Street—the ability to make a lot of money.

With Tom on board, we quickly zeroed in on what the problems were. First and foremost, there was too much capacity—at Merrill Lynch and throughout our industry. Too many bankers, too many traders, too many brokers chasing too little opportunity. We needed to trim down, and that meant shedding people, real estate, and equipment, all of which costs money in the short run. But we had to do something. Earnings in 1988 of $460 million–on revenues approaching $10 billion–just weren't cutting it.

As we worked through the numbers, the magnitude of the problem became clear. We needed a major restructuring of the company, and that meant taking a very substantial charge against our 1989 earnings. On January 22, 1990, at the close of the market, we announced our plan: We were taking a $470 million charge against earnings as a reserve for restructuring costs. This would result in a loss for the year of $213 million.

If there is a Schreyer descendant or other curious soul reading these words a hundred years from now, you may reasonably ask, "Was this a big deal?" You bet it was a big deal! We had just reported the first loss in Merrill Lynch's eighteen-year history as a public company. There were a lot of risks involved. Clients entrusted us with their money, and there was always the possibility that they would decide en masse that they didn't want to put their hard-earned assets with a money-losing organization. We were financially strong–with unencumbered capital well in excess of any regulatory requirement–but an emotion-driven run on the bank, however remote the possibility, could have been fatal to us.

Then there were the shareholders. Would they buy our story that this restructuring would lead to substantially higher earnings over time, or would they vote with their feet and drive our stock into the ground? Ditto the bondholders. The press would be brutal, the employees angry and upset, and critics would come out of the woodwork, demanding my head.

I factored all of this into the decision to take the charge, and went ahead, anyway. I had a high level of confidence that it was the right thing to do, that it would work. And if it didn't work? I figured I would cross that bridge when I came to it. If all else failed, well, what the hell, there was always that house on the golf course in California. Maybe I could learn to like golf.

Within weeks of our announcement, the dire straits our entire industry was in claimed a major casualty. Drexel Burnham Lambert, the house that junk bonds built, declared bankruptcy, went out of business, and started liquidating itself. It turned out that Drexel had been overly dependent on short-term debt—commercial paper—to fund its operations. Every thirty days or so, its paper would mature and it would have to roll it over, or sell it anew to the same or different creditors.

There was generally very little risk in commercial paper, but as the value of Drexel's junk-bond portfolio plummeted and its genius superstar, Michael Milken, faced criminal prosecution, nobody would roll over its paper. As the end neared, its CEO made a round of desperate calls to other Wall Street houses, including Merrill Lynch, asking for credit. But no one wanted to come to the rescue of the firm that was known to have possessed the sharpest elbows of the 1980s.

Milken, who masterminded the art of corporate takeovers funded by junk bonds and made billions in the process, ended up sentenced to federal prison. The investigation that ultimately led to his downfall was sparked by Steve Hammerman's law and compliance department at Merrill Lynch, after one of our lawyers received an anonymous letter from someone in our Caracas, Venezuela, office, alleging suspicious trading in an offshore account.

Once investigated and referred to the Securities and Exchange Commission, the trading was traced to a Drexel banker named Dennis Levine. Through a circuitous route, the financial operator Ivan Boesky was implicated and, ultimately, so was Milken himself. While he was never found guilty of insider trading, Milken was ultimately convicted of market manipulation and securities fraud. I took no personal satisfaction in the downfall of Milken and his firm, and Lord knows, we lost hundreds of millions ourselves through our own exposure to junk bonds and junk loans. But in an odd and unexpected way, the destruction of Drexel Burnham Lambert validated the drastic actions we had taken to put the excesses of the 1980s behind us.

In taking the charge against earnings, I was strongly advised by the board of directors to capture everything possible and not do it in a piecemeal fashion. The worst thing for our credibility as a management would be to have to come back a year later for another bite of the apple. As I told our employees in a video broadcast, "Although no one can predict the future with one hundred percent certainty, based on the environment we envision, we've done what we need to do."

Dan Tully, Tom Patrick, and the managers under them set about implementing our cost-cutting and restructuring. Tully began a highly symbolic "red dot" campaign. He roamed the building placing red dot stickers on pieces of equipment that were "nice but not necessary" to have. The joke was that people quickly started hiding from him because they were afraid he'd put a red dot on their forehead, but the message was clear: Cost-cutting was everyone's business.

Tom Patrick and the finance staff undertook what we called a "burden of proof" review of something like fifty different business units. They were divided into three categories—those producing at least a 15 percent return on equity, those under 15 percent with little hope of ever reaching it, and those under 15 percent that, with the right changes, might realistically be expected to reach the important ROE hurdle within a foreseeable timeframe. We eliminated those businesses that could show no hope of producing a minimum acceptable return.

Around this time I was giving serious thought to fundamentally changing the structure of the company. I wanted to change the structure of two sectors: Consumer Markets, which served the individual investor or "retail" marketplace, and Capital Markets, which included all of our institutional businesses: trading, investment banking, and so on. The two sectors reported to the holding company, or "management company," as I preferred to call it, Merrill Lynch & Co., Inc.

My thought was to break down the sectors and organize them as six separate businesses, each reporting to the management company through the chief operating officer, Dan Tully. This would elevate the visibility of each of our main businesses, but I also had an ulterior motive. I said to myself, "I think Dan Tully is the right guy to take over this place when I retire, but how do I know for sure?" This new structure would give him a more complex organization to manage, and I and the board could watch how well he did it. Also, with six highly visible business heads, other potential succession candidates might surface as well.

I thought it would be best to get out of the office to talk about this, so one afternoon I took Dan over to Peter Luger's steakhouse in Brooklyn. We had a pop, and of course their great steaks and French fries, everything bad for us, and then I pulled out a piece of paper from my pocket and said, "Dan, I think we have to bite the bullet and blow out the sectors." I outlined what I had in mind and who the key players were, and I said, "You think about it."

Dan got it immediately, and shortly after that we announced our new organization. Henceforth we would be organized into six large businesses: private client (the retail business), insurance (which needed some serious fixing, so we gave it to Tom Patrick), asset management, and then our institutional businesses, equity, debt, and investment banking. Dan did a great job managing this new organization, handling the budgeting process, making difficult compensation decisions, and so on. By the time I was ready to retire, I knew he was the right guy to take over.

As 1990 progressed, it became increasingly clear to me that our restructuring would work exactly as planned. Our private client business was, and is to this day, the crown jewel of its kind on Wall Street. Merrill Lynch revolutionized the industry in 1977 when we introduced the Cash Management Account, which combined a securities brokerage account with a money market fund for cash balances, checking privileges, and a debit charge card. The first account in which clients could conveniently combine their investment and banking activity brilliantly foresaw the direction in which the personal finance industry was heading, and helped lead it there.

The CMA allowed us to gather assets from individual investors at a rate far exceeding anyone else in the industry. By the summer of 1997, less than four years after I retired, we had become the first Wall Street firm to surpass $1 trillion in client assets. John "Launny" Steffens was a visionary in designing and executing the asset-gathering strategy. He ran that business for about fourteen years, but frankly, we let him run it for far too long. As good as he was, his overly long tenure did not allow new talent to develop and rise up through the ranks, as it should have. Organizations benefit from change at the top. There's a good reason U.S. presidents are limited to two terms.

Equally impressive strides were being made on the institutional side. By the late 1980s we were consistently topping the so-called league tables—the tally that gave investment banks bragging rights for being number one in various stock and bond underwriting categories. By the mid-1990s we were also a consistent top contender in the glamorous merger and acquisition advisory business, an investment banking specialty traditionally led by Morgan Stanley and Goldman Sachs.

The progress we were making was recognized in a November 25, 1991, *Business Week* feature article headlined "Raging Bull: The Trimmer New Look of Merrill Lynch." The magazine made this assessment: "Today, there are clear indications that Merrill Lynch is remaking itself. Led by Chief Executive Officer William A. Schreyer, an ebullient, unpretentious former stockbroker...the giant firm is busily trying to change its lax, free-spending culture.... More fundamentally, the firm is pushing employees to focus on profits instead of size."

One of the securities analysts covering us was quoted as still harboring some skepticism–"They have gotten some religion. Whether they're born again, I don't know"–but our results began speaking for themselves. Our restructuring and our determination to build our most profitable businesses paid off where it counted–on the bottom line. We swung from a $200 million loss in 1989 to a $200 million profit in 1990, which grew to $700 million in 1992 and nearly $900 million in 1993, a record at the time. Our stock price soared as well.

That *Business Week* article included a profile of me, accompanied by a photo of my dad and me. It quoted friends Joe Paterno–"Bill is a very dynamic guy, but in a different way. He's not filled up with himself"–and Charlie Sanders, who said of me, "He is the spirit of Merrill Lynch, from Wall Street to Main Street." The writer concluded, "The man who made Merrill get its act together may not be an easy act to follow."

Around the time of my retirement, *Forbes* magazine editorialized, "If ever a chairman deserved well of his shareholders, Schreyer does. The great bull market in stocks and underwriting was not, of course, of his making. What he did accomplish was to bring–and keep–Merrill's costs under control." Given all the opprobrium directed at me during the difficult years by *The New York Times, The Wall Street Journal, Fortune* magazine, and others, it was gratifying, to say the least, to have the last laugh.

CHAPTER 16

Travels with Chairman Bill

During the last three years of my tenure as chairman and CEO, I was able to spend a good deal of my time on a part of the business I loved: developing our international activities. I went countless times to Japan, including a trip in 1991 when we took our entire board to celebrate our thirtieth anniversary in that country. Mike McCarthy, one of our former chairmen and a great mentor to me over the years, joined us on that trip. Mike had had the foresight to establish a representative office in Tokyo in 1961, long before Japan had become the third-largest economy in the world. Despite his advanced age, Mike had a great time on that trip.

A lot of people don't particularly enjoy going to Japan, but I always did. I'd call on a succession of clients, and the routine was always the same. You'd meet the head guy, the chairman or president, and you'd carry on a conversation with the help of a translator. Invariably you'd get tea—sometimes green tea, which I hated, or yellow tea, all kinds of tea. (I would be so up to my hoo-hoo in tea by the time the day was over, I could hardly stand it.) You'd talk with the client, lay out the facts, the relationship, the business we were doing or trying to do, and at the end of the meeting they'd bow. It was all very polite and formal, and everything ran like clockwork—in at nine, out by 9:45, and on to the next meeting.

In the evenings, after a dinner with clients or internal folks, we'd go to the Ginza district to my favorite geisha bar, which was run by a pretty young girl named Aki. She had borrowed money from the Mob to start the place—they'd financed her because she was so successful. She staffed the place with all these beautiful gals, and it was great entertainment. They couldn't pronounce Schreyer, so when I came in, they'd jump up and down and say, "Chairman Bill, Chairman Bill." Then they'd make a big fuss over us, serving us drinks, and we would sing karaoke. Usually it was men only, but once we brought our wives along just to let them see how innocent the whole thing was.

I always stayed at the Hotel Okura, at that time one of the two or three great hotels in Tokyo. The service was unbelievable, and they had all kinds of different food. On one trip, Joan was with me, and I said, "God, I'm tired. I really feel like a massage."

She said, "I'll call down and they'll send someone up."

I had visions of a beautiful young masseuse, but when the girl they'd sent arrived at the room, I saw that she could have been a linebacker for the Chicago Bears. She spoke very little English, and she started giving me a massage. She noticed the scar down my chest and said, "Ooh, bypass."

"Yes," I replied.

And then she remarked, "Just like Henry Kissinger."

"Yes," I said, "same doctor, too."

"Oh. I do Henry Kissinger last week."

"Good. I'll tell him I met you."

Kissinger, of course, was world famous as Richard Nixon's globe-trotting secretary of state. Second secretary of state, that is, after Bill Rogers.

The scene changes. I'm in New York at a dinner about a month later, and Kissinger was sitting on my left. I told him about having the same masseuse he had. Another guest at the table overheard us and asked, "What are you two guys talking about?"

I said, "Can I tell him, Henry?"

He said, "Yes, but don't tell him she was as big as a linebacker. I've got my image to protect. Tell him she was a beautiful young thing." It was funny as hell. That Kissinger is quite a character.

Nixon, Rogers, and Kissinger had been instrumental in reestablishing diplomatic relations between the U.S. and China in the early 1970s. By the 1990s it was clear that the Soviet Union and China, the old Communist bloc, were both on their way to embracing capitalism. I was a member of New York Stock Exchange delegations that traveled to both China and Russia; of the two, it was obvious to me that the Chinese were the ones who really "got" capitalism.

In fact, I'd go so far as to say that in two millennia of Chinese history, Communism was nothing more than a brief aberration. Wherever you traveled in Asia, there was a business class that seemed to control a lot of the local commercial and financial activity, and invariably, that business class was Chinese. Unlike the Japanese, who tended to be formal and reserved, the Chinese struck me as warm, open, and gregarious. Early in 1993 we learned that Merrill Lynch would become the first U.S. investment bank to be granted permission to open a representative office in the People's Republic of China. This would involve the equivalent of a "state visit" to Shanghai and Beijing.

Joan and I landed at the Shanghai International Airport in March 1993 and were whisked by motorcade to the official state guesthouse, a compound of classically designed Chinese buildings on elaborately landscaped grounds on the outskirts of Shanghai. There was an elaborate welcoming ceremony upon our arrival, where we were presented with a big bouquet of flowers by a pair of little girls–twins. They were six or seven, as cute as could be, and later I was told it was quite unusual to see female twins in a country where boys were favored and there was still a "one child per family" policy in place.

The guesthouse was a lush and elegant place. After I learned years later that it had been the final residence of Deng Xiaoping, the premier who changed the course of history by reversing Mao Tse-tung and putting modern China on its road to capitalism, I've often thought it's highly likely he was living somewhere on the grounds when we were there. I would have liked to have met him.

If Beijing is China's equivalent of Washington, D.C., the political capital, then Shanghai is definitely the equivalent of New York, the capital of finance and commerce. It is a vast city, and when we were there, skyscrapers were being constructed as far out on the horizon as the eye could see. It was said at that time, with good reason, that the national bird of China was the "building crane."

While we were there, we met with local officials and had receptions and a traditional, multi-course Chinese banquet to celebrate the opening of our office. There was lots of toasting with the traditional Chinese liqueur called Maotai, a sorghum-based drink that was an acquired taste, to say the least. Someone once described its flavor as that of "melted, burning tires," which wasn't too far off. I was concerned that one of our traveling party, Jim Wiggins, was truly on the verge of "going native" when he admitted to me that the taste was growing on him. Come to think of it, it was growing on me, too! Wiggs was handling our public relations on the trip, and somehow he managed to transmit video footage of our office opening back to the States, where it was picked up by CNN International.

We visited the floor of the Shanghai Stock Exchange, where the stock quotes were displayed on a big electronic board in Chinese characters, and were taken to a retail brokerage office, which resembled a curbside betting window and at the time we visited was surrounded by a big throng of people milling about on the sidewalk. Our escorts cleared the way for us to enter the building, and as we passed through, one of our Chinese speakers overheard someone in the crowd say, "They must have inside information."

We were ushered upstairs to an area where the high rollers did their trading. It doubled as a restaurant, complete with live-fish tanks. "Billy Boy," I thought to myself, "you've come a long way from the Merrill Lynch office in Williamsport, Pennsylvania."

From Shanghai we flew to Beijing, where the government put us up in another state guesthouse, Diao Yu Tai, a walled compound of elegant Chinese architecture and gardens; in ancient times it had been the emperors' fishing grounds. Joan and I stayed in the same suite that had been occupied by President Reagan on his visit to China. It was filled with exquisite hand-carved furniture, intricate jade screens, and an adjoining terrace on which we could have entertained two or three hundred of our closest friends.

The guesthouse was staffed by a bevy of extremely tall and attractive Chinese women, dressed in identical silk dresses with a slit up the side that showed off their long legs. They were charming and solicitous, and told us they all came from the same province in Northern China. They were always asking if we needed anything, and once or twice I ordered a beer, not so much because I wanted one, but because I liked to watch them come and go.

At the appointed hour we were ushered into the Great Hall of the People for our audience with the premier, Li Peng. He shook hands with everyone in our delegation and we had our photos taken; then we were seated in a large semicircle, with Li and me at the apex, separated by an elaborate floral arrangement set on a low table, with two translators behind us on stools. The reception room in which we sat was decorated with two extraordinary ceramic vases in the corners behind us, giants, probably ten feet high.

It struck me that a meeting between a capitalist like the

chairman of Merrill Lynch and a Communist like the premier of China was a pretty momentous occasion. So after the usual pleasantries, I opened the conversation as follows: "This meeting reminds me of what the astronaut Neil Armstrong said when he set foot on the moon: 'One small step for man, one giant leap for mankind.'"

Premier Li replied, "As I recall, when you Americans traveled to the moon, all you returned with was a bag of rocks. I hope this meeting results in something much more valuable." Now he was talking my language! Soon we were discussing China's desire to enter the global capital markets, and Merrill Lynch's desire to help them do so.

At one point in our conversation I mentioned that I had just been in Shanghai, and that my Uncle Wilk had lived there in the 1930s and was responsible for building the Shanghai power plant. (My Aunt Helen remembered that she could watch from their apartment window as he went out to the plant by boat.)

It turned out Li Peng was an engineer himself, and just loved power plants. "Well, did you go over to see it?" he asked.

Of course, I wouldn't have thought to go see the goddamn power plant. But fortunately, I had enough wits to say, "I really wanted to, but your people kept us so busy that I didn't have a minute to be able to do it. But when I go back I'm certainly going to do that." Now, what the hell would I do at a power plant in the middle of an island off the coast of Shanghai?

The following day we were taken deep into the heart of the Forbidden City for a meeting with Jiang Zemin, the Chinese president. He also headed the military, and was a bit younger than Li Peng. In fact, he eventually succeeded Li as the head of government. It was the same deal—big semicircle, flower arrangement, two translators. As I recall, Jiang was more personable than Li Peng. He talked at length about how difficult it was for the central government to collect taxes in a country the size of China.

So, I had paid a state visit to the two top leaders of China. Later I learned from our people who were close to Beijing that after my trip the government adopted what was known informally as the "Schreyer Rule": Visiting potentates from Wall Street could meet with one or the other of the two top leaders, but not both!

Clearly at the time of my visit, the Chinese were eager to tap the international capital markets to help propel their growing economy. Our cultivation efforts were rewarded when, several months after my visit, Merrill Lynch was awarded the coveted role as lead underwriter for China's first-ever global bond issue. Their timing, as it turned out, was impeccable. The issue hit the market in early February 1994, right before Alan Greenspan and the Federal Reserve Board began a year-long series of interest rate increases that threw the fixed-income markets for a loop.

From Beijing we flew to Dubai, in the Middle East, to visit our office there, which was managed by Johnny Morris, the son of Mack and Janelle Morris, our good friends from Princeton. At one point our jet had to zig and zag to skirt Vietnamese airspace, which still wasn't open to any U.S. traffic. Like any good local manager, Johnny was going to take full advantage of a visit by the chairman and CEO, and while we were in Beijing, we learned that he had scheduled two extra public speeches for me. I put Jim Wiggins to work, and I'll never forget the sight of him sitting in the back of the jet, banging out the speeches on his laptop computer as we soared southwest across Asia and India to the Persian Gulf.

I still believe that globalization is the way the world will continue to go, though sometimes you do get discouraged watching the news every night, but we've gone through this sort of thing before. It just seems to get meaner. You can't get anything done in Washington, either. The two parties aren't getting along very well. But I can't help but be an optimist over the long term, given all the positive things I've seen over a half-century career in finance.

People have asked me, did I have some over-arching vision of where I wanted to take Merrill Lynch, or did I just kind of let things happen? The answer would be: a little bit of both. I knew where I wanted to take the company: continue to be the preeminent private client firm, build the capital markets side, better integrate the two, and then globalize. That was the vision. Then you have to make it happen. You can't just be beating a drum. You set the wheels in motion, get the people in place and the plans laid out, and let it happen. You call an audible every once in a while, to speed it up or slow it down, depending on which part of the firm we are talking about. The bottom line is it all worked out pretty well.

As I prepared for my retirement at age sixty-five, as required by Merrill Lynch's bylaws, I turned over the CEO role in May 1992 to Dan Tully, while remaining chairman of the board for another year. Tully was the clear choice to succeed me. He was a great salesman, in the right sense of the word. People like to downgrade salesmen, but we're all in the business of selling something. He had great people skills. He was a warm, enthusiastic leader.

My public advice to him was pretty short and to the point. At one of our big managers' meetings I said, "Danny Boy, we've got a pretty good thing going here. All I can say is, don't screw it up!" I was kidding…but maybe a little bit serious.

I wanted to have my last board meeting in Germany, the country where I got my first international experience as a young Air Force lieutenant in the 1950s. During an earlier trip there I'd met with the U.S. ambassador and told him of my intentions. He asked me where I was going to have the meeting, and I said Frankfurt, probably, since that was the financial capital.

He said, "Would you consider having it in Berlin? They just got East and West together, and companies don't think about going there. It would mean a lot. I think it would be good for Merrill Lynch, too. It would be a symbol." Sounded good to me, so we picked Berlin.

Steve Hammerman, our vice chairman and general counsel, who is Jewish, didn't like the idea of going to Germany in the first place, but I told him it would be good for him to go back and look at the places where all the atrocities took place—it would be an educational experience.

As the meeting was getting under way, I asked him where my gavel was. He said, "Geez, I don't know."

"How soon you guys forget, for cripes sake," I said. "I can't believe you forgot my gavel for my last meeting!"

He couldn't tell me, but the gavel was part of a beautiful, three-dimensional collage of mementos from my career, enclosed in a glass case, that they were going to present me at the meeting. I displayed it in my office until 2008, when I donated it to the Schreyer Honors College.

I figured that as long as I had the board in Berlin, I might as well take them over to London, too, so I had a kind of round-the-world retirement party. I officially stepped down as chairman on June 28, 1993—exactly forty-five years to the day after I started out as a junior executive trainee.

A lot of the parties and festivities around my retirement, including a memorable "roast" at the 21 Club presided over by Dan Tully, had been organized by Lee Roselle, a long-time Merrill Lynch employee who, as the head of "employee relations," looked after the human side of things. He had a terrific sense of humor and always made sure that as tough as things got from time to time, we always remembered to laugh at things a little bit and not take ourselves too seriously. He and our advertising director, Charlie Mangano, were geniuses at putting together funny videos that spoofed the executive team and the situations we were involved in. Lee was particularly close to Don Regan, and kept in touch with him and all of the other retired partners, organizing periodic reunions. In this way he was a great caretaker of the culture that made Merrill Lynch such a special place.

Another loyal Merrill Lynch colleague who was tremendously helpful to me over the years was Claudia Kahn. She had been a student of Jill Conway's at Smith College and came to Merrill Lynch through that connection. As I recall, she started out in Human Resources and later worked for Paul Critchlow in Corporate Communications, where she ran our events area for a number of years.

When you gave Claudia an assignment, you didn't have to worry about follow-up because it would be done. After I chose Berlin for that last board meeting, they sent Claudia over to scope it out. She never complained, just got on an airplane with her briefcase and bag, and took care of the planning. All the arrangements were perfect; we had a great spot for the meeting, and the whole thing went like clockwork. Whatever you asked her to do, she'd just get the job done and do it well. She's a great asset to the company.

During the meeting in Berlin, the board granted me the title of "Chairman Emeritus," of which I was rightly proud. Of course, that didn't prevent me from joking about it.

"What's *emeritus* mean, Bill?" people would ask me.

"Oh," I'd say, "it's Latin for 'no pay and no say.'"

What a tremendous journey, by any measure. From 1948 to 1993, our growth was astonishing:

- Annual revenues: from $27 million to $17 billion
- Net profit: from $5.5 million to $1.36 billion
- Offices: from 98 in the U.S. to 510 around the world
- Employees: from 2,800 to 42,000
- Clients: from 100,000 to 7 million
- Capital: from $14 million to $153 billion

And yet after all those years one thing had remained the same: Merrill Lynch was still a meritocracy, a place where talent and hard work were rewarded, and integrity and client service were the two most important principles; where every employee could be proud of our global reputation.

Behind me was a career that was more successful and fulfilling than I ever could have reasonably hoped for. Ahead of me lay a very busy retirement.

CHAPTER 17

"Chairman Emeritus"

On June 28, 1993, the official date of my retirement, my successor, Dan Tully, and other Merrill Lynch colleagues presented me with a wonderful book of letters—tributes and messages from sixty-six people, representing all walks of life, with whom I had worked in various capacities over the course of my business career.

Harold Burson, founder of Burson-Marsteller, the public relations firm that has represented Merrill Lynch for decades, started his letter this way: "Merrill Lynch without Bill Schreyer? That's tantamount to saying corned beef without cabbage, or bagels without cream cheese, or Mom without apple pie." Those words struck a chord with me. They echoed my own sense of disbelief that I would no longer be officially associated with the company that had been at the center of my life for forty-five years.

Intellectually, I was ready to move on. Emotionally, I knew this new phase of life would take some getting used to. President George Bush (the first), himself "retired" as of the 1992 election, shared in his letter some warm reflections on his own transition:

We hope the withdrawal pains will not be too acute. As one who

198

is now a noted expert on retirement, I can recommend it. For the first few days I sat around wondering why the phone didn't ring. I waited for someone to bring in an option paper, waited for a decision that needed to be made. No, no one came along. Then the joys of my new life began to overtake the thinking about what used to be. Time helps. Family helps a lot.

The White House speechwriter Ray Price, who had worked with me on some of my own speeches during my years as CEO, offered a valuable perspective on how to approach this whole retirement thing. Ray wrote:

Having helped Richard Nixon adjust to life after the presidency, and Bill Paley to life after the chairmanship of CBS, I've seen quite a bit of the readjustment process. But those two transitions were, to put no finer point on it, of the somewhat reluctant variety. So it's a special pleasure to salute a retiree who's not only planned the transition and looked forward to it, but prepared the way with consummate skill and sensitivity. I'm sure you'll find the readjustment a lot more fun than they did.

Ray was correct in his observation that I had put a fair amount of thought and planning into the direction I would take after leaving Merrill Lynch. Readers may recognize by now that this is a pattern in my life. Sure, luck and chance play a part in everyone's life—maybe a big part. But I have never been one to leave things entirely to chance. Thinking ahead, positioning myself to do the things I wanted to do, and doing them on my own terms—that has always been my approach. Does this make me a calculating SOB? You can draw your own conclusions, but I don't think so.

Here's how I look at it. Preparation, planning, and foresight can make a big difference in life. Setting a goal and figuring out what it will take to get there. Flicking on the high beams once in a while to see what's up ahead on the road of life. That's been my philosophy. And you know what? It hasn't worked out half badly!

One post-retirement option I had been contemplating—or at least a potential option—had been foreclosed to me by Bill Clinton's defeat of George Bush. I had gotten to know Bush when he was vice president, and I'd worked hard for his election as president, and also his reelection. Quite frankly, I had indicated that I didn't want to become an ambassador to just anywhere, but if the Court of St. James were to have an opening, well, that was one I would certainly be fascinated in having.

There were no promises, but he knew I was interested. Merrill Lynch had a strong presence in London, and I was told that certainly I'd have been considered to be a natural candidate. But when Clinton beat him, that killed my plan. At least it was a nice dream as I was entering my final days at Merrill Lynch. Clinton gave the job to Admiral William J. Crowe, a former chairman of the Joint Chiefs of Staff who had supported him in the election. To add a touch of irony, I had been involved a few years earlier in recruiting the admiral for the Merrill Lynch board.

I've kept in touch with President George and Barbara, seeing them occasionally at affairs down in Washington, and serving on the board of his presidential library foundation. Let me tell you, you've never been hugged until you've been hugged by Barbara Bush. She's a very warm and gracious lady. When I recently took my grandson down to the black-tie Alfalfa Club dinner in Washington, they both spent a lot of time with him. That made a big impression on young Charles William.

Joan and I kept the house out in California, but frankly, we haven't used it all that much. It's nice to relax in the great desert climate, but the time difference puts you out of the loop. You get up at seven or eight in the morning, read the papers, then pick up the phone and try to get someone in New York, only to find that they're all out to lunch. So then you do some fussing around, take a walk or get a massage, then go to lunch and come back and try to make your phone calls, but they're all gone for the day. Over in London, you're on top of your game. But when you're out on the West Coast, you miss out on almost a whole day of activity.

To keep a foot in the business world, I started going on some corporate boards. I had joined the Schering Plough board, chaired by my friend and fellow Merrill Lynch director Bob Luciano, a few years before I retired. After that I joined the John Deere board with Bob Hanson, and the Foote Cone & Belding board—Foote was an advertising company based out in Chicago. There was also Willis Corroon, the Anglo-American insurance company, and, later, Callaway Golf. That was the last board I joined. I also served on the boards of Iridium, an ill-fated telecommunications venture started by Motorola, and AEA Investors.

I continued to do board work until a few years ago, when I turned seventy-five. They were fun to serve on and weren't too demanding in terms of time. You met a different group of directors at each company, and though as individuals they represented different aspects of the private sector, I found that we all had a great deal in common, and shared a basic set of principles for running a major public corporation.

Each CEO had a different style. Bob Luciano was very good. He was extremely well organized at board meetings. His president would give the operating report. He'd give the strategic report, then open it up to questions. He'd answer them all himself unless it was some odd-lot thing he didn't have the answer to.

Bob Hanson, running Deere & Co., was a little more expansive. He had more of a sales orientation. He was selling John Deere—in a good way. He was the consummate people person, getting everyone involved in the board discussions. That could be a problem once in a while if you had a director who was a pain in the neck.

Of course, being on a corporate board is different today. In the old days, and I'm exaggerating to make a point, the CEO felt he had to be in total charge of the whole thing and run a very tight meeting, with brief, detailed reports. At the end he'd ask, "Have you any questions?" The old-timers didn't like to raise anything that would interfere with the smooth running of the meeting.

Today you can't have too regimented an atmosphere. As a director, you have to follow the business pretty closely, do your due diligence, ask tough questions. That's the world we're living in. Sometimes it isn't as much fun, but it's probably better.

It's important that a company have a great chief financial officer who can give a good report on the finances. And then you need to have your key executives participating in the board meeting, so that the directors can be looking to succession down the road a piece.

The kind of corporate scandals we've seen in recent years—Enron, WorldCom, that sort of thing, with phony accounting and questionable activities to inflate the price of the stock—these things occur when a world of excess starts to open up. Excess in compensation. Excess in fringe benefits. Sloppiness about fiscal discipline. Looking the other way with a wink and a nod. Rationalizing, "Well, it's really not such a bad thing to do."

I think until we get proud of being conservatives—conservative fiscally, conservative morally—we're going to have these kinds of scandals. Values—a clear sense of right and wrong—have to come from people themselves, the people in charge. They've got to be instilled by our social institutions—the honors colleges of this world, or the business schools or medical schools. There's got to be a sense of fairness and integrity. We have to have high standards and hold people accountable. I'm not entirely pessimistic. The capitalistic system has a way of straightening itself out, and I still think it will.

❀

I've been fortunate in retirement to have the resources to be a philanthropist, with Penn State as a major focus. At the request of Bryce Jordan, one of the university's most dynamic presidents, I chaired the first-ever capital campaign in the mid-1980s: The Campaign for Penn State. Though we got off to a rocky start—one of our first organizational meetings was held a day or two after the 1987 crash—the campaign was a great success. From an initial goal of $200 million, we raised over $350 million in six years.

Dave Gearhart, a great guy from Arkansas who was the university's top development officer—Joe Paterno and I worked very closely with him on that campaign—paid me a great compliment. "Bill Schreyer," he said, "has a leadership style that makes people want to work themselves to the bone for him. I found working with Bill a little bit like dancing with a bear. You don't stop when *you* get tired. You stop when the *bear* gets tired." Dave worked tirelessly on the campaign and was a major reason it was so successful.

One of the great benefactors of the campaign was a fellow Wall Streeter, Frank P. Smeal, who gave $10 million in 1989 to endow the college of business administration, which now bears his name. At the time, it was the largest gift the university had ever received.

Frank was born out in the small town of Sykesville, Pennsylvania, near Punxsutawney, and he attended the Dubois campus for two years before he came to State College, where he got his degree in economics right on the eve of World War II. After serving in the Army he got an MBA at Harvard and, eventually, a law degree from New York University.

He began his Wall Street career at Guaranty Trust Company, which later became Morgan Guaranty, and worked there for thirty years, eventually becoming executive vice president and treasurer. He joined Goldman Sachs in 1977 and became a partner and member of the management committee before retiring in 1985.

Frank's specialty was municipal bonds. According to his 2003 obituary in *The New York Times,* he was among the first to warn New York City Mayor Abraham Beame that the city's borrowing practices were leading to disaster. After the city's brush with bankruptcy in 1975, Frank was part of the team that counseled it through its fiscal crisis. By the end of his career, many people in the industry regarded him as the "dean" of the municipal bond market. And after he retired from Goldman Sachs, he served for a number of years on the Citizens Budget Commission, a volunteer watchdog group that had been formed to keep an eye on what the politicians were doing with the public's money.

Frank was an informal, down-to-earth kind of guy, not at all the epitome of the stuffy type that you expect when you think of a Goldman Sachs partner. I'll never forget the day he was honored for his gift to Penn State. He didn't even have a suit on at the ceremony; he was dressed in his usual open shirt and sports jacket. He looked around at the crowd and said, "You know, I just bought a college for ten million bucks. That's a pretty good deal!"

As a partner of Goldman Sachs, Frank was a natural competitor, and we both thoroughly enjoyed that competition over the years. We always enjoyed needling each other, and there wasn't a session that went by at Penn State when we were together where we didn't get the competitive juices going. We'd let the whole Penn State world know that we were arch competitors, but we were also bound together by our love for and loyalty to Penn State. So it was always great fun.

I used that competitive strategy when I asked him for his campaign gift. Bryce Jordan and I took him to dinner at a restaurant in Bucks County, and at one point I took him outside and said, "My job is to ask you for a big gift."

He said, "You can ask, and you know I'm going to do something, but I'm not going to tell you tonight what I'm going to give."

I responded, "Don't be so stubborn, for cripes sake. Frank Smeal. Isn't that who I'm talking to, Frank Smeal? That's right."

So we played the competitive "I'm going to one-up you" game for quite a while. But when he came through, he didn't let anybody down.

In 1986 I was appointed to the Penn State board of trustees by Governor Dick Thornburgh and was later reelected by delegates of Industrial Societies, serving as board president from 1993 to 1995. I was fortunate to serve on the board with some very distinguished individuals. Lloyd Huck, a former CEO of Merck, served a term as president before me. An outstanding executive and individual, Lloyd and his wife, Dottie, have since moved to State College, and we consider them two of our closest friends in Happy Valley.

Bill Weiss, the former CEO of Ameritech, one of the Baby Bells, served on both the Penn State and Merrill Lynch boards. He and his wife, Jo, are both Penn State graduates. He and Lloyd Huck are exactly the kind of people we want on the board at Penn State. They come from the private sector, they've been successful in their business lives as well as their personal lives, and they represent the very best of Penn State graduates.

Jesse Arnelle is another long-serving trustee who epitomizes Penn State excellence. He was an all-American athlete, a star in both football and basketball, and he went on to have a highly successful career as a lawyer. In fact, he founded the first African-American law firm in San Francisco. He succeeded me as president of the board, and he always called me "Chief." He's a towering guy, physically and otherwise, and he'd always come up to me, pat me on the shoulder, and say, "How ya doin', Chief?" I always got a kick out of that.

Another great friend on the board, and otherwise, is Mimi Coppersmith, who also served a term as president. She's a State College institution, runs a publishing company up there, and nobody is a bigger Penn State booster than Mimi. She's helped countless students over the years by giving them part-time jobs at her magazine, *Town and Gown,* and other publications.

During my time on the board, nobody was more helpful to me than Carol Herrmann, who served as secretary to the board. In advance of the meetings, she'd have everything laid out, all the agendas, and she'd give me the background of whatever the problems were–not suggesting the right answer, but what the alternatives might be.

When she retired from Penn State, I strongly recommended to Bob Poole that he hire her at S&A Homes, our real estate development company. She's doing a great job for us there just as she did at Penn State. She may get frustrated if she doesn't get things changed or done as fast as she'd like, but that's an asset, not a problem. She gets it done by sticking to it. She's got a great, quiet sense of humor and she's just a wonderful lady.

Before, during, and after my service as an active trustee, Joan and I had a great many opportunities to contribute to the university, among them an endowed chair in Global Management Policies and Planning at the Smeal College of Business Administration, and a million-dollar challenge grant as part of the Paterno Library campaign.

I'll never forget the day Joab Thomas, who was president at the time, asked me for another million to renovate the grand old house north of campus that Penn State had just purchased to serve as the official president's residence. Joab had announced his retirement, and the new home would be occupied by his successor. Not only wouldn't it have been appropriate otherwise, but the board of trustees wouldn't have approved spending money on a new house for a sitting president.

Joab was a great golfer–loved the game of golf. He called me out in California, on a day when I just happened to have shot the best round of golf I ever played out there. I had broken 100, which is normal for most people, but for me was a major deal. I was two-thirds of the way through a good, celebratory martini when Joab called.

"What's on your mind, Joab?" I asked.

He said, "Well, I wonder if you would consider fixing up the house we just bought for future presidents. We'd like to call it Schreyer House. It's going to cost a million dollars."

"Joab, I had the best round of golf I've ever had in my life today. You got it!"

He damn near fainted. "I what?!"

"You got it."

"What should I do now?" he asked.

"You better hang up before I change my mind."

I went out and told Joan, "I just gave Joab Thomas a million dollars."

"You what?!"

"Well, I shot a ninety-nine today and just poured myself a drink. It seemed like a sensible thing to do."

Joan had a great time decorating the place, and it's beautiful now. I think it's one of the nicer president's houses in the country.

We always knew that in setting up our family foundation, Penn State would be a major beneficiary. We wanted to come up with something that was special or unusual. I didn't want to build a gymnasium or anything like that. I wanted to come up with something that would be of particular interest to me.

STILL BULLISH ON AMERICA

One thing that always bugged me was that, in the search for young talent that is always so intense on Wall Street, Penn State wasn't even on the list that Merrill Lynch recruited from. I thought that if the business school couldn't make that happen, maybe there was some other approach. We had to have a school here that had the capability to attract and turn out kids who could be as well-qualified as those at any Ivy League school, whether it be Harvard, Yale, Princeton, or Cornell. That's where the idea of an honors college came from. We needed a place where Penn State students would get an education as good as—in fact, better than—they would get at any of those Ivies.

Graham Spanier, who had succeeded Thomas as president, was thinking about a similar type of thing. I'll never forget, as long as I live, the day he and John Brighton, the provost, brought me the idea. It was a hot summer night, a Friday, and I was staying at the Nittany Lion Inn. They laid out the concept over dinner.

The first question I asked was this: "Is this going to be a bunch of bookworms, or nerds, who spend all their time getting straight A's? If that's what they are, I'm not interested. I want them to be leaders. Yes, to be good academics and scholars, but also to be able to make a real difference out in the world, no matter what field they go into—business, biochemistry, or whatever. To be the best."

They told me that's exactly what their goal was.

So I said to them, "How much are you talking about?"

"It's in the proposal document, on the last page."

"I won't read it now," I said, and took it up to my room. I decided I wouldn't read it that night, either, but wait until I got home.

Back home in Princeton on Saturday, I started to read it in the library. At one point, Joan walked in, but I wasn't quite prepared to tell her what I was thinking about.

"You seem to be deep in thought," she said. That woman has an uncanny ability to instantly size up any situation.

"Just catching up on some homework," I said, and put it aside. The next day, Sunday, I went over to my office at the Merrill Lynch campus and really read it. That's when I saw they were asking for $30 million.

On Monday, I met with Tom Koslowski, my financial advisor in the Merrill Lynch family office, who was starting to do the planning on our foundation. "Here," I said. "Take this proposal home, study it, then call me back and tell me why I *can't* do this. It's just too much."

He came back in a few days and handed me the proposal. "You can do it if you want to," he said.

"Oh, come on."

So we sat down and he went through the whole exercise with me to show how I could afford to do it. I kicked it around with Joan, and she said, "Whatever you want to do. This is the major thing you want to do, and I think it's terrific." That's how it all got started, and so far it's exceeded, not my hopes, but surely my realistic expectations.

The way it works is, students in the Schreyer Honors College can choose any major, any line of study, and they take intensive honors courses. They're also supposed to write a thesis. That's the toughest part. It's hard work doing an honors thesis at the end of their four years, but that's part of the requirement.

There's also an international component. Part of our endowment goes to fund international study by students in the college who are known as Schreyer Ambassadors. From my days in the Air Force in Germany, I know what a broadening experience international living can be.

Our programs involve more than just going to school in a foreign country. They involve spending enough time there to really get to know the people. The students come back with an experience that will last forever. So I think if you combine the scholarly development with the travel, with getting to know people around the world, maybe someday down the road, we'll prefer to get along with one another instead of fighting. International experience can make a difference. There has to be more of it around the world, though.

I'm told there's great pride among students at the Schreyer Honors College. They call it "Schreyer," and I get a kick out of that. You can't help but get a kick out of hearing a student say, "I go to Schreyer." As long as they don't say, "Go to hell, Schreyer," it's OK.

In December 2000, when the Pennsylvania Society recognized me with its gold medal for endowing the college, I got one of the best examples of what we have accomplished. At the black-tie dinner at the Waldorf-Astoria, where the society holds its big annual event every December, two couples came up to me separately. They didn't even know each other.

One of them said, "We have twins. A boy and a girl. The boy goes to Cornell, the girl goes to the honors college."

Then another couple came up a few minutes later. This one had two boys—brothers, not twins. One went to Yale and the other went to the honors college.

Both of those couples told me that their kids who were going to the honors college were getting a far better education than the ones who were going to Cornell and Yale.

"Tell me why," I said.

They explained that their children were getting individual attention from brilliant scholars who would spend time with them, but who were also very demanding in terms of performance. And the kids had never been happier. They were enjoying the big life, the joy of going to a big university, with all the excitement of Penn State football and things like that, but one with a little academic jewel right in the middle of campus.

That sure was music to my ears. I knew we were going in the right direction, and since then it has only gotten better and better. I get letters from the kids, about what it has meant to them to get an honors education. I took a stack home a couple of weeks ago and read them all for about an hour. Joan walked in and said, "Do you mind if I read them?"

"No, they're addressed to you, too, for cripes sake!"

She read them and said, "That tells the whole story of why we're doing it. Because of what it's meant for each of these kids who could not afford to have gotten an Ivy League education, to get this kind of education. That's it in a nutshell."

In November 2006, we announced we were committing another $25 million to the college. I was quoted in the press as saying that Joan and I consider it the best investment we've ever made. We really believe that.

Aside from my philanthropic activities and involvement with the university as a trustee emeritus, I also have a couple of business investments in State College. One was more or less for fun, and the other has turned into a serious investment.

The fun one is Carnegie House. I had gotten to know Phil Sieg, who was behind the very successful Toftrees residential development in State College. His son Phil Jr. works for Merrill Lynch, managed the State College office for a while. Another son, Andy, was with Merrill for a while, and his third son, Doug, who played football at Penn State, works for the asset management firm Lord Abbett.

I'd been thinking that I didn't want to come up to State College just for board meetings. It would be nice to make a buck, too. Joe Paterno was also looking for something to invest in. I'd met Phil and liked him, so one day I said to him, "You know, Paterno and I want to do something. How can we have some fun and invest in something?"

Phil, the Ayatollah—his sons had nicknamed him that because he was so strict when they were growing up, "The Ayatollah of Bellefonte"—said, "I'm building an inn. I hadn't planned on taking any partners, but if you'd like to take a twenty-five percent

STILL BULLISH ON AMERICA

interest, you and Joe can divide it." So Joe took ten percent and I took fifteen percent. I said, "I've always wanted to own an inn. I'm a frustrated bartender, anyhow. I would love it."

We patterned it after Skibo Castle, this place in Scotland that dates back to the twelfth century and was owned for a while by Andrew Carnegie. In fact, the land we built our inn on was once owned by him, too, so naturally we named it Carnegie House. It's just a fine country inn, with a warm feeling to it–and the food has always been good, too! We have twenty guest rooms, a couple of suites, a cozy little bar, and a nice meeting room. I've had many meetings there over the years. We're making money, but it was never intended to be a home run, just a solid single. I might retire *in* it, but not *on* it.

It's run by this wonderful German couple, Peter and Helga Schmid, who also own a piece of it. When I'm in town for a visit, my daughter, Drue, her husband, Rod Frazier, and the kids say, "Why don't you stay out at the house with us?" I kid them that I get better service at Carnegie House. So it's worked out great.

I'd always hoped that Drue and Rod would go back to State College someday. I couldn't think of a better place to raise a family. Rod's a very good chef, and a bartender, too. He worked at the Nittany Lion Inn for a while, for Matty Mateer, one of the great old guys around Penn State in the old days. Then Joan and I decided we'd do something to set them up and get them going in business, maybe buy an apartment building or something.

That turned out not to be necessary after I met a couple Drue and Rod had met socially and become great friends with, Bob and Sandy Poole. When we met them, we just clicked. Bob owned a real estate development company called S&A Homes. He had been in business with his brother-in-law, but they had had a falling-out, and Bob bought him out. He was looking to diversify, and I was planning to do the same thing. I didn't want to keep everything in Merrill Lynch stock.

So I bought half of S&A Homes. That got Bob some money, so he, too, was able to diversify into other things. We satisfied each other's needs, and my son-in-law, Rod, went to work for the company. I'm about two years younger than Bob's father, so it's a nice relationship. He and Sandy are like a big brother and sister to Rod and Drue. I have an office in the company's building and I spend time there when I do go up to State College. Bob and I have a good working relationship. We're good personal friends as well as business partners.

S&A Homes. I always joke that it stands for "Schreyer and all others." It's maybe the third- or fourth-largest home-building company in Pennsylvania. We have a subsidiary that builds industrial buildings as well. Our business extends out to Pittsburgh, to Eastern Pennsylvania, down into Maryland and West Virginia. We haven't gone into Ohio yet. We may or may not.

Rod is doing the thing that he particularly likes in the land area for S&A Homes. You can't build a house unless you buy the land first, and he's in charge of looking for new land. That's the lifeblood of the company. A lot of that work he does right on the computer. You can spot a lot of information online, which is what he does, then he goes out and takes a look. For example, he talks to the farmer who might be interested in selling his land, to see if he can encourage it. It's quite a process. He loves it and he's good at it.

As an investment, S&A Homes is a real winner. The question is what we want to do next. I don't think we want to become a public corporation. We may want to merge with someone else at some point, but I don't see that happening in the immediate future. It's growing so rapidly by itself. And we have good people working there. Bob has had the same guys in there for the last fifteen years, and they work as a team. Bob is clearly the boss, but he works collaboratively, and they all love working for him. He's a really thoughtful, considerate guy.

❋

Another institution that has been important to me in my retirement years has been the Center for Strategic and International Studies (CSIS). Government and public policy have always been a great interest of mine, the whole Washington scene, and I've been able to stay very much engaged in that through CSIS.

CSIS is a nonpartisan think tank, though I like to call it a "do tank," because they don't just think, they do. They work with the agencies of government, with Congress–both sides of the aisle–to solve problems facing the world, domestically, internationally, economically, and so forth.

CEOs from different companies are on the board, along with distinguished government figures, often people who've been leaders in both worlds–people like Henry Kissinger, Brent Scowcroft, Harold Brown, and Felix Rohatyn. It was founded by a fellow named David Abshire, a West Point graduate who had been an ambassador to NATO.

We attract learned scholars at CSIS. Some are Democrats, some Republicans, but all are problem solvers. It's supported by the private sector. The center takes on assignments for major corporations, to study something that's of particular interest to a company and its business. It's not a lobbying organization at all. CSIS stresses that the solution should be found not by government but by private enterprise–corporations, foundations, and individuals. We think across borders about ways to protect and promulgate the free-enterprise system. It's globalization at its best.

And it's stimulating. You get some pretty good debates down there. One of the challenges now is to raise enough capital to ensure our operations going forward, and I've been very much involved with that. We hope to create a conference center, owned by CSIS, that would permit various parties–

governments, NGOs, and private sector corporations–to come together to solve problems. We want to be an honest broker–a place not under the influence of our government or any other, but clearly in line with the free-enterprise philosophy. We want to differentiate ourselves by choosing a location away from K Street, where all the lobbyists are.

Sam Nunn is currently the chairman. Formerly a senator from Georgia, and an acknowledged expert on foreign policy, Sam is a Democrat–but a Southern Democrat, so I consider him acceptable. In fact, I kid him that when I look at the 2008 crop of presidential candidates, all I can think is "Nunn of the above."

On December 18, 2006, he sent a memo to the CSIS board of trustees, the subject of which was "New Chairman of the CSIS Executive Committee." He wrote that "Anne Armstrong has informed me of her desire to step down as Chair…a position she has so well stewarded for the past 19 years…I am pleased to inform you that I have asked Bill Schreyer to serve as the next Chair…and I am delighted to be able to tell you that Bill has graciously accepted."

At the risk of seeming immodest, let me quote one more line from Sam's memo: "Recognizing a need and helping to find a way to fill it has long been one of Bill's many strong suits."

Anne, a gracious Texas lady who had served as ambassador to Great Britain and was very close to the Bushes, had called me a few days earlier and asked me to do this. She said that at age seventy-nine, she was ready to step down.

I said, "OK, I'll do it for a month, because in January I'm turning seventy-nine, too." We both got a good laugh out of that one. Early in 2008, CSIS held a big eightieth birthday bash at the Willard Hotel for Anne and me. A whole bunch of Washington luminaries attended, including Vice President Dick Cheney and Karl Rove, who was George W. Bush's political strategist. My grandchildren, Charlie and Kelly, got up and made a speech together, and I couldn't have been prouder. It was a great night. Sadly, Anne passed away not long after that night.

So the saga continues. I'm lucky in that I've got a great zest for life. Oh sure, I've had my share of health challenges as I've gotten older. But as the saying goes—and it happens to be true—growing old is not for sissies. Still, my zest for living is undiminished, and I think I know where it came from.

I had an outstanding early role model in my father, who taught me to take life's twists and turns with humor, but also to set my course with a moral compass that would not waver. I've been sustained over all my years by loyalty to three great institutions: the Catholic Church, Penn State, and Merrill Lynch. And my life has been immeasurably enriched by the love of family—an extraordinary wife, a wise and loving daughter, a terrific son-in-law, and grandchildren whom I love and cherish, and whom I've been privileged to watch grow up.

It's been a wonderful life. And, thank goodness, it's not over yet.

CHAPTER 18

After the Flood

In September 2008, the substantial leverage that Wall Street's investment banks had been using to generate profits finally caught up with itself, and Wall Street as it had been structured since the 1930s ceased to exist.

The stage had been set six months earlier, on March 17, when Bear Stearns, the smallest of the "big five" investment banks, collapsed under the weight of its leveraged inventory of mortgage-backed securities and was forced into the arms of J.P. Morgan, which received government backing to limit any losses it would incur in absorbing Bear.

By September, it was Lehman's turn. Also over-concentrated in a portfolio of mortgage-backed securities of questionable worth, with no rescuers in sight in the form of a "white knight" acquirer or government bailout, Lehman filed for bankruptcy on September 14. This set off a tidal wave of panic in the markets, and in short order, events came to pass that were unthinkable only a few months earlier.

Goldman Sachs and Morgan Stanley, generally regarded as the number one and number two pure investment banks, announced that they would become financial holding companies under the primary regulation of the Federal Reserve. Each received a substantial capital injection, Goldman from the investor Warren Buffet and Morgan Stanley from Japan's largest bank, Mitsubishi, and both also received capital (along with seven other major banks) from the U.S. Treasury. As financial holding companies, their business models will evolve in ways yet to be determined, but one thing is clear: With the Federal Reserve, whose primary concern is the safety and soundness of the U.S. financial system, looking over their shoulders, the days of swashbuckling trading strategies, fueled by a balance sheet leveraged thirty-or-more-times equity, are over.

After the Lehman bankruptcy, Merrill Lynch was viewed as headed for a similar fate. Despite efforts by the CEO, former Goldman and New York Stock Exchange executive John Thain, to right the ship, the company had by the third quarter of 2008 reported five consecutive quarters of losses that together were approaching $40 billion on a pretax basis. The problem was pretty basic. The company had gone hog wild manufacturing securities that were based on subprime mortgages, and when it couldn't sell the things, it piled them onto its balance sheet. Under the rules of "mark to market" accounting, as the securities plummeted in value, these "paper" losses became real as they had to be written off against earnings. This eroded equity capital and, with the company finally unable to raise additional capital, put Merrill Lynch into a death spiral. Everyone in the markets knew it.

At this point it is natural to ask how we got into this state of affairs. It boiled down to the execution of whatever the business plans were at the time. And then you'd have to ask, "Well, who was running the show?" There's no second-guessing on that. The results spoke for themselves and they weren't good. Stan O'Neal, to his credit in this case, resigned as CEO of the firm when he found out the results were not what he had hoped they would be. It was the only honorable course for him to take, but by that point the damage had been done.

I never believed in staying involved in the firm's day-today business after I retired because that's up to the generations that follow, and you don't want to be sitting there second-guessing everything they do. But I've always said, "Beware of mortgage-backed securities." Because we had our own little incident twenty-one years ago when that trader came in and hid some tickets in his desk drawer, and caused us a big loss. I've always hated the damn things ever since. And sure enough, they got us again. So, fool me once, shame on you, fool me twice, shame on me—or us, collectively, as a company.

News accounts have reported that on the weekend of the Lehman bankruptcy, John Thain was told by the Federal Reserve chairman, Ben Bernanke, and the treasury secretary, Henry Paulson, that he needed to find a partner, and fast. He apparently took that advice to heart, and in a matter of hours, on September 15, Merrill Lynch announced that it would be acquired by Bank of America.

The company that had been founded in 1914 by Charles E. Merrill, that after the Depression of the 1930s had helped lead the resurgence of the American economy by bringing "Wall Street to Main Street," that became, in 1971, one of the first Wall Street firms to go public, and that climbed to the pinnacle of the global capital markets in the 1980s and 1990s, would now become a division of a larger commercial bank. A new era was about to begin.

During my time as CEO, my goal was never to sell out to someone else. In fact, I wanted to take a very hard look at anybody we might consider acquiring because I thought that most of the natural candidates were actually not that attractive for us to want to buy. If we were going to diversify, we might do it in different ways, but not through the acquisition of any of our regular competitors. I was "Bullish on America," but I was more bullish on Merrill Lynch than I was on anyone else in the industry. But obviously, times had changed.

The Bank of America announcement was certainly an emotional one for everyone who has known and loved Merrill

Lynch. At the company's final shareholder meeting on December 5, 2008, when the acquisition was officially ratified, Win Smith Jr. gave an impassioned speech. He recounted the successes of the company under the leadership of people like Charles Merrill and his father, quoted the thoughts of a former colleague, "What a wonderful collection of character and talent; those years we had at Merrill Lynch were like catching lightning in a bottle," and went on to reflect, "Lightning in a bottle. That captures so much of what our culture created, and what we felt, and why Merrill was so successful. We were not about bricks and mortar. We were about character, spirit, leadership, ethics, and pride."

With that, I certainly agree. But I am not much for looking backward for very long. I prefer to look forward, and after the emotion of it all, my reaction to the Bank of America deal was that it had to happen sometime, with somebody, and from what I had learned in a quick study after the announcement, it seemed like a good fit from the standpoint of where they're from, what their values are, and what their success has been.

I initially got a lot of good reports about the company. So that, of course, made me feel much better. Now, obviously, if I could have written the script myself, I would have preferred being the acquirer. Somehow there's just a little more joy in that than there is in being acquired. But on the other hand, I can't help but believe that if they're going to invest that kind of money in us, they recognize the value of the brand and they're going to do everything they possibly can for the people of Merrill Lynch. They want it to be successful.

So, being a basic bull at heart, I'm positive that the outcome will eventually prove to be successful. I don't like to call it an acquisition, I like to call it a merger, but you can call it anything you want, as long as it works.

In the days after the merger was announced, there were some conspiracy theorists who reasoned that as a former Goldman guy, Thain had really hoped for an outcome that would chop up Merrill Lynch and sell its crown jewel, the retail division, to Goldman Sachs.

I don't give credence to that conspiracy theory, but in this day and age, and with the business that Goldman Sachs has been in all their lives, it would be a natural thing for them to look around, and it would make sense that they might want to combine what Merrill had to offer with what they did. They're the leaders on the capital markets or investment banking side, and we're the leaders on the retail side, which Goldman didn't have at all, so it would have been a natural merger by itself.

But from what I understand, Greg Fleming, who was on the investment banking side of our business, was close to Bank of America CEO Ken Lewis and thought it was a good natural fit, so he was well on the road to talking to them before it all happened. I have a lot of confidence in Greg Fleming. I think he's an outstanding guy and his interests were always in the right spot.

I also like what I have seen of Ken Lewis. Shortly after the Merrill deal was announced, he was profiled on the TV program *Sixty Minutes*. The correspondent, Leslie Stahl, went down to their headquarters in North Carolina and tried to make a big deal about how all the power in the financial world had shifted away from New York. She tried on multiple occasions to bait Lewis into saying, "Charlotte conquered Wall Street." That's a lot of crap, trying to pull that stuff.

He didn't fall for it. Finally he just said, "This particular game we won." I like the way he handled himself, refusing to indulge in triumphalism. He seemed like a down-to-earth guy. I hope I'm right. I think I am, from all I hear and read, but you never know until you find out. So far, so good, but we'll see. Besides, the truth is that there has never been that much of a divide between Merrill Lynch and the Charlottes and the Main Streets of the world. We've been right there for fifty years or longer.

The only thing that might throw up a warning signal is that I've never known a bank yet to be successful in our business. In some ways the two cultures are like mixing oil and water. It was that way when my uncle worked at the commercial bank and Dad worked at the Merrill Lynch brokerage all those many years ago in Williamsport. One is a risk-averse culture, and the other embraces risk in things like commodities trading.

If Bank of America lets Merrill run its business, tries to make a little synergy work, but sits back and enjoys being the stockholder, it could be well worthwhile, a terrific thing. But if they pull an "I'm in charge here" routine, "you listen to us," it could be trouble.

I'm told that has been their philosophy all along. They're not big payers; they're very tight with the buck in terms of the help. Everybody's afraid of massive cuts in compensation. But you know, everyone always gets nervous when somebody new takes over. They're not going to screw around with the big producers, I wouldn't think. So I am going to continue to be Bullish on America, Bullish on Charlotte, Bullish on New York, Bullish on anything that is Merrill Lynch-related.

❋

The cataclysmic events of 2008 have raised anew the age-old questions about risk-taking in the capitalist system and the proper role of government regulation. The good old news media have gone to the usual extremes of finger-pointing—in this case, at the bad, greedy guys on Wall Street.

I think the guys and gals on Wall Street have been pretty good overall since 1929 when the going got tough, so I don't think we have to be doing a mea culpa for the rest of our lives because of what's happened in the last few months. It's part of the financial world we live in—it's risky. So I guess I just take it in stride. I don't like it particularly, when I look at my monthly statements, but I don't really take it that seriously. In fact, as one wise old man says, "Schreyer, remember you came into this world with nothing and certainly you shall take nothing with you when you go." I never much cared for that assessment. I've always thought I'd try to take a little with me —just in case they're all wrong!

On the subject of regulation, the federal government makes the rules, and if they get too loose, the players in the world will say, "Well, the government says it's OK to do this, this, and this; let's go ahead and do it. Let's take greater risk." Then they get hurt. Fannie Mae and Freddie Mac are a case in point. These agencies supercharged the subprime mortgage market to support a social policy, endorsed by both the Republicans and Democrats over many years, of increasing home ownership in America. A laudable goal, no question, but the devil is in the details of how it's carried out. This does not excuse the excessive risk-taking that ensued, but it certainly helps explain it.

It's right to vilify greed, but it isn't just on Wall Street. It could be right next door to where you're living. Sure, there are greedy people on Wall Street, but there are greedy people everywhere. It comes down to a question of character, and the Bernard Madoff affair is a case in point.

When I think about my mentors in life, people like my dad and Howard Roth, they would no more steal from their customers than they would commit armed robbery at high noon in the public square. Yet here you have this guy Madoff running a Ponzi scheme for decades and stealing, by his own admission, upward of $50 billion of other people's money. Some saw through his scam. They looked at his alleged consistent returns and supposed trading strategies and took to heart that old proverb "If it looks too good to be true, it probably is." Yet, whether out of ignorance or greed, others went along with it, and they paid the price.

People ask me, with all that's gone on, how do I advise

young people who are thinking about a career in finance? Well, I think it's still a worthy profession, and when I go up to Penn State, to the honors college or with the board of visitors of the business school, they sit me at a table with all honors students who are studying finance. They're always loaded with questions. I give them encouragement on which direction to go, what firms they might want to talk to. Needless to say, they're all interested in talking to Merrill Lynch, but they're also interested in Wall Street in general, and their values seem very high.

They still want to go to Wall Street—whether they're greedy, whether they think they can make more money there, or they think that's where the action's going to be, or whether they look upon it as an honorable place to go, and try to make it a better place, I don't know. There's a little of each in everybody I talk to. But they are always a very positive group of young students who are very bullish on going to Wall Street.

They're all much more positive in their outlook for the future than they are negative. Sure, you run into a sourpuss once in a while, but most of them figure they're going to be part of the solution as opposed to being part of the problem. It's just what you want a Penn Stater to be like—and they're fun.

There were a lot of Obama meetings the last time I was up at Penn State. The young folks in America are excited about having a younger person as president. Obama is not a dope. He's a pretty sharp guy, and with the pessimism probably way overdone at this point, that creates a real opportunity for him. Over the near term we're likely to see some pretty heavy sliding, and Obama will make mistakes—he's just as human as everybody else. But he won by a decisive amount, and he has the personality to get something done, at least in the first couple of years.

The people may get tired of him if he doesn't get results, but if he does, and I think he's likely to get results, we could have a pretty good market. Most Republicans, I guess, would say, "We're going to have a tough time; they're going to do dumb things," but I think that's probably not going to happen. I think we'll have a pretty good market. But we'll see.

Yes. I'm an optimist. The pessimists are correct at given points in history, but never over the long term. I believe in the regenerative powers of capitalism, as long as there are people at work with intelligence, imagination, courage, character, and the desire to make a better life. I don't see any of those human qualities going away anytime soon.

People I Have Known

If you're fortunate in life, you meet some extraordinary people who become great friends or otherwise profoundly affect your life. I've been particularly blessed in this regard. Here, in no particular order, are reminiscences of some of the wonderful people I have known.

Pope John Paul II

My involvement with the Vatican began around 1981, out of concern for the way the Church, which was such an important part of my life, was mismanaging its finances. Working for Merrill Lynch, with some of the best financial minds in the world, I thought we had something to offer.

A group of us who had been benefactors to the Vatican Museum were invited to Rome for a show of appreciation, and we arranged a meeting with Archbishop Paulius Casimir Marcinkus, the head of the Vatican Bank. Paul Marcinkus had been born in Cicero, Illinois, the son of a Lithuanian immigrant. As a young priest he went to Rome to study canon law and, through his friendship with the man who would become Pope Paul VI, he rose to become the third most powerful official in the Vatican, behind the Pope and the secretary of state.

I don't remember many of the details of the meeting in which we broached the subject of offering our expertise to help the Vatican manage its money, except for one: During the course of the evening, Marcinkus drank an entire bottle of Scotch. Not much came of that first meeting, and it was followed by countless others in which we continued to press our case. Meanwhile, the Vatican Bank scandal grew.

The bank has been the main shareholder in Banco Ambrosiano, which collapsed spectacularly to the tune of $3.5 billion in 1982. Rumors arose of the bank having been involved in money laundering for the Mafia and an outlawed neofascist organization, among other unsavory activities. The body of Banco Ambrosiano's chairman was found hanging under a bridge in London, and a journalist investigating Marcinkus, the Vatican Bank, and ties to organized crime was also found murdered, according to contemporary accounts.

Marcinkus himself was indicted in 1982 as an accessory to the Ambrosiano bank collapse, but the Italian courts later ruled that as a Vatican employee, he was immune from prosecution. He retired to Sun City, Arizona, as a simple parish priest, and died in 2006.

We continued to meet with Vatican officials, including Cardinal Castillo Lara, president of the Administration of the Patrimony of the Apostolic See, to offer Merrill Lynch's professional services. Joe Vullo, our office manager in Rome, went on a lot of those visits. He had been in Naval intelligence and spoke several languages, including good Italian. He married a girl from Naples; they were a wonderful couple. We'd call once a year, sometimes twice. Bill Rogers joined us on some of those trips. The Vatican officials kept counseling patience: "We've been here for two thousand years. Things don't happen overnight."

Finally, Merrill Lynch did get some money to manage, and we did a superb job of it—and do to this day, as far as I know. Joe got high marks over there for his follow-up and dedication to maintaining the relationship. He was a man with the highest personal integrity and a great sense of humor—just a joy to work with.

Under John Paul II, experts were brought in to manage the Vatican Bank, and they created an advisory board of financial professionals from around the world, which I was invited to join. We'd meet once or twice a year. At one of those meetings we had a report on how the various money managers were doing. Most were up 10 percent, down 5 percent—in that range—but the Merrill Lynch money was up something like 30 percent! A fellow on the board named Ferrari—he was part of the automobile family—said, "Why don't we just cancel all the others and give the whole thing to Merrill Lynch?"

I turned to the cardinal in charge and said, "Those were his words, not mine. But it's not a bad idea."

It was through this advisory council that I asked for and received a private audience with the Pope. I had decided to tell him frankly how I thought things were going with the Vatican's financial management. After the first advisory board meeting, I did not come away with a high degree of confidence, but subsequent meetings were more encouraging, and as I headed to my audience in the Pope's private residence, I felt I could give a positive report.

I was ushered into his study, and, dressed in his white gown and skull cap, he greeted me warmly. My mouth suddenly went dry. What do you say to the Holy Father?

I opened the conversation with a question. "How's your tennis game?"

A look of surprise came over his face, followed by a slight rueful smile. "Not so good since that guy shot me," he replied.

William A. Schreyer
Official Merrill Lynch portrait, 1980s

(Left) Visionary founder Charles E. Merrill, one of Wall Street's truly great men, with *(Below)* his partner, Winthrop H. Smith. *(Right)* Dedicating the building named for my Dad in Williamsport on May 13, 1987. Win Smith Jr. is at left.

(Left) Tully and I with Steve Hammerman and Gen. "Stormin' Norman Schwarzkopf, who was about to be honored in a tickertape parade. (Above and Right) Merrill Lynch directors, fellow CEOs and good friends Bob Hanson and Bob Luciano.

(Left, Clockwise from Top) Don Regan
in his Merrill years; Director, author
and professor Jill Ker Conway; Bob
Magowan, executive extraordinaire
and Merrill son-in-law. *(Above)*
Merrill Lynch director Jim Lorie in
a University of Chicago classroom.

(Above) Presenting a bull to Gen. Lou
Wilson on his retirement from the
Merrill Lynch board. *(Right)* Greeting
dignitaries in Tokyo with counselor,
friend and Merrill Lynch director Bill
Rogers, who is also pictured below.

(Left) Merrill Lynch directors Bill Bourke and *(Below)* Bryan Smith. *(Right)* Greeting Russian President Mikhail Gorbachev with a New York Stock Exchange delegation.

(Above) Six generations of Merrill Lynch CEOs
at a 1995 company leadership conference. To
the right are Dave Komansky, Dan Tully, Mike
McCarthy, Don Regan and Roger Birk. *(Above
Right)* Roger Birk in his CEO years. *(Below
Right)* Friend and gifted executive Tom Patrick.

(Above) Makram Zaccour in his Merrill Lynch
Beirut office. The bullet hole is genuine. *(Right)*
Meeting with the Chinese leaders on my 1993
trip to Beijing, including Premier Li Peng, above,
and President Jiang Zemin, below.

(Above) In London for "Christmas Calls," a
Merrill Lynch charitable tradition I started
that connects the elderly with distant
loved-ones at Christmastime.

"I had hoped to challenge you to a game of doubles. You with your Jewish lawyer friend, and me with my general counsel, who also happens to be Jewish." He was surprised I knew about his favorite tennis partner, but I had done a little homework.

"We thought we'd give you a pretty good match," I continued, and he responded, very papal-like, "I'm sure you would have." He was probably thinking to himself, "In my prime, I could whip you bucks anytime."

Now the ice was broken, and I was feeling much more at ease. We proceeded to have a thorough discussion about the Vatican's financial affairs. He was very engaged, totally aware of what was going on. While certainly no financial expert, he was a brilliant man and had a clear grasp of the fundamentals. He understood the various asset classes—stocks versus bonds, for example—and how they differed in terms of risk, return, and performance characteristics. I made a few suggestions about things I thought they should do, and he listened intently.

At one point in our conversation, I mentioned my relationship with Theodore Cardinal McCarrick—"Father Ted"—at the time the Archbishop of Newark, and another brilliant and inspirational man of the Church with whom I have been blessed to have a warm relationship. He recently retired as the cardinal in Washington, D.C.

"McCarrick," the Pope said. "McCarrick. I always do what McCarrick tells me to do."

Toward the end of our meeting, which lasted nearly an hour, I looked over and saw my associates peeking through the doorway—Joe Vullo, Vince Murphy, another Merrill Lyncher who worked on the Vatican account, and Vinnie Morrelli, our security man.

"Are those men with you?" the Pope asked. I nodded yes, and he motioned for them to come in. He greeted them all warmly, and when he got to Vinnie, he said, "Morrelli. Morrelli—a good *Italian* name." Just as natural and down to earth as could be. His warmth, his humanity, his charisma—these are things I will never forget.

I had the privilege of meeting Pope John Paul II three times in my life—once at a small private Mass that Joan also attended, once at the meeting I just described, and one final time at another small Mass he conducted when he was already sick. He persevered to the very end. And in doing so, he taught people not only how to live with dignity—but also how to die with dignity.

The first Polish Pope, miraculously surviving an assassination attempt, presiding over momentous events in human history such as the fall of the Soviet Union, traveling the world spreading the gospel in the dozen or more languages he spoke, he was truly a towering figure of his time. A man I will never forget.

Joan Legg Schreyer

It's hard to know exactly why you fall in love. What makes you decide you want to spend the rest of your life with someone? As a young man I could always go out with this girl or that girl and have a good time dancing—just dance all night long—"Billy Butterfly," as they nicknamed me over in Beirut.

Joan is a beautiful and stylish woman. That goes without saying. I think the key was when I took her home to meet the folks for the first time. She was the only girl my mother ever really approved of. She thought she was terrific, and my dad did, too. If you're close to your parents, as I was, that always makes a bit of an impression.

Joan has a good sense of humor. After we got married and went to Germany together, we just clicked as a team. Socializing with the senior officers and their wives, she was always a great asset as my partner and my wife. You couldn't have asked anyone to do a better job with all the people I have worked with, all the clients we've met over the years.

She has never, ever disappointed me in any way in terms of being my wife and doing the things we expected her to do. Never, "Oh, I don't want to do that." Because she genuinely likes people—entertaining them, being around them—she's totally blended into every situation—with the generals' and colonels' wives in the Air Force, throughout my career on Wall Street, over the years at Penn State, with all the friendships we've made, nationally and locally.

Still, she is a pretty private person. I mean, she's open, but really private. She doesn't sit down and share a bunch of private things with people she doesn't know. And she's a real watchdog. She'll see you put on a tie with a spot on it and, by gad, that tie comes off before you know it.

Joan is about as shrewd a judge of character as there is. It's almost scary sometimes. She can size up the phonies pretty quickly. When she spots one, it's always a little something that bothers her. Sometimes I'll get mad at her. "You don't even know the guy," I'll say. "What are you laying down a judgment for?"

She doesn't dwell on it. "Just not my cup of tea," she'll say. More often that not, she's right.

When we've disagreed, it's generally been about matters of little or no importance. Putting arguments on a scale of one to ten, we've probably had some eights or nines. There are certain things you just can't solve; if she feels a certain way about something, my views won't change her basic opinion. You can't roll her over and she can't roll me over, either. So we've had some "Mexican stand-offs," I guess you would say, but they've been about inconsequential things. "Don't sweat the small stuff," as I always say.

Sometimes, say, after I've had a disagreement with Drue, I'll come to bed and get a performance evaluation on the spot. "You didn't handle that one particularly well," Joan tells me. I'll give her her own performance evaluation once in a while, too. That's part of a good relationship—the give-and-take. I like the making-up part the best. That's even more fun.

Yes, she can spend a little money once in a while. You know, women do that. "Can you leave me a little money, dear?" she'll say.

"Oh sure," I'll say. "Just don't run out, because you don't want to worry about going into debt in your old age."

She'll come right back at me. "I'm not the one who bought two Bentleys in three months."

She doesn't buy things just for the sake of buying them. It's pretty good when you want to get her a new car, and she prefers the eleven-year-old car she's already got—just fine for her, thanks. She lets me take the new cars for myself. She's got her priorities and I've got mine. We've never had a real problem in this regard. She buys good things and appreciates quality.

Come to think if it, we've never had a real problem at all. It's been fifty-five years and counting—a great partnership, a great love affair.

Drue and Rodney Frazier

I can't say enough about what wonderful parents Drue and Rodney have been. It's easy to downplay Rodney, because he's such a quiet guy, but he's always there for Charlie and Kelly. He's not one of those parents who just says, "Don't, don't, don't, don't," he supports them in all their studies, sports activities, and so forth, encourages them, and fills the role of a father as well as a good friend and a strong supporter.

Drue and Rod met in Texas, when they were both attending SMU. They were each out with friends one night, and they met at a bar.

To his credit, when she finally brought him home, he handled himself very well. He was very respectful—he always is. I was prepared not to like the SOB, just naturally, but as it turned out, you couldn't help but like him. He was just a likable guy. He didn't talk much, but that suited me fine, too. I don't want a talker on my hands—a yakker. But he's now vastly improved in the art of conversation, better than he was even a year ago. So, at this moment in time, I think they're doing pretty darn well together.

Rod started out his career in the food service industry. When he and Drue moved from Texas to State College, I asked Matty Mateer to look him over, and Matty hired him in the Nittany Lion Inn as a bartender to start out, and then later he worked in the kitchen. He's a great cook. My God, he can put together a weekend breakfast that you'd kill for. I have trouble just getting myself a piece of toast and a hard-boiled egg, but Rod is really good at that. He also had a good sense for real estate and thought he might like to buy an apartment building, and then they met the Pooles. As I mentioned earlier, it was through Drue and Rod that I met Bob Poole and got involved in S&A Homes.

Now, as far as parenting is concerned, Drue is the taskmaster. She figures she has to be tough, and she is. Rodney's great with the kids, but he's not the disciplinarian, so Drue gives them hell when they deserve hell, and when she starts to give me hell like she gives the kids hell, that's when we go head-to-head.

The other night Joan said to me, "Now, when we see Drue, don't lash out at her like you did a week ago."

I said, "I'm not going to lash out at her."

And she said, "Well, you did. You really lashed out when she was just trying to be helpful to you."

I had said, "Quit treating me like an eighty-year-old invalid, for Christ's sake. When I want your help I'll ask for it." That's just a man's independence. On the other hand, I'd have been plenty ticked off if she *hadn't* looked after me. I just didn't want her to be too overt about it.

She shows that she cares. She doesn't make a big deal out of it. Not long ago when I had to go up to Boston for some medical treatment, she just said, "When are you going to go to Boston? Can the plane pick me up on the way?" She just knows Mass General Hospital inside out. She has a great sense of direction, she knows where everything is. She went up there and had some surgery a couple of years ago, and she's just in love with Mass General. Of course, Charlie Sanders ran the hospital for a number of years, so she has a strong feeling for it. So when I went for my treatment, she went along. She asked a lot of questions, and just made sure that everything was going right.

Joan and I are just so proud of Drue and the woman she has become, because the truth of it is, she was a difficult teenager. Joan thinks, and I agree, that the turning point was when she got married, and had Kelly. She had a responsibility to take care of a little girl, and that really changed her life. We're all the more impressed that she didn't have any difficulty with her own children; she handled it better than we did.

The teenage years were rough on all of us. Frankly, when I was working, I'd get home late at night, and she would have already gone to bed, so I'd just go in and kiss her good night. Then I'd leave in the morning at six o'clock, five-thirty sometimes, before she was even up. So I was an absentee parent during the week. It's one of those things that you just have to overcome, and you do. It's not a "poor me" sort of thing–that's life!

She didn't want to study, and we didn't realize she had a reading problem. She was absolutely brilliant. She was rated as a genius actually, her IQ was so high, but she had dyslexia and we didn't know it. There was nothing to indicate that at the time.

This was when she was a young teenager. She never liked to read at all, and we just could not understand it, because we were great readers. But nobody knew about dyslexia at the time. We didn't discover it until she was in her twenties. We took her up to Boston. A specialist tested her and said, "She'll peak when she's forty." He was a doctor of psychology at Harvard, and a lot of kids went to him for scholastic problems.

It pretty well worked out for Drue the way he said it would. Today she can stand up and give a speech extemporaneously. She'll stand up in front of a whole group in an auditorium and just talk naturally on a particular subject. She doesn't bother with notes, because it's still painful for her to read. Now she listens to books on tape. She's doing beautifully–she and Rod are doing beautifully as a couple, too. If you have your choice of peaking early or later in life, it probably makes sense to do it later.

Much later.

I don't worry about Drue. She's a happy camper and is doing well. You can always make up problems, things you wished your kids would do differently. But she's strong in loyalty, she's strong and caring about following up, just checking in without appearing to be checking in, and she always has a good sense of humor. What the hell, you can't ask for more than that.

She's really developed into a strong leader in the world of Scouting in the state of Pennsylvania. She's also spending more time with S&A Homes, with stuff that she's good at and interested in. Drue never did graduate from college, and her goal now is to get a degree. I said, "Well, lots of people get their degrees when they're fifty years old. There's nothing wrong with that. Get it whenever you want–what the hell difference does it make?" I think she'd like to be an architectural engineer, take a shot at that. Might take three or four years, but it doesn't make any difference. So she's turned out beautifully. A lot better than most kids.

Now that we're making plans to move to State College, we have a little joke between us. I ask her, "What are you going to say to people when they inquire, 'Whatever happened to your father?'"

She says she'll tell them, "Oh, he's fine. He's older now. In fact, he lives in a little barn right below my house, behind the woods here somewhere. He pops up once in a while."

Then Joan says, "You'll pop up plenty, don't worry." So we're having a lot of fun getting ready for all of this.

Kelly Anne Frazier

Kelly Anne is my first grandchild, and for that, she will always occupy a special place in my heart. She was born in Texas, before Drue and Rod moved to State College. There's a story Joe Paterno likes to tell about when she was born. Drue had gone into early labor, and Joan was keeping tabs on the whole thing by telephone, telling me about the progress.

At one point she excitedly relayed the news that "Drue has broken her water."

I was alarmed. "She what?!" I exclaimed. "What do you mean, she broke her water?" I thought that was a bad thing.

Joe was there in the room with a couple of other people and he overheard the conversation. He started to laugh at my reaction. "That's good, that's good. Don't worry about it."

I admit I didn't know much about this whole birthing procedure, and I just figured it was reasonable to assume that if something broke, it couldn't be good. Paterno laughs like hell about that to this day.

So Kelly Anne came into this world as a healthy infant, to be followed a couple of years later by her brother. They sure

were cute when they were little, and I got to enjoy them more
and more as they got a little older. Joan tells people that I really
started to like them when they got to be about four. She's just
kidding about that, she says, but you know, there may be a
little bit of truth to it.

But the years have flown by and Kelly is now a student at
Bucknell, in her junior year. She thought it would be good to
go away for college, but not too far away. Bucknell's right down
the road from State College. Kelly's a serious young woman. I
don't mean that in the sense of being heavy or dull, but she's
not a hell-raiser or a heavy drinker—she drinks a glass of wine,
and that's about it. She doesn't admire the girls who live in the
wild sorority houses, but she joined a very good sorority
herself, Chi Omega.

She is majoring in classics and religious studies, with
minors in art history and dance. She's also president of the
Young Episcopal Club at Bucknell. It wouldn't surprise me if
she wound up as an Episcopal minister; it wouldn't shock me
one bit. She's got quite a social conscience. She goes down and
works with the homeless and the poor in Tennessee, and helps
put new roofs on their houses. Works with a group of people
who do it every year—a group mostly from the Methodist
Church, called Mountain T.O.P., that goes out from State
College. She's so conscientious and responsible that this year
they've asked her to help lead the group, and they're paying
her for it.

Kelly's developing a very good sense of humor, and she's
a good dancer—especially at classical dancing. She's thoroughly
enjoying sorority life now, and you can see her maturing, so
I'm getting a bigger kick out of her. You see, I wasn't good with
a little girl. What the hell do you say to a little girl? The usual
stuff, of course, but boys and men bond more easily than men
and women or men and little girls.

But as she gets older, you can see her really coming along.
And I thoroughly enjoy her. She laughs easily, readily. She's a

very generous person with her time. She's been in a couple of shows up at Bucknell, and she's doing great there. That's what college is supposed to be all about. It's working, as far as she is concerned.

Her success in college is really no surprise because she was quite accomplished in high school, too. She was active in Scouting, just like her brother, and achieved the Gold Scout award, which is the highest award in Girl Scouts–the equivalent of Eagle Scout for boys. As a high schooler she won an "Outstanding Young Woman in Centre County" award, coming in first in poise and presentation. She's very good on her feet, very articulate.

Kelly is just an outstanding young woman. She's very loving, very demonstrative of her love, and she's smart and pretty, all of the above. Joan and I are very proud of her and her brother. They're nice kids, they really are, tap wood. They weren't into all the crazy things that some kids get into in high school. They were very circumspect about the way they conducted themselves. They weren't into the drinking and the other high-flying stuff that some kids get involved with. They were removed from all that, and Joan thinks that their involvement in Scouting was a big part of it. It gave them something to focus their youthful energy on.

Drue and Rod had a lot to do with it, too. They did a beautiful job. They're wonderful parents. They're very hands-on, just terrific parents. We enjoyed traveling with Kelly as we did with Charlie. We took her to Paris for her thirteenth birthday and had dinner at Maxim's, which she thought was fabulous. She also thought that the South of France was just a wonderful place.

We took them to Disneyworld at the appropriate age; I think they were six and five. And we took them on the *Curt-C* a couple of times–our friend Curt Carlson's boat–once in Florida, and once down in the Bahamas.

We also took them to Scotland and they loved that. We

took them twice and they want to go again. They did everything that Skibo Castle had to offer—golf, horseback riding, skeet shooting, tennis—all the things that Joan and I can't do much of anymore. Kelly thought she might like to visit Scotland for her junior year abroad, but she ended up picking Athens because of her Greek classics studies.

The study of religion and the classics is pretty serious stuff, but she has a great sense of humor about it, she's not heavy about it or anything like that. People ask me how I, as a dyed-in-the-wool Catholic, feel about having a wife and now a granddaughter who are such avid Episcopalians. Joan, of course, says, "Amen, brother." And me? Well, I tell people I'm just hedging my position, that's all.

Judging from how they've developed into young adults, I think both of my grandchildren are going to be very successful in whatever they decide to do in their lives. I think Charlie is going to be a great businessman, because that seems to be his forte.

And Kelly? I'm just so impressed with the way she's maturing—more impressed every year. Whatever she decides to do, she'll do it well. Joan and I are very proud of her.

Charles William Frazier

Charles William Frazier is my grandson. Sometimes I call him Prince Charles, but his real nickname growing up was Buddy. I couldn't argue about that because I was known as Buddy until I went to college. I don't think that's where his nickname came from, though. I think it was just coincidental.

Here's what I like about Buddy. He takes his work, his studies, and his grades very seriously. He's competitive about grades; if he's third, he'd rather be second. He's a competitor naturally. He takes all these things seriously, but he doesn't take himself seriously, which is what I like about him. He doesn't have "bigshot-itis," he doesn't want the glare of publicity, but he's not exactly an "Aw, shucks" kind of a kid, either.

He's an Eagle Scout, and he's climbed every mountain in the country, I think. I ask, "Why do you climb those mountains?" His answer is always along the lines of, "Because they're there." He's a good all-around athlete, but he's a particularly good tennis player. He plays golf, but his attention span isn't as great in golf as it is in tennis.

Buddy has a great sense of humor about himself; he has the ability to laugh at himself, which I admire. This showed up recently in the college application process. He had applied to the University of Pennsylvania's Wharton School, and that was the only rejection he got. According to his parents, his reaction was, "I guess I'm not as smart as I thought I was." He wasn't feeling sorry for himself. He was accepted at the University of North Carolina, the University of Texas business school, and the Honors College at Penn State. He reviewed all of those options in great detail, wanting to know what the courses were, what the opportunities were. Ultimately he chose Penn State. One of the things he likes about it is the fact that they do lots of things in Germany, and he'd like to spend his semester abroad there, because he's been studying German, and that way he would get to use the language more.

Lately he's been involved in all the typical things a young man of eighteen, getting ready to graduate from high school, is naturally involved in. We were together at Easter, and he had a bunch of his male friends over, playing poker and so forth.

I asked him, "What about the prom?"

"I got a date," he said.

"Who've you been dating?"

"Oh, so-and-so," he said. "She's an Indian girl. Her parents were born in India, but she's a U.S. citizen, she was born here."

I said, "I think that sounds great. Do you have a picture of her?"

So he took me upstairs and showed me a picture he got off the computer. I don't know how the hell they do all these things, but there she was on the screen—a very pretty girl.

I said as much, and Buddy responded, "We're just going to the prom together, Big Daddy. This isn't any romance. I asked her to go to the prom, and she said yes, and that's all there is to it."

I said, "OK. Well, if you need any further advice on the subject, don't hesitate to ask."

I mentioned he's an Eagle Scout. Ever since he was a kid he loved Scouting. He loved the Cub Scouts, and of course his mother's been deeply involved in Scouting herself all her married life, on the Girl Scout side. He's learned a lot about leadership, so I think it's been a good program.

But I also told him that man does not live by Eagles alone, and he maybe ought to think about getting a job that pays a little income. Wouldn't hurt, one summer. He got the message. But what I like is his demeanor and sense of humor. He has this dry sense of humor, which is terrific. We laugh together a lot, and we thoroughly enjoy each other's company, just as people. I think we have a great rapport.

I was telling a friend about Buddy and he said, "He seems to take a little bit after you. He's interested in Germany, and tennis. Do you think he got those from you, or did he just pick them up on his own?" I really think he got them on his own, but he knew I played tennis and he talked with me about it when he was growing up. And he saw me play plenty of times. I used to play reasonably decent tennis.

Even with a good kid, you find it hard to keep from lecturing. Sometimes that isn't easy; in fact, most of the time it isn't easy. But our relationship is like the one I had with my own father. He rarely if ever lectured me, and we just had a great relationship, like a friendship.

You can't deliberately make it work out that way. It either does or it doesn't. I imagine in some cases it would be very difficult to do, with some kids. I think Buddy likes to excel for himself, but I also think he takes pride in excelling and seeing how proud we all are of his success. We don't gush over it, but we sure let him know we're very proud of him. He likes that and responds to it.

About a year ago we had lunch up at the River Club in New York City. The women went holiday shopping, and it was just he and I together. He said, "Hey, I've been wanting to ask you a question. Would you be offended if I didn't go to Penn State, to the honors college, and went to some other school?"

I said, "No, no, you can go anyplace you want to...as long as you've got the money to pay for it."

He said, "Aw, come on, Big Daddy. Let me at least explain why I'm thinking about it."

I said, "Go ahead, give me your best shot." And he made a very convincing argument that because he had been born and raised in State College, he just thought it would make sense to see what some of the colleges in other parts of the country would be like.

So he made his tours, and it boiled down to the honors college being one of his final choices. He made the decision on his own, based on what he wants to study and the quality of the program they have. And of course I was delighted when he finally settled on Penn State.

It won't be like living at home for him. They keep them so busy there, he'll be lucky if he goes by the house once a week to pick up clean laundry or something, run in and run out. And he's not a baby-at-home type of guy. He's very independent.

One of the great pleasures Joan and I have had is traveling with our grandkids. The first time we took them over to Europe, we ended up down in the South of France. Buddy was about fourteen then, and of course, a bunch of us men were hanging out, watching all the beautiful girls, appreciating this one and that one. He wondered what the heck these old guys were fussing about. He didn't really care that much about it. Anything to do with sports or things like that, he was very interested in. But women were not a particularly strong interest for him at that age.

I'm glad to see I don't have to worry about him on that score, because there's been a noticeable change in the last year. He's now starting to look around a bit and see what nice "butterflies" are out there. But he just loved to travel abroad, he loved all the stuff we did together over there, and the things we saw and the places we went. He especially loved going down to Monaco. We got down there once for the car races, which we could watch from the boat, and he really got a bang out of that.

He's planning to climb a couple mountains this summer somewhere. What I hope is that at the end of this year, having accomplished all there is to accomplish in Scouts, it will be the end of that phase and he'll move on to other stuff.

In fact, he's already indicated that's what he's going to do. As I said before, you can enjoy it, but you can't go through life being a perpetual Boy Scout. I have to be careful how I say that, because it sounds like I'm anti-Boy Scout, but I'm not. It's just that life is a progression—get on to doing something else.

I think Buddy's developing a great sense of taking personal responsibility for his own actions and figuring out what his plans are going to be. And he doesn't just do something because it's the thing to do, or because his parents say, "You really ought to do this." He thinks it all out pretty carefully.

He's been an excellent student—he's not a fast reader, but he spends the time that's required. With homework, it may take him an extra half hour to get it done, but he just does it. And that's why, out of a class of, I don't know the exact number, but I think there's six hundred in the class, he ranks fourth or fifth. That's pretty good.

243

As for a career, he's interested in the broad field of business and finance. He doesn't want to be an engineer, though he'd probably be a pretty good one. One summer he worked at the Center for Strategic and International Studies in Washington, and I got rave reviews about him from the folks down there. Of course, you expect them to say nice things about your grandson, but Buddy really worked hard, kept his mouth shut. He was much younger than the rest of the students, and they'd have him back anytime because he gets along with people so well.

He has great people skills, and he doesn't complain about anything. When he said he didn't think he should go back to CSIS for another year right now, that he wanted to do other things, how can you argue with that? Just because he did it last year doesn't mean he has to do it again this year.

So I admire the fact that he doesn't just roll over and play dead—"Yeah, I'll do that." He thinks it through for himself. Or if you make a suggestion to him, he'll say, "Let me think about that." He'll chew on it, follow up on it, then he'll come back in three days and say, "I've thought this through, and I don't think this is right for me," or "I think it's a good idea," whatever the case may be. He's very thoughtful.

Oh yeah, I'm very proud of the kid. I think I'll keep him. At least a while longer.

Postscript: Shortly after I wrote those words, I received a phone call from my young grandson. He was right in the middle of all his high school graduation activities and I was happy to hear from him.

"Big Daddy," he said, "I have a problem that I need to talk to you about."

"Sure, what's the problem?" I said.

It seems that the boy was involved in a senior prank. He

and some others unbolted all of the dividers between the toilets in one of the high school lavatories and hid them away. The kids did leave a map showing where the dividers could be found, but I guess they didn't cover their tracks too well because they all got caught. The punishment? They would not be allowed to attend the senior prom.

"What should I do, Big Daddy? I've got a date, and she's gone to all the trouble of getting a fancy dress, and now I can't go to the prom."

"Heck, have your own party," I suggested. "Get some refreshments, some music, invite the kids over to your house, and have your own party."

That's exactly what he did. He and the other pranksters took their dates by the prom—the girls all wanted to go in and spend some time showing off their dresses and checking out everyone else's—then they went and had their own party.

What was I saying about being so proud of this kid, about him being so responsible? Well, boys will be boys.

Ruth Rempe

I had lunch with Dan Tully recently. It was the first time we'd been together in a while, and near the end of the lunch, he said, "You know, I've been meaning to tell you that I think Ruth Rempe is the best senior secretarial assistant of anybody I've ever known. She doesn't let her personal feelings interfere with the way she does her job. She's a real pro." He was just lavish in his praise of Ruth, and he's not alone. Anyone who knows her feels that way, too. She has a legion of fans after our thirty-six years together—and still counting.

Ruth originally worked for E. A. Pierce, the name partner of Merrill Lynch, Pierce, Fenner & Smith. He came into the office regularly until he was in his mid-nineties, and died at the age of one hundred. I'm told that when he died, she was very protective of his office. She examined everything before Human Resources removed any of it, and she separated out what personal papers would be offered to the family. She made sure it was done just the way Mr. Pierce would have wanted it done.

Ruth came to work for me in 1972, after I had come back to New York City from Buffalo to work in the Metropolitan Region. I had a high school gal for my secretary, young and inexperienced, and one day Sam Mothner, who ran the "SD" office, came up and said to me, "Billy, you ought to get yourself a first-class secretary."

I agreed. "But where am I going to find one?"

He said, "I have this lady in SD who used to be E. A. Pierce's secretary. She's one of the best I've ever seen."

"Well, if she's so good, why doesn't she work for you?"

"I've had my secretary for twenty years. She does a good enough job, and besides, I'm retiring in a couple of years. I really think you ought to interview her."

"Sure," I said.

So Ruth came in, we talked a little bit, and then I said, "Before you decide on your part whether you'd like to work for me, you can call Natalie Kubera, my old secretary in Buffalo, and compare notes. She can tell you about any idiosyncrasies that might make you decide you wouldn't want to work for me."

I liked Natalie. She was quite a character. She had been Howard Roth's secretary before she was mine, and she ended up marrying him. To this day I do not know what she said to Ruth about me, but she must have expressed the opinion that while I might be a challenge, I was manageable, because Ruth came back to me and said, "I'll take a chance if you will." So that's the way it happened—all those years ago. Worked out pretty well for both of us.

I've gotten compliments about Ruth from everybody I've ever dealt with all over the world. They all feel comfortable talking to her and laying things out. In fact, to this day, I don't write letters anymore. I'll say, "You know what I want to say," and Ruth will write a perfect letter of congratulations or sympathy, or so forth. She knows how I feel about things–about people or whatever–and she can express it and write an absolutely fantastic letter. I never have to change very much, if anything. That's just one example of how good she is at what she does.

There is a particular chemistry that has made our partnership work so well: We argue like hell–and it's gotten a little more fierce during these later years. She's so damned efficient; her efficiency sometimes drives you nuts instead of the other way around, but obviously it's been to my great benefit to have her be exceptionally efficient rather than not efficient at all.

Ruth is too professional to ever admit it publicly, but I'm sure she could tell you I drive her nuts sometimes, just as she drives me nuts sometimes. She's so meticulous. To this day, I'm not sure I've ever heard her admit that she was wrong or made a mistake. Granted, she hasn't made many–but there must have been one or two of them along the way! As I always say, "Not always right, but never in doubt."

In fact, her attention to detail and following up on things is just unbelievable. I'll ask her something and she'll say, "Well, if you look at your schedule or in the pile of papers on your desk, you'll find it right there." I love to catch her when she forgets to put something in–but it doesn't happen very often, I can tell you that.

Ruth is extraordinarily conscientious. She spends the time. She never leaves the office until she's good and ready–in her own time and her own way–though I'm sure she breathes a sigh of relief when *I* leave for the day: "He's gone; now I can get my work done."

She's not one to watch the clock, thinking, "When can I get out of here?" Sometimes I'll say, "Why don't you take off at three o'clock. Just get out of here, hit the beach." Then I'll call at five o'clock and she's still there, getting things done just the way she wants them done. I come in in the morning and it's all laid out–a schedule, something to sign, maybe something I need to read. It's just been good.

She is also very, very discreet. I think it was the way she was brought up. She went to Holy Angels Academy and the Katharine Gibbs School. When you're the CEO of a large corporation, a lot of information flows through your office, and people are always trying to find out about this or that. But whenever people tried to pry some information out of her, she'd just say, "I don't know. You'll have to ask Mr. Schreyer."

She is very much a leader among her peers. For many years, she has been active in the Seraphic Society, an elite organization of the top executive assistants to the top CEOs in corporate America. She's always been a role model for others.

And she's always shown grace under fire. I think back to the October '87 stock market crash–information and calls were pouring in from all over the place. Ruth never batted an eye, just gave me the details and information I needed and always perfectly prioritized. So she's a source of calm and confidence in a crisis.

And as gatekeeper, she has had a certain power and has always exercised it well–firmly when necessary, but always judiciously and graciously.

One day she asked me, "Am I ever going to be allowed to call you Bill?" I'm kind of old school, and I said, "You bet. The day you retire." So I've maintained that formal aspect of our relationship, and she's been very professional about it. Eventually she did narrow it down to "Mr. S." I think as a result more people know me as "Mr. S" than as anything else. Of course, you can take that "S" and use it for whatever you want to. Probably for some people it's short for SOB!

We all have our idiosyncrasies. One of hers is that she is frugal as hell. If she were in politics, some would call her a fiscal conservative. She's managed her own finances quite well, but she always thinks she's going broke any minute, and so she doesn't spend money foolishly. Likewise, she watches my affairs very carefully. She wants to make sure I don't get overcharged for anything, which is good! Probably saved me thousands of dollars over the years.

Ruth has a rare and wonderful ability to connect with people and make friends. At Merrill, she had great strengths for dealing on the telephone with employees, business associates, clients, and people she knew we were trying to develop a business relationship with. She's so open and approachable. People are not afraid to come in and talk with her and see if they can get together with me.

This doesn't mean that everyone gets through the door. She spots the phony-baloneys pretty fast, and she can tell just by the tone of my voice who I want to hear from and who I don't want to hear from.

Not too long ago I made what turned out to be a big mistake when I said hello to someone when I was attending a dinner up in State College. He waved and came over and introduced himself, said he was a retired military man who was participating in a Penn State leadership institute.

He mentioned different companies he was going to talk to about a job, and one of them was one where I had served as a director. I said, "Well, I used to be on the board there and one of my friends is still on the board now. Send me a copy of your résumé and I'll ask them to take a look."

Now he calls constantly, wherever I go. He's been a pain in the ass, to tell you the truth. Finally I said to Ruth, "After this, I won't talk to him anymore. Make sure you screen his calls." I was only being a nice guy, offering to do a favor for a former military man. Good thing he's retired, because if he's an example of leadership, I wouldn't want him fighting the next war. But you can bet that one front he'll never penetrate is the one guarded by Ruth Rempe!

When you have two people working together as closely and as long as we have, it requires a lot of give-and-take on both people's part to make it successful. Almost like a marriage but not quite—because you do maintain a little bit of distance. We don't try to mix everything together in one big pot. Otherwise it would be impossible for me—surrounded by women. Between her and Joan, they'd have me outnumbered. It's tough enough as it is.

Joan will say, "We're lucky to have her."

I'll agree. "Yes, *I'm* lucky to have her."

Then she'll say, "I wouldn't work for you for anything."

And I'll say, "I wouldn't *want* you to work with me for anything."

So it goes with Ruth and Joan. We all want to get in the last word.

But we *are* lucky to have Ruth. She doesn't forget things and she follows up on everything. She speaks with Joan and apprises her of the things she should know that I would probably forget to tell her.

Ruth is also entirely at ease socially. She's quite sophisticated in any setting and can handle herself on any occasion. When we have a party down at the beach, she comes and she doesn't have to have her hand held. People all know her for who she is, and if someone doesn't know her, they soon will. She can go on a trip to Italy with a dozen people she's never met before, make new friends while she's there and have a wonderful time. She moves around very easily, very graciously. People not only respect her but like her.

She loves Merrill Lynch, and she loves the people she's met while being a part of it. Whether in the Metropolitan Region, government securities, or everything that came after, Ruth just blended right in and made the running of things a lot easier. She's been a wonderful asset—a partner in many

respects, an important part of my life and my family—and I am
grateful to this day that Sam Mothner brought us together.

Bob Adam and Claude Shuchter

Bob Adam was a neighbor of ours in Buffalo who lived
a half-dozen houses down the street from us. He was from
a merchant family who had set up a department store
years before, called Adam, Meldrum and Anderson—AM&A—
which he carried on. It was the leading department store
in Buffalo.

Claude Shuchter was another close Buffalo friend. He was
with U.S. Trust in New York City when he was asked to come
to Buffalo to be the number two guy at M&T Bank, with a
promise that he'd eventually be the number one guy, which
he became in relatively short order, and he did a great job.

Bob loved the department store business. He was a
Scotsman by background, and Scotsmen were historically good
merchants. Tight with a nickel. He knew something about cost
control. Bob didn't try to be an outgoing guy. He was just
himself—low key, with a great winning smile and a great sense
of humor. He had the ability to laugh at himself and his whole
family. They had an island up in Canada that Claude and I
were frequently invited to with our families, so we got to know
everyone. We all became part of one big family, really.

Bob's wife was named Ann. She had a funny nickname—
everyone called her Feedie. Her mother, who lived right next
door to us, had outlived her first husband and married a fellow
who was a leading syndicated writer on hunting and fishing, a
marvelous man. He was from Canada and, I think, England
before that. They were great neighbors. In fact, when we used
to discipline Drue when she was a "bad girl," we'd send her

up to her room. What we didn't know was that Gramps, as we called him, and his wife would be next door in their backyard, and would entertain Drue from the terrace. She was just a little girl then, and Gramps would throw his hat up to the window for her to try to catch. So, she didn't mind being sent to her room for punishment, unbeknownst to us. They were just terrific people, and we got to know Bob and Feedie through them.

Claude's wife had a funny nickname, too. They called her Tix. Damned if we knew where it came from. We'd see them often socially, either together or separately. Claude was president of the bank, Bob ran the biggest department store in town, and I was running the Merrill Lynch office. We each had different business challenges, and it was just fun to sit around and talk about them.

Claude and I worked in the same office building and parked in the same lot. We'd head out together at the end of the day. Both of us had Mustangs, and we would race up Delaware Avenue and stop off at the Buffalo Club for a little cocktail on the way home. That was a great life. People kid about Buffalo, but it was a great place to live. People were great to be with, and when you had the job I had, it couldn't have been better, just meeting everybody and being part of their lives.

Together, Bob, Claude, and I had a damn good time. We'd play golf. Claude's game was a little bit better than mine, but not much. Bob was a pretty good golfer–Scotsmen have to be. He was also a great Scotch drinker. He could drink Scotch, or vodka martinis, and never show it. We all traveled together, and I'll never forget a trip we took to Sardinia with the Adams, the Shuchters, and the Sanderses.

On the flight over, Bob was playing cards–gin–with Claude and Charlie. Well, Bob had a drink every hour, and he just drank the whole way over there. Finally, after we landed, we got into a van that the hotel had sent to pick us up, and poor Charlie must have been hit with motion sickness or something, because he got sick to his stomach. Bob said to Claude, "What in the world is wrong with him? He didn't even have a drink!" Bob had all those drinks and never folded at all. He could hold it better than any man I had ever seen in my life. We just had nothing but fun with those people.

We traveled everywhere with the Adams. One night we were over in Switzerland, and Feedie and I got into an argument about something. Somehow I would always argue with the guys' wives—my nature, having a little fun. They were usually good-natured arguments, but this time she got really mad at me.

When I woke up the next morning, I said to Joan, "God, at breakfast I'll bet she won't even speak to me."

She came into breakfast just as if nothing had happened. Later I said to Bob, "Gee, Feedie was really mad at me last night, but today she didn't seem to be mad at all."

"Oh," he said, "she just had one of her bourbon attacks. She doesn't remember anything that happens when she has a bourbon attack," and he roared with laughter. "So don't worry about it. In fact, I'm glad you do give her hell once in a while. I can't get away with it the way you can." They were really very special people.

Bob and Feedie Adam had four daughters, and we've been fortunate to have remained close to them over the years. Bonnie married Nick Hopkins, one of the leading neurosurgeons in this country. Robby married Leonard Hall, who had a very successful career with Merrill Lynch before he retired. Trudy married Van Mollenberg, and Wendy married Keith Alford, both great guys. The Adam family was a special family, and we've been blessed to be friends with them for so many years.

Bob and Claude were a little bit older than I, and they're both gone now. I miss them a lot. I last had lunch with Bob about three months before he died. He liked to wear certain old sweaters, with holes at the bottom and so forth, and they buried him with a bottle of his favorite Scotch, Chivas Regal, and one of his old sweaters. It was typical Bob, and he would have loved it.

You know, in your lifetime you meet, if you're lucky, a handful of really special people, and both these guys were very special people. Their wives were fun, too. Obviously, men have more in common with other men than they have with the wives, but we always had great times with them as a family. Those were good days–good memories and great friends.

Joe Paterno

I first got to know Joe Paterno probably in the late 1970s, but not on a close basis. We got to be close in the mid-1980s, after I agreed to chair the Campaign for Penn State. Bryce Jordan, who was university president at that time, came to see me about chairing the campaign. It was a few months after I'd gotten the CEO job.

I listened to Jordan's pitch about the realities of shrinking state financial aid and the need to attract more private support through a capital campaign–really, the first serious capital campaign in Penn State's history. He made a compelling case that we had to do it if we wanted to keep Penn State at the forefront of public universities.

I told him, "I really don't have time to do this. But if you convince me that you have a top-notch development staff, I'll consider it."

"I think we've got the best," Jordan replied. "We just brought in a guy from Arkansas–his name is Dave Gearhart." I think he was the best, as it turned out.

"Also," I said, "I've got to have Joe Paterno as vice chairman. Because a lot of people with money may not particularly want to see me, but everybody wants to talk to Joe Paterno."

So Jordan convinced him to take a leadership role in the campaign. Joe said he'd be happy to do it. And that's when we started traveling together to make calls on prospects we thought would be supportive of the campaign. We got to know each other really well.

I'll never forget we had a campaign meeting right during the week of the October 1987 market crash. We had everyone there in one of the conference rooms at Merrill Lynch. At one point I had something to deal with, so I excused myself. "I'll be back in thirty minutes. You go ahead and start the meeting," I told Joe.

When I got back, Joe said, right in front of everyone, "How in the world can you be so calm? I mean, it's the biggest market crash that anyone can remember, and you're still here focused on this business!"

I said, "Well, I've done all that I can do. Now, let's get back to raising money for Penn State. It'll take my mind off today's problems, which I can't do anything else about, anyway." So he liked that, I guess, and we just got to be very close fiends.

I think Joe has been the single most important contributor to Penn State in so many ways. Not only has he been an outstanding football coach, a real leader, but he develops the kids to be more than just football players: to be better students, better men, better leaders who want to do things with their lives and have successful professions—doctors, lawyers, and so forth. He doesn't just turn out jocks—he turns out full, complete men. And he's very proud of the professional success so many of his players have had outside of football.

He's also given generously to Penn State financially from his coach's compensation. He's in a class by himself. Of all the people I have ever known who have been involved with the university, he represents the very best of what we like to think Penn State is.

Over the years I've invited Joe to speak at a number of Merrill Lynch meetings. Nobody could give a better motivational talk than Paterno. He could talk to a women's group on their stuff. He could talk to Merrill Lynch account executives or managers. The first meeting he attended–I think it was down in Florida–he participated not only as a speaker, but he joined in all the games and activities on the beach–the tug-of-war, this, that, and the other thing. In fact, he captained one team and I captained the other, and my team beat his team, which I enjoyed immensely. (I knew how to pick the stronger competitors, because I already knew some of the guys.) We just had a natural relationship. I would needle him, he would needle me, and we just had great fun together.

With Joe, what you see is what he is. There's nothing devious about him. He just calls it as he sees it. He'll say, "Don't mess with me. I grew up in Brooklyn. We know how to take care of things."

His wife, Sue, has been a great partner. They met when she was a cheerleader and he was a young assistant coach. They have a wonderful family, and they're very close. She's had some health problems recently because of falls, breaks. She's never complained. She just goes and gets it fixed up and then comes back again. You never hear Joe complain, either. He just tries to encourage people.

When he asked me about my rebuilding from my own recent health problems–weakness in the legs, and so forth–I told him about my trainer. I said that the guy told me that I was in the freshman class–he was just starting off easy. But then, one week, he decided to move me up, and it was like going from freshman to senior in one big jump. "Cripes," I said, "I could hardly walk for two days."

"He's doing the right thing. You just listen to him," Joe advised me. Then. of course, he's had to take a dose of his own medicine as he recovered from breaking his leg after he got hit on the sidelines in the 2006 season. He admitted to me that when he stood up after taking that hit–he knew he was on national television and he was determined to stand up–it hurt a lot more than he let on. He's tough, I'm telling you.

His record as one of the winningest coaches in the history of college football speaks for itself. But in the losing seasons, he's never blamed anyone but himself. If his coaches failed, it was his responsibility. If the players were not the right players and not playing in the right spots, that was his ultimate decision.

In the 2004 season, when the Nittany Lions started their losing streak, losing seven games that season, Joe never complained or didn't try to explain. He just said, "We've got good kids. We've got to get them playing closer together."

It was after that season that Graham Spanier, the university's president, and three others from the administration came to see him. He invited them to his home to talk about how the next season was going to be, share any thoughts they had, and so forth. They suggested that maybe he should think about announcing his retirement. His response to the president was, "You play in your sandbox and I'll play in mine. I'll know when it's time to go, and I'll make that decision." As well it should be—because the overall good he's done for Penn State far exceeds the contribution that any other coach could make.

"Furthermore," he said, "you don't announce your retirement right at the end of the recruiting season. That would be a dumb thing to do. People came because I recruited them."

Then, of course, he came back in 2005 and had an almost perfect season, losing only to Michigan in the final second of the game, and going on to win the Orange Bowl against Bobby Bowden and Florida State in triple overtime. So anybody who discounts Joe Paterno, takes him out of the picture, doesn't know what the hell they're talking about. It's not a case of misplaced loyalty on my part, just because he's a close friend. If I ever really thought that Joe was doing the wrong thing— we're close enough friends—I'd tell him, "Maybe you ought to consider retiring." But you don't have to tell him that. He'll know when the time is right.

Both Joe and Bobby Bowden were recently elected to the

College Football Hall of Fame, which is highly unusual for living coaches. They're great friends, and Bobby Bowden told him how surprised he was, because he always thought you had to die to get in there. "I wasn't ready to die, so I'm glad they changed the rules," Bobby told him. Joe agrees with that 100 percent!

In 1998, *The Wall Street Journal* published a guide to "Who's Who and What's What" on Wall Street. The entry for Merrill Lynch contained this passage: "Merrill rarely hires stars from rivals, preferring to train its own brokers and investment bankers. Employees are expected to sublimate their egos to 'Mother Merrill.' Merrill executives often have compared the firm to the Penn State football team, which doesn't put names on its jerseys—and whose coach, Joe Paterno, is an old friend of former Chairman Bill Schreyer. The result is a firm that sports few superstars, but that can field a team of excellent people working together as a firm." I think that captures it pretty well.

Of course, having a living legend for a friend is not without its trying moments. We both have places at the Jersey Shore. One day Joe paid me a visit and we went out for a walk on the beach. A kid spotted him and said, "If I run and get my football, will you sign it for me?"

"Sure, I'd be happy to," Joe said.

Word spread, and soon a whole flock of kids came running down the beach. We were just about back to the house, and the kids surrounded him. "Mr. Paterno! Mr. Paterno!" He was autographing pieces of paper, books, footballs, you name it.

Frankly, I was getting a little sick of it. Finally this guy came down the beach and said, "Bill Schreyer, remember me? I used to work for you. I was stationed in Boston." I could have kissed that guy. Seems Joe Paterno wasn't the only one with a fan club.

A little while later, just as we were sitting down to lunch, the doorbell rang. I got up to answer it, and it was one of our local town officials.

"To what do I owe the honor, Mr. Councilman?" I said. Then I saw his young son, carrying a football. The boy looked up with wide eyes. "Is Joe Paterno here?"

He is just a very special person, not only in my life, but in the lives of everyone who loves Penn State. He should be there, if nothing else, as a goodwill ambassador for the rest of his life, and I'm sure he will be.

The Morrises

We first met the Morrises, Mac, Janelle, and their family, back in 1963, when I became manager of the Trenton office and we moved to Princeton, where they were living. Mac, who worked for the Newspaper Advertising Bureau, was a friend of a friend in Buffalo, and when this friend found out I was going to move to Princeton, he called Mac and made sure we all got together.

He was a guy you liked almost instantly. When we were both working in the city, we'd commute together frequently, by car and, later, sometimes by helicopter. We always had a little bar in the helicopter, or if we were traveling by car, we'd stop at Phil's Grill, or whatever it was, on the other side of the Holland Tunnel, where we'd have a vodka, a cocktail on the way home. We got to be good friends just from commuting together. Joan and Janelle clicked, too.

Mac was the kind of guy who was a genuine friend. He never asked for anything. He was never one of these guys who was always saying, "Could you do me a favor, do this or that for me?" All he wanted to be was a good friend. Then they started to travel with us. We'd go out to California and spend some time, and they were always a pleasure to have as houseguests because they didn't just sit around and wait to be entertained. They pitched right in, just like part of the family. We've been to Europe with them, the South of France, all over the place.

Both Joan and Janelle are strong, outspoken women, and often Janelle and I would disagree about things. Mac would get a big kick out of the two of us having a hell of a fight about something–he would just sit back and watch me do all the arguing, so he didn't have to do that sort of thing.

Knowing that Janelle was from Texas and had been raised as a Democrat, once I deliberately provoked her by saying something negative about Franklin Roosevelt. That really got her going.

"How could you? How could you say that about the greatest president?" she demanded.

I said, "Listen. You think Pearl Harbor just happened? They had this big Depression, then he put all the Navy right there in Pearl Harbor to invite the Japanese to attack so he could build up the economy."

Of course, it was all tongue in cheek, but over the years I've always pulled Roosevelt out of the bag once in a while to get a spirited conversation going with Janelle. Now, of course, she's become a full-fledged Reagan Republican, which, as I've told her, I consider a sign that she's truly become more mature.

The Morrises love Santa Fe and have vacationed there for many years. Janelle's big on Indian jewelry. She collects it and started a little business selling it to the ladies in Princeton. She likes to tell the story about the time she and Joan had gone out there ahead of time, and came to pick me up at the Albuquerque airport.

On our way back to Santa Fe, we stopped off at an Indian reservation to buy some jewelry from an old Indian woman. We got there and Janelle said to me, "I don't think you want to come in, because the lady is quite sick and it will probably make you uncomfortable."

"OK, I'll wait out here," I said. So I'm standing outside

the car, and this little old squaw comes up to me and starts trying to sell me jewelry. "No, no, I don't want to buy any jewelry," I said. Finally the girls came back to the car, and I made sure we got out of there just as fast as we could. "God," I said. "I hate poverty!" That statement is one Janelle has never forgotten.

As we were leaving the reservation we saw a truck that had a BULLISH ON AMERICA sticker on it. Janelle pointed it out to me. "Look at that," she said. "They can't be all bad." But to this day, the phrase "I hate poverty" is a private joke between us.

The Morrises have four children we're close to, too. Steve, the oldest, lived out in Irvine, California, for many years and is now back East, living over in Bucks County and doing very well with his business. Janelle, their oldest daughter, married a Frenchman, Eric Thibau, who has been a wonderful addition to the family. They have three children, and their oldest son, Alex, became a brother of mine in Sigma Phi Epsilon. Janelle has worked for many years at Merrill Lynch, in our Government Relations Office in Washington. I can tell you that to this day, she gets rave notices about her work.

Johnny Morris was with Merrill Lynch for a number of years, too, first as a successful financial advisor in our international business in London, then as a manager there and in Dubai, and back in New York. He left a few years ago to start his own business in the area of money management. Another daughter, Pat Harris, also works for Merrill Lynch—in training, the human resources department—what we used to call "Personnel."

They're a great family. Every Christmas Eve we have a big party together, which is always fun—lots and lots of people, all the neighbors and extended family members. We've been doing it for years, and now we're on the third generation.

Mac has always been the kind of a guy who enjoys everything in life. He takes the good and the bad together.

We like to relax together; he loves sports and we watch all the games together, and he's always enjoyed following Penn State.

If you get just a few friendships like this in life, you're lucky. The Morrises are a great clan. It's been a mutually happy relationship, and it's stood the test of time.

Dr. Charles A. Sanders

I first met Charlie Sanders when he was a senior executive at Squibb, the medical and pharmaceutical company. He and his wife, Ann, were renting the house next door to us in Princeton while the one they bought was being renovated. Our driveway ran right past their bedroom window. Charlie recalls that he was awakened more than once at some god-awful hour when I'd walk out my door on the way to work and announce loudly, "Good morning, world. I'm ready for you. Are you ready for me?"

"Who is this egotistical guy?" he'd think sleepily to himself.

When I came back to Princeton from my second stint in Buffalo, the Sanderses had become good friends of the Morrises—Charlie and Janelle were fellow Texans and really hit it off.

One night I was returning from a trip, and when I got home, I headed over to Mac and Janelle's house for dinner. I could see through the dining room window that they were already starting to sit down to eat, and I noticed that Charlie had taken the seat I always sat in—my seat! "Hmm," I thought.

I went in, people got up to say hello, and I quickly went over and sat down in my old seat. I wanted to let this new-comer know who was boss around here. Charlie was good-natured about it, and they just quietly moved him to another spot at the table. An inauspicious start to a friendship, perhaps, but later we got to talking and I liked him right away. All these decades later, Charlie and Ann are two of our closest friends.

Charlie has had as distinguished a career in medicine as anyone could have. A cardiologist by training, he graduated from the University of Texas medical school and served as the general director of Massachusetts General Hospital. He was also a professor of medicine at Harvard Medical School and, after Squibb, served as chairman and CEO of Glaxo, another global leader in pharmaceuticals.

It was through Charlie that I met my cardiologist, Dr. Roman DeSanctis. I was talking to Charlie one day about having had heart problems since I was about thirty-five years old. He asked me a few questions and said, "Well, I'd like you to go up to Mass General and see Roman. He and I were cardiologists together and we set up this stress laboratory." Later, when I had my bypass operation, Charlie stayed with me every step of the way—and beyond.

Once I asked him why he stopped being a practicing physician to become a hospital administrator and then a business executive. He said, "I realized I'd never be the dedicated doctor that Roman is, that I'd never be able to compete with him and the way he does it, and that I didn't really want to. I decided I'd try to run the hospital instead."

That's exactly what he did, and he was probably the most successful doctor-administrator they ever had.

To this day, when I go to the hospital's blood lab, I'll say to some of the older ladies who work there, "Do you remember Dr. Sanders?"

"Oh, Dr. Sanders!" they say. "Best boss we ever had. He cared about the people here more than anybody before or after." They all rave about him. He was a great boss, but he was also a very good businessman, too.

I continue to go to Roman to this day; he is still the head doctor on my account. With his ongoing involvement, we set up the Schreyer Chair of Medicine and Cardiology at Massachusetts General. I meet all these kids–young doctors– when I go up there every year for a dinner. Roman is their mentor. He's a superb doctor and a superb human being.

Charlie's wife, Ann, is a beautiful person. A most attractive, very caring woman. She does things in her own way and on her own time, that's for sure. Charlie jokes that he'll give her a list of ten things to do, and while they may not get done as quickly or neatly as he would like, they do get done, and they get done Ann's way, which in the end is just fine. She's fun to be with–a lively, vivacious person. Joan and Ann enjoy each other's company very much. We enjoy the two of them together just as much as I enjoy being with Charlie.

In 1996, Charlie got the political bug and decided to run for the U.S. Senate in North Carolina, for the seat then held by the conservative Republican, Jesse Helms. One night he told me, "I'm going to run against Jesse Helms."

"Well, given his popularity down there, you'll probably get about two votes in the Republican primary," I said.

"No, I'm a Democrat."

"You're a what?!" I replied. "I never knew that. Southern Democrat, I hope. I might be able to forgive you a little bit if you're a conservative Southern Democrat and not some New England Democrat." We all gave him money, though we kidded him that if he did end up winning the primary and running against Jesse Helms, we probably wouldn't recommend that anyone in North Carolina vote for him.

Charlie campaigned hard in the primary, going all over the state, into the black churches and so on. He ended up losing to a black candidate who was the mayor of one of the cities down there, and that guy lost to Helms.

I don't think he'll do it again, run for office. He gave it a good shot and had a good experience doing it, and got it out of his system. Now he's one of the most respected people in the state—Mr. Integrity. He was asked by the governor to serve as the first chairman of the state lottery system they were setting up. When he agreed to do it, he said that while he personally opposed the idea of a state lottery, it deserved to be done right. That about sums up the selflessness and sense of duty of Charles Sanders.

I appreciated having him as a friend and confidant on the Merrill Lynch board, and he's served as a director for a lot of other companies—Genentech, Fisher Scientific, and so on. We've worked together on the CSIS board and the external advisory board of the Schreyer Honors College, which he graciously agreed to chair. Since his retirement, he's also devoted himself to philanthropic endeavors such as Project Hope and the Foundation for the National Institutes of Health.

Charlie has been among the best friends I've had. He is certainly among the top three with whom I am very close, like I used to be close to Bob Adam and Claude Shuchter. And that's as good as I can say about anybody.

William P. Rogers

No CEO could have asked for a better advisor and counselor than Bill Rogers. An internationally known lawyer who had served as attorney general under President Dwight Eisenhower and secretary of state under President Richard Nixon, he knew his way around business, government, and diplomacy at the highest levels, and was comfortable in the corridors of power. Some say that by counseling Nixon through the famous "Checkers" episode, Bill Rogers saved the future president's career.

He was one of the most impressive gentlemen—and I stress that, *gentleman*—I have ever met. He had a great career in the Navy during World War II, serving on the aircraft carrier *Intrepid* and surviving two Japanese kamikaze attacks during the Battle of Okinawa. Then he worked for Thomas E. Dewey when he was the district attorney in New York City, crusading against organized crime.

As a member of the Merrill Lynch board, he showed such great common sense about any issue that came up. He never exaggerated something into a bigger deal, a bigger problem, than it had to be. We got to be friendly even before I became CEO. We'd have lunch, and he always gave me advice about not being too impatient about moving up the corporate ladder: "You're doing fine. Just keep doing your job, and I'm sure everything will work out just the way you hope it will." He was always an encouraging guy.

There are so many stories I could tell you about Bill Rogers. One that tickled me the most was the one he told about Dwight Eisenhower and Lyndon B. Johnson.

As attorney general, Bill was meeting with President Eisenhower one day, and Ike told him he wanted him to stay for the next meeting. It was with LBJ, at the time the majority leader of the Senate.

"Bill," Eisenhower said, "I want you to do me a favor. When Johnson comes in here, just be sure that he can't get close to me."

Bill looked at him quizzically. "Why do you say that?"

"Well, he's always grabbing me, holding on to my lapel, just touching me. I can't stand that. Maybe just sort of block his way, and we'll carry on the meeting and get it over with."

So LBJ came in, and he kept trying to make his moves. Big diplomat Bill Rogers just kept quietly and smoothly moving around in such a way that LBJ could not physically get to Eisenhower.

He finally left, and Ike said, "Thank you very much, Bill.

That went just fine. You made it a lot more pleasant for me."

LBJ called Eisenhower later and said, "That attorney general of yours sure is a pushy fellow. I felt like I couldn't really talk to you with him around."

Eisenhower brushed it off. "Oh, he probably just got immersed in the conversation and didn't realize what he was doing." Ike just didn't care for people who would pat him on the back or grab his lapel or whatever the case might be.

As a counselor and advisor in the best sense, Bill would never tell you what to do. He'd say, "Have you thought about this, have you thought about that." He'd get you to try to look at things from a different perspective. He had a great knack for appealing to people's better instincts. If they had positive instincts in any way, shape, or form, he'd bring them out somehow and make the people feel like they were bringing them out themselves. And he gave them full credit.

During the Nixon years, the feud he had with Henry Kissinger was well known. Henry was always trying to upstage Bill. But I never heard any complaints about the effectiveness of Bill Rogers's work as secretary of state. Kissinger had a different style and a different flair. I'm sure that in many ways Henry might be more like Bill Rogers today than he was twenty-five years ago. Maturity, it's called.

I was deeply honored when Bill's daughter, Dale Rogers Marshall, asked me to deliver one of the eulogies at Bill's memorial service at the National Presbyterian Church in Washington, D.C. Jim Baker, another great counselor and diplomat, was also one of the speakers. My remarks are reprinted in these pages. They are filled with humor and admiration. Bill Rogers was truly a great man whom I was proud to call a friend.

The Sieg Family

I became acquainted with Phil Sieg through mutual
acquaintances in State College and got to know him even
better after his oldest son, Phil Jr., became the manager of the
Merrill Lynch office in town. I was up there one day giving a
talk to an executive group of some sort, and at the end of it, one
guy said, "Mr. Schreyer, you talk a lot about Merrill Lynch, but
do you recommend it as an investment? Do you suggest buying
the stock?"

I said, "Well, I know the rules of the New York Stock
Exchange. We are not allowed to give an opinion on our own
stock." Then, as I often did when I got this question, I concluded
with a one-liner that never failed to get a chuckle from
the audience.

"But I will tell you this. My wife thinks it's a hell of a buy."

Phil Sieg Sr. was in the audience, and later I ran into him
at another event at one of the hotels in town. He said, "I just
called my son at the Merrill Lynch office and told him to buy
me some Merrill Lynch stock."

"You did what?" I said. "I was just kidding."

"I heard you," was all he said. So I got to know Phil
through that.

(As an aside, Dan Tully heard me tell that joke on frequent
occasions, but when he told it himself down in New Orleans,
he actually got in trouble with the regulators. The SEC or
someone chewed him out. So we had to stop using that, but I
still think it's a damn good joke.)

Over time I met Phil's two other sons. Andy, the middle
boy, worked at the White House for the first President
Bush and then came to work for us at Merrill Lynch in
a variety of jobs. Now he's at Smith Barney, part of Citigroup. The youngest son, Doug, works for Lord Abbett, the
money management firm. He played football at Penn State,
and I said to him once, "Boy, it must be tough being on

a football team coached by Joe Paterno–he's so tough, so demanding."

Doug just shrugged. "He's not so tough. Not if you've been raised by the Ayatollah of Bellefonte." I laughed like hell, and that's how Phil Sr. got his nickname–the Ayatollah. The boys like to kid about how particular he is, how everything has to be just so. For example, growing up, if they read the newspaper before he did, they'd catch hell if they didn't fold it back up neatly, almost iron it, and put it back just the way it was. He hated getting a rumpled newspaper.

Phil's wife, Judy, is a great gal who's got to be a saint. That's another thing we all kid about: You have to be a saint to live with the Ayatollah of Bellefonte. She's very much of a lady, and she has a great sense of humor. She and Joan have become great friends. They talk on the phone regularly to keep up. Judy gets a kick out of the Ayatollah, too. They spend the winter down in Florida, and Judy would love to come home a month or two sooner, but the Ayatollah loves his golf. He plays just about every day of his life.

Golf played a big part in the first trip we ever took together. One day Phil said, "Maybe you and Joan would like to come over with us to Skibo Castle. I swear by it." Well, you know if the Ayatollah swears by it, it's got to be pretty good, he's so darned fussy. So we met him and Judy over there. It was a beautiful castle, and we had nice accommodations.

No sooner do we get settled in than Phil tells me, "Now, the good news is that I've got us a tee time tomorrow morning at nine o'clock."

"Okay, good," I said, all the time thinking to myself, "Oh, hell, I was hoping he'd forget about playing golf."

The course was about ten miles away. They had a beautiful course right there at Skibo, but this other one was the one he wanted to play. We got over there, and we had one caddie. I knew I'd be spraying all over the place, and he'd be hitting right down the middle, so I said, "Phil, since you'll be hitting it straight down the middle, do you mind if I take the caddie?"

"No, you go ahead," he said. So I had the caddie, and sure enough, I'm spraying shots to the right and the left, and he's hitting right down the middle. After nine holes, I said, "Are you tired?"

"Oh, God no," said Phil. "We've got nine more beautiful holes to play."

So we played nine more holes. My first real experience of going away with him and getting to know him. Finally we got off the golf course and I said, "Can you get a drink anywhere in this firetrap?"

"Sure," he said. So we went into the clubhouse for a bite of lunch and a good martini. I raised my glass and proposed a toast: "Here's to the closest thing to the Bataan Death March that I've ever experienced!" Phil laughed, but I'm telling you, playing golf with him was tough work.

But he's always a gentleman, and he always goes out of his way to please people. It's been great being a partner with him in Carnegie House. The Sieg family are terrific friends and a wonderful part of our life.

Makram Zaccour

I first met Makram Zaccour when Joan and I first visited Beirut about six months before Israel invaded Lebanon in the 1980s. Don Regan had stopped there once, too, when he was CEO, but he could only stay about half a day, and we wanted to spend a little more time. We fell in love with Beirut.

Makram wasn't the manager of the office at that time, as he would be later. He was the biggest producer, and we spent a fair amount of time with him. The Lebanese were just terrific people, very hospitable. They wouldn't just take you out to dinner; they would take you to their homes. One night I was dancing with all the young wives of our customers, and one of the Merrill Lynch guys said, "Boy, Mr. Schreyer, he sure likes to dance, doesn't he?"

"Yeah, like a butterfly," someone else said. And so they nicknamed me "Billy Butterfly." We just had a ball.

When the civil war between the Syrian-backed Muslims and the Christians aligned with Israel intensified, we had one office in the Christian sector and one in the Muslim territory. So while the city was politically divided, everyone was still able to do business with one of the offices of Merrill Lynch. By that time Makram had become the head of the office, and I had a direct line to him from my office in New York so I could keep close tabs on what was going on over there. He kept the office open the entire time, and there's a famous picture of him in the Merrill Lynch archives—a photo of him at his desk, shot through a window with a bullet hole in it.

Makram went on to become regional director for the Middle East. One part of his reputation that was almost legendary was his ability to judge people. Anybody who wanted to know about someone before they took him on as a client would check it out with Makram. He had a sniffer; he could smell out a phony faster than anybody I've ever known in my life, which is why losses from business done with unsavory people never happened on his watch. He was one of the best managers—tough but fair. And he ran the office in London the same way.

He's an astute businessman and just a very caring guy. He enjoys a good life without carrying it to excess. He loves cars; he has Porsches and a Rolls-Royce. I was speaking to him during the summer of 2006, right after hostilities had broken out again in Beirut between the Israelis and the Palestinians, and I told him that one of those bad guys was going to steal his cars. "It looks too hot," I said. "Go to France and wait for things to cool off." I was worried about his safety.

STILL BULLISH ON AMERICA

He said, "No, this is my country. I love it and I don't
intend to leave it." He appreciated the call, though, and we still
talk frequently. He has a great sense of humor and he's very
loyal; loves Merrill Lynch. I don't know anyone he has a bad
relationship with.

It was through Makram that I met Rafik Hariri, who
helped negotiate the 1989 agreement that brought peace to
Lebanon and served twice as prime minister before he was
assassinated in 2005. It is generally believed that the Syrians
were behind it. Hariri was born in Lebanon to a poor Sunni
Muslim family, but he was well-educated and went to Saudi
Arabia first as a schoolteacher and eventually to work in the
construction business. He got a job managing construction of
the first major conference center in Saudi Arabia, hiring a
construction company in London to take the job at the prices he
recommended. The Saudis wanted to have the first Pan-Arab
summit at this new hotel and convention center, and by gad, he
got it in on time and under budget.

The government was so pleased with the quality and
timeliness of his work that after that he got a lot more business,
made some good money, and ended up owning his own
construction company. He was very successful and became the
personal contractor to Prince Fahd. At one time he bought a
large position in Merrill Lynch stock, which ran up pretty high
before he sold it. We developed a friendship. I visited his home
in Switzerland and we went out on his big, beautiful boat–
about the size of Saudi Arabia.

For a while I served as a trustee of the Hariri Foundation,
whose purpose was to give Lebanese kids a good education at
top schools in the U.S. and Europe so they could return to
Lebanon to be better, more successful people. They were
supposed to pay back what they borrowed from the Hariri
Foundation at no interest. I think that some of them did and
some of them didn't, but he was like that. He just wanted to
get a large group of Lebanese kids educated.

After the civil war, Hariri invested a lot of money in downtown Beirut and, with his construction background, rebuilt the whole place. Merrill Lynch helped by underwriting some of the reconstruction bonds. He was just a very gracious man, but also very tough minded. He didn't suffer fools gladly. And, of course, eventually he was elected prime minister for two terms.

It was a real tragedy the day he was killed by an enormous car bomb. He was a highly independent guy, who wouldn't take any crap from the Syrians, who were trying to control the country. Now we know what has been going on, and it's pretty bad.

Makram has always maintained a close relationship with Hariri's family, including his son, Saad, who succeeded his father as leader of the faction in parliament opposed to Syrian domination. There is a general view that this government was weak, and that while Hariri's son was a very able young man, he wasn't his father, didn't have the experience of his father, probably wasn't as tough as his father. They were difficult shoes to fill. Rafik Hariri was a remarkable man, almost like the George Washington of Lebanon.

Stephen L. Hammerman

Another trusted advisor and friend over the years has been Steve Hammerman, who served as my general counsel when I was chairman and CEO. Before I retired, we made him vice chairman of the board.

Steve had joined Merrill Lynch as part of the White Weld acquisition, and I got to know him when I was executive vice president of the Capital Markets Group. I knew that compliance was a big problem in the industry. We'd always been known for our compliance stature, but with the large number of people we had, producers in trading and sales and the branch offices, you always wondered which one out there might be peeing in your pool at any given time.

Steve had spent some time as the New York regional administrator of the Securities and Exchange Commission, and as I got to know him, I saw that he knew the rules and regulations and was tough. That's the way I was brought up in the business, particularly with Howard Roth, who, as I mentioned earlier, told me from the start, "If you ever make a trade in a client's account that you can't justify to me is in the client's best interest, you're fired!" Steve knew that's how I felt about it, and I asked him to be my general counsel, to take overall responsibility for enforcing our rules.

It was a great relief to be able to go home at night and know you had a guy who was right on top of things and would take steps if necessary to deal with someone who had done something that was not in the best interests of the customer or of Merrill Lynch. Steve had a motto, "No one's personal bottom line is more important than the reputation of the firm," and that became one of the mottos of Merrill Lynch, right up there with Charlie Merrill's famous first commandment: "The customer's interest MUST come first."

So Steve was a dedicated guy. He had his own set of personal rules as a Conservative Jew: He would never do anything at work, or socially, between sundown on Friday and Saturday night. I greatly admire a guy who is dedicated to the principles of his faith. But that never got in the way of his doing his job, and doing it to the best of his ability.

The Merrill Lynch compliance department under Steve was responsible for uncovering one of the biggest Wall Street scandals of the 1980s. In 1985 one of our compliance officers received a badly typed letter, sent anonymously from our office in Caracas, Venezuela, that called attention to some suspicious trading. It seemed that someone was making trades through an offshore account in advance of public merger announcements that sent the shares soaring.

Our compliance people looked into what was being alleged and decided there was indeed something suspicious going on. They turned the information over to the SEC, whose investigators used their subpoena power to trace the account. It turned out the beneficial owner was a banker at Drexel Burnham Lambert by the name of Dennis Levine. As they traced the matter further, they discovered that Levine was in cahoots with the big Wall Street arbitrageur Ivan Boesky, who in turn had connections with the Drexel junk-bond star Michael Milken, who was notorious as the highest-paid Wall Street executive of his era. All three of them ended up going to jail.

On June 12, 1986, I received a letter from John Shad, chairman of the Securities and Exchange Commission. I reprint it here in its entirety:

> Dear Bill,
>
> On behalf of the Commission, I want to thank you and your organization, particularly the Law and Compliance Department and Robert Romano, for their outstanding work in identifying the suspicious trading patterns which led to the discovery of the illegal trading by Dennis Levine.
>
> The prompt recognition and disclosure of this potentially illegal conduct to the Commission's staff was a critical element in this case.
>
> Congratulations to all concerned.
>
> Sincerely,
>
> John Shad

Needless to say, it was enormously gratifying as CEO for me to get this kind of letter from the SEC, rather than one advising me to show up at the courthouse with my lawyer on such and such a date, and that I had the right to remain silent. Because of Steve Hammerman's diligence and no-nonsense approach, it was a proud moment for Merrill Lynch.

Steve's wife, Elly, is a pistol–opinionated, strong-willed, and a lot of fun to be with. Like Joan, she is fiercely loyal to her husband, her faith, her family–and Merrill Lynch. Steve was a morning person, Elly an evening person–how they make it work is a mystery. But they do and are a beautiful couple to have as friends and colleagues.

Steve went on to serve both Dan Tully and Dave Komansky, my successors as CEO, as vice chairman and general counsel. After the terrible attack of 9/11 that destroyed the World Trade Center, Steve left Merrill Lynch to become deputy commissioner and counsel for the New York City Police Department, helping in the fight against terrorism. I will always be grateful for Steve's leadership, personal counsel, and friendship, which continues to this day.

Stan O'Neal

Wall Street can be a brutal place. Markets move suddenly and oftentimes unpredictably, and if you're caught with a big position on the wrong side of a trend, the results can be devastating. All market professionals know this in theory; in reality, however, this knowledge does not prevent some from getting good and clobbered. It's a story as old as the markets themselves, and in the fall of 2007, it became the story of Stan O'Neal.

I remember first hearing about Stan from Bob Luciano and Tom Patrick sometime in the year 2000. Bob was a senior member of the Merrill Lynch board and Tom was serving once again as CFO, brought in by Dave Komansky to try to restore financial discipline after a wave of acquisitions.

Tom had become impressed by Stan's performance as president of the Global Private Client Group, a position he was appointed to in February of 2000, and one in which he wasted no time streamlining operations and putting his own strategic stamp on what had always been the firm's core business. This business serving individual investors was in many ways Merrill Lynch's crown jewel, but it had become loaded down with costs and was struggling to produce decent profit margins. Stan really roiled the waters in a business traditionally held sacrosanct from change.

He refocused the field on higher-net-worth customers and moved smaller accounts to call centers. He cut costs. He wasn't at all deterred by complaints from some quarters that he was being too abrupt, taking too much risk. Instead, he made big changes in key management positions, and anybody not with his program had to leave.

And most important, he quickly began to achieve some very significant improvements in operating performance.

As a result of all this, Tom and Bob were convinced that Stan was the best candidate to become the next president and COO. The previous president, Herb Allison, had been dismissed by Dave in the summer of 1999, touching off a very public and bitter two-year horse race among three or four key executives.

I probably had met Stan at previous Merrill Lynch events, but it wasn't until January of 2000 that I had the chance to see him in action, at an awards dinner for the firm's annual CEO golf outing at the Eldorado Country Club in California. Stan spoke off-the-cuff about what he was trying to do in Private Client and it was impressive as hell. He was understated, not necessarily showing the dramatic flair of some executives, but his logic was unassailable and he exuded determination and quiet strength.

It occurred to me that his style and approach might be just what the doctor ordered for the whole company, which as a result of the tech stock boom was struggling with high costs and over-capacity. This would only become worse when the market started to implode later that year. And so I was happy when in July 2001 Dave named Stan president and COO–in effect, his successor.

Right out of the box, Stan seemed the right choice for the job. His role in leading Merrill Lynch through the traumatic events of 9/11, and its aftermath, was amazing. He rose to the challenge. Even as the company struggled to recover, he had the courage to make the decision to restructure–a decision that positioned Merrill Lynch for success. He subsequently provided superb leadership to guide the company through the twin scandals of stock research and Enron. With him at the helm as CEO, a streamlined, better diversified Merrill Lynch produced four years of record profits.

To this day, I have no regrets about my decision to support Stan. For a time, he was an effective leader. He brought the same brand of tough-minded management and leadership to the entire company that he had brought to Private Client.

There was tremendous complaining from the "old guard," though. Much was made of what was viewed as his assault on Merrill Lynch's people-oriented culture, but against all this he stood his ground. He was criticized publicly as being "ruthless." His defenders would say that he was just being "objective"– clear-eyed about analyzing performance, deciding what needed to be done, and then doing it, without looking back. They would argue that a lot of executives who had some pretty good people skills couldn't make the tough decisions that needed to be made.

It was, however, his lack of people skills and his inability to trust anybody other than himself that ultimately did him in. Through the summer and into the fall of 2007, the global credit markets deteriorated steadily. Worst hit was the so-called subprime sector, where Merrill Lynch had a very substantial exposure. What had seemed a smart business strategy to produce revenues and profits became a massive liability.

At some point, it became clear that the company was facing billions of dollars of unexpected losses. And then I think Stan panicked. Unbeknownst to his board of directors, he approached Wachovia Bank about a possible merger. Faced with a massive hit to the balance sheet and an unauthorized merger overture, the board had no alternative but to seek a new CEO.

There is irony, of course, in the fact that the same broad class of securities—debt instruments backed by home mortgages—that bedeviled me early in my tenure as CEO ultimately undid Stan. And while his mortgage-backed problem had a lot more bells and whistles and the losses he faced eclipsed mine by far, I believe he could have survived even this. Had he included more people, called together a brain trust of the best minds in and out of the company, confided early and often with his board, maybe, just maybe, he could have worked his way through his problems. But collaboration was not his style. Instead, he fell back on his own worst instincts to act unilaterally and alone. At the end he had very little support within the company, having ousted some of his strongest supporters, people like Tom Patrick, who could have helped him.

Stan is a remarkable, self-made man. He blazed a trail as the first African-American CEO of a major Wall Street firm. He had almost every quality needed to be a great leader in the best tradition of Merrill Lynch—except for the ability to value, trust, and inspire other people. It turned out to be a fatal flaw. And that, ultimately, is the tragedy of Stan O'Neal.

Curt Carlson

I met Curt Carlson because we both happened to have been members of the same college fraternity–Sigma Phi Epsilon. He'd been part of Sig Ep at the University of Minnesota, and of course, I had at Penn State. The national fraternity wanted to get me involved in fund-raising for its foundation. I wasn't all that eager to do it, but they sicced Curt Carlson on me. He was considered the number one Sig Ep in the country; he had given a lot of money to the fraternity.

He called and asked if I could meet him for a drink at the Plaza Hotel. I was interested in meeting him from a Merrill Lynch point of view, to try to get some business with him. After all, he was the founder and chief executive of the Carlson Companies, one of the largest privately held corporations in the world, with a personal net worth estimated by *Forbes* magazine at $1.7 billion. So I agreed to meet him.

We sat down on the appointed date and ordered a drink. He gave me his pitch, then he said, "I have to catch an air-plane now, good-bye." The whole thing lasted about twenty minutes. But somehow or other it just clicked, and we got to be great friends.

He was a big Swede. The Swedes are hardworking, dedicated people. He had a vision of what he wanted to do at a young age, and when Curt Carlson set his mind to do something, it got done. It's all about organization and determination. He's going to do it, there's just no question about it. Not in his mind. And he doesn't make a big deal about it; he doesn't wave his own flag.

Curt caddied at the local country club at age nine, and by eleven, he had shown his entrepreneurial skills by putting together a network of newspaper delivery boys. After gradu-ating from the University of Minnesota in 1937, he went to work selling soap and such for Proctor and Gamble. But he wanted his own company, and about a year later, he scraped together enough money to start the Gold Bond Stamp Company. He'd convince merchants to buy his stamps and give them to customers to reward their loyalty; after the customers got enough stamps, they could redeem them for merchandise.

The thing was a tremendous success. Then Curt bought the Radisson Hotel in downtown Minneapolis, and started acquiring hundreds of hotels and restaurants and travel agencies across the country. By the time he retired, he had built a diversified $20 billion company.

A couple of years before he passed away—in 1999, at age eighty-four—he gave an interview to Minnesota Public Radio in which he recalled the best piece of business advice he ever got. "I was a fairly young fellow," Curt said, "and one of my customers on the paper route made the statement to me—he had a drugstore—and he said, 'You know, I work six days.' And he said, 'I feel that five days is when I stay even. It's the sixth day when I get ahead.' And I have never forgotten that. Practically all my life, Saturday was my day to get ahead."

Boy, can I relate to that advice. Working Saturdays—or at least Saturday mornings—was a habit I got into for most of my own business career. Particularly when I was CEO, I'd go into the office on Saturday to clear the desk, catch up on some reading, do a little thinking when the phones were quiet and other people weren't around. It gave you an edge—a jump on the week.

Along with his capacity for hard work, Curt also had a great way with people. I tell you, if somebody came into his office and tried to give him a bunch of excuses for failure—well, you didn't do that to Curt Carlson, because he just wouldn't tolerate failure. He'd beat the heck out of somebody, and after that he'd pick him up off the ground, clean him up, dust him off, make him understand the reason he was angry. He wouldn't just throw him down a flight of stairs; he'd make the person understand where he had goofed, take the time to give him another opportunity—"Why don't you try it this way..."—and send him on his way. And those people were so indebted to him, so grateful for the second opportunity, that they'd knock themselves out. They wouldn't make the same mistake twice. Curt was in many ways a teacher, and he was willing to teach.

Merrill Lynch became a great client of his—we gave him all our travel business, sales recognition meetings, the credit card rewards program and that sort of thing. I, of course, was always trying to get his financial business—both personally and for his company. He'd give me that old patience routine: "You just keep working on it, young fellow, keep working on it. You'll probably eventually get there." In the meantime, he wanted *all* of our business with him—immediately. Nobody could say no to Curt Carlson. You didn't want to. He was a guy of great integrity; he wasn't a B.S. artist at all. He was a marketing genius—though sometimes there's a fine line between the two.

He had this beautiful boat, the *Curt-C,* which he used to entertain clients and prospects. So we were invited on that boat a number of times. You always had the availability of fishing if you wanted to fish. We'd pull into a place and they docked that big boat. Then they'd get out the fishing gear. I wasn't a great fisherman, but I faked it the best I could. Curt didn't enjoy fishing that much, either. It was there if you wanted to do it, but he'd rather sit around and discuss sales, tell stories, talk about experiences. He wasn't a heavy drinker, either. He'd have one light drink and nurse it. He was a guy you just enjoyed being with. You loved to see him come, and you hated to see him go.

Curt was a fierce competitor, and he could energize a group of people when they were just gathered around him. He had all the right stuff. Not an ounce of phoniness in his body at all. We did a lot together on behalf of the fraternity. He always did his share of the work, but he'd push you out front—whoever he was working with, he would just build them up. He wasn't doing it for his own aggrandizement. You can see why his people always admired him so much, because he always gave them full credit for what was accomplished. He would say things like, "If you want to be successful like Bill Schreyer, then you'll do such and such." He would never talk about himself. And he was revered. You mentioned Curt Carlson in the fraternity and everyone knew him. Even if they'd never met him, they'd all heard of Curt Carlson.

You wouldn't know Curt had all the money he had; he wasn't that kind of a guy. In fact, I think he let me pick up the check more often than he picked up the check. We'd both try to outdo each other a little bit. Of course, he was generous in all the ways that really mattered. He endowed the Carlson School of Management at the University of Minnesota and led one of their capital campaigns. Since Minnesota and Penn State compete for prestige and students, not to mention football, I guess we'll be trying to outdo each other for eternity.

Bob and Sandy Poole

I first came in contact with Bob and Sandy Poole through my daughter and son-in-law. They had met them socially and kept telling me what great people they were. There was a mutual interest because Bob was in real estate and Drue and Rod were interested in starting up their own business by buying some buildings in State College.

They said, "We'd like to find out more about the market up there."

I said, "Well, why don't we all get together with Bob and Sandy Poole, have a social evening, and we'll just talk."

So we talked. What struck me immediately was that Bob clearly knew the real estate market, period. But he also knew it in State College in particular, inside and out. In fact, he's done extremely well there. We had a great time that evening and we said, "We'll have to get together again."

When we got together the next time, I had a thought in my mind. I said, "Bob, it seems to me that we have a mutual problem. I have all of my money invested in Merrill Lynch–not all of it, but a large percentage–and you have most of your money, I would gather, in S&A Homes. If you want to diversify and I want to diversify, why don't I buy half the company and make it a family affair? After all, you and Sandy hit it off so well with Drue and Rod."

"Well, I'll have to think about that," he said. He did, and decided it was a pretty good idea, and we ended up buying half his company. He took the proceeds and invested them with Merrill Lynch, primarily, but with others as well, and diversified his estate. Now the guy who takes care of my estate planning takes care of Bob's, too, so it's a very close association.

Bob grew up in the Philadelphia area. He went to school in Bucks County somewhere before he went to Penn State, and he played all the major sports except football, I guess. He wasn't big enough for that. But he played baseball, tennis–good tennis–he's just a good all-around athlete. He's really a terrific guy. He doesn't pat himself on the back all the time. He's very low-key, and he gets very involved at Penn State. He's a Distinguished Alumnus now, at a relatively young age, which is good.

I met his mother and father, and they're very proud of him. His father was a milkman–a damned good milkman, I'm sure of that–and his mother could not have been sweeter. He just looks up to them; they're very close. So he's got all the right values, and a good sense of humor. Works like hell.

Bob started out working for one of the big accounting firms, and then he decided he'd use his skill with figures to go into the real estate business. He decided to operate out of State College, which he saw as a ripe area, and he certainly was right on. Now we're accumulating land, and just over the last seven years or so, the market valuation is probably up two and a half to three times. So when I fly into Penn State now on "Bull Air," I look out the jet window and joke, "It's all mine." So I think

we've got a real winner here, and maybe someday someone—
one of the majors—will buy us out.

Bob's just a workaholic. I mean, that's the only thing that
worries me about him. We'll go out to dinner and break it up
around ten o'clock, saying, "We're going to hit the sack." But he
won't go back to his house. He'll go back to the office, which is
only two blocks from his house, and work until two or three in
the morning. Hell, I couldn't do that. Even at his age, I couldn't
do it. But he's got that energy level that keeps him going.

We've got a lot going on. We're moving into West
Virginia, Western Pennsylvania outside of Pittsburgh, maybe
down as far as North Carolina, but maybe not. It'll take us a
while, but it's a good business. S&A has gotten into the storage
facility business, too. We have seven units across different parts
of the state, and that's a terrific return on investment. You
couldn't have a better situation, as far as I'm concerned.

Paul Critchlow

Paul Critchlow worked for me as head of marketing and
communications when I was CEO, and has become a great
friend over the years. When he first joined Merrill Lynch he
worked for a man named Jim Murphy, and then for Larry
Speakes, who was President Reagan's press secretary before
we hired him.

The story Paul always tells about getting to know me was
when I was just starting to organize the Campaign for Penn
State, the university's first capital campaign which I chaired,
and he was working with me on that. We'd be talking about
Penn State, and he'd always start to talk about how he had
played football at Nebraska. I'd talk about Penn State; he'd
bring up Nebraska. I'd change the subject to Penn State, and

he'd bring the conversation back to Nebraska. Finally I had enough of that, and said to him, "You know, all this Nebraska crap is starting to get on my nerves." Paul was smart enough to change the subject pretty quickly, and that was about the last I heard about Nebraska.

I was recently reminded of that story, and I have to say it's reasonably true. I hated Nebraska. I also remember what was probably the very first time I met Paul. I walked into Jim Murphy's office one day—it was either late in 1984 or early in 1985—and he was sitting outside waiting to go in for an interview.

I said hello to him, and he said he was going to meet with Mr. Murphy for a job interview. I looked him over and said, "By the way, when you're through, and assuming you get recruited, the first stop ought to be the barbershop. You probably ought to go up and get yourself a haircut."

Oh God, he never got over that. He talked about that for years. But he went somewhere and got a haircut right away. The next time I saw him he said, "How do I look?"

I said, "You look much better, you look great."

Paul was a decorated Vietnam veteran. He had been wounded pretty badly over there, and after he came back he got a graduate degree in journalism at Columbia. He worked for *The Philadelphia Inquirer* and then went to work for Dick Thornburgh, first as a key aide in his successful campaign for governor of Pennsylvania, then as press secretary and communications director. That experience made him invaluable to me as CEO.

One of Paul's great strengths is his ability to size up a situation, whether it be a political or communications situation, and suggest the best way to handle it, how to deal with it— either head-on or go behind the scenes and talk to somebody. He was frequently in favor of the direct approach, rather than playing games with it, and I think most of the time that was the best approach.

He also had a good way of sizing up what the press would think, or what the investors would think, or what the branch offices would think. He was good at judging what people would say or feel about things. He wouldn't always be right, but very seldom was he grossly wrong.

I'd say, "What do you think about this?" And sometimes he'd say, "Well, let me take some time to think about that." He wouldn't give you a right-from-the-hip answer all the time. He'd give you an immediate reaction, but he'd say, "Let me think about that overnight," which I liked. He knew the importance of good decision-making. He had helped Thornburgh manage the Three Mile Island nuclear crisis in Pennsylvania, when they were faced with some real life-and-death decisions, and his experience in that crisis sure was a big help to me during the 1987 stock market crash. He did a pretty good job of juggling all those egos on the Merrill Lynch executive committee, too.

Another thing I like about him is that he has the ability to poke fun at himself, which is always a great trait. One example of that was another Nebraska football story that he liked to tell about himself.

He'd recall the times when he was in the backfield, waiting to return the opposing team's kickoff. Right before the ball was kicked, he recalled, "I'd say a little prayer."

"What did you pray for, Paul?" we'd ask him.

"'Oh Lord, please don't let the ball come to me.'"

And when he was still drinking, of course, he was a lot of fun. I'll never forget the trip we took to Japan. He and I decided to sit together up in the front of the jet cabin, because that way we could drink. Joan and Paul's wife, Patty, were sitting in the back, probably thinking, "Look at the old fools up there."

They'd come up and stare at us from time to time, and we'd cut back a little bit. But the point was, he was really a fun-loving guy, particularly after he had a couple of snoots.

He took his work seriously, but he didn't take himself too damn seriously. People generally liked him and respected him. He's still at Merrill Lynch, working as a vice chairman in the municipal finance area, looking after relationships with the issuers of municipal bonds.

I think it's a job that's absolutely right for him. He can schmooze as well as anybody I know in that world of municipal finance, because people like him. How can you get mad at Paul indefinitely? When he comes in he's pleasant, he doesn't make a pain in the ass out of himself; he just has a way of charming the secretary or the assistant, whoever it is. He doesn't look angry or mad when the person says no, the boss can't see you right now. He just handles it. And that takes patience and persistence.

I know that when he was younger and I was the active CEO, he returned phone calls immediately. And when I asked for a piece of paper, or a report on something, I could get the answer before the end of the day, or at least a progress report on how long it would take and when it would get there. Now sometimes it takes him days to return phone calls, if at all. I like to kid him about that. The truth is, I know that Paul will always be there for me when I need him.

Patty is a pistol—Irish, charming, and independent-minded as can be. She's a talented writer and has become a popular author of young-adult novels. She likes to poke fun, and we both enjoy teasing Paul. They've both been great friends to Joan and me over the years; we've had so many great times together, both as couples and individually. It's a friendship that we cherish very, very much.

Jim Wiggins

Boy, this guy's something. He was always very proud of the fact that he went to work at Merrill Lynch, where the CEO was a fellow Penn Stater. He used to tell people, "Some people go to Harvard or Yale to get connected on Wall Street. I went to Penn State."

These days he works for a competitor—which I wasn't too crazy about, but I understand the situation. At Merrill and even before—in Governor Thornburgh's administration—he worked closely with Paul Critchlow, and they made a great team. They were even better than—who? Abbott and Costello? They didn't compete with each other; they complemented each other. Wiggins is a master of words, a master communicator—that's a great skill, and he must have learned it at Penn State.

He was also a master at crisis management. From the crash of '87 all the way up through 9/11 in 2001, Jim could size up the facts of any situation, and quick as lightning develop a sound response. During the crash of '87, he and Paul wrote the scripts for the famous "Still Bullish on America" commercial. I never saw anyone work so fast or with such unerring instincts as Jim. Nobody was better at projecting the qualities and character of Merrill Lynch than "Wiggs."

He could deal with the press, too, sometimes using sweetness and light, sometimes being a tough, miserable old goat. However he mixed it up, the reporters he had to deal with couldn't take him for granted, because they weren't quite sure what they were going to be getting, based upon the questions they asked him. My guess is that the reporters felt that they'd better ask reasonably intelligent questions, because if they didn't, this guy was going to burn them up.

Jim's wife, Chris Fleming, is a Penn Stater, too, and a strong and delightful gal. Joan and I have enjoyed her company at various social events over the years—and, of course, when we all go to Penn State events it's really special.

Wiggins is a guy of many talents. He worked with me a lot on various speeches over the years, and it's amazing how I could tell him what I wanted to say, and he'd find a way to say it better than I could. Over time, he learned to capture my voice—but I think he actually improved on it. In fact, I may have captured his voice. Wiggs has been instrumental in helping me prepare this book. It's been a project that we've both enjoyed a great deal.

Still Bullish
—on—
America

A MEMOIR

——— by ———

WILLIAM A. SCHREYER

Appendix

Appendix:
Selected Speeches

Gold Medalist Acceptance Speech

The Pennsylvania Society
102nd Annual Dinner: December 9, 2000
The Waldorf-Astoria
New York, NY

My philanthropic activities with Penn State led to my being awarded a Gold Medal by the Pennsylvania Society, an organization that was founded in 1899 to, according to its constitution, "cultivate social intercourse among its members, and to promote their best interest; to collect historical material relating to the State of Pennsylvania, and to keep alive its memory in New York."

For many Pennsylvanians, the Society's annual gala black-tie dinner in New York City inaugurates the Christmas season. Joan and I attended and were greeted by so many fine Pennsylvania friends as we prepared to accept the award. As he introduced me, the Society's president, Sam McCullough, really took me by surprise. He brought to the

podium two students from the Schreyer Honors College.
Their brief remarks are worth reprinting here:

✻

*Hello, my name is Maureen Gramaglia. I went to high school
at Thomas Jefferson High School for Science and Technology in
Alexandria, Virginia. After I decided to go to Penn State, my whole
family moved here because they said, "She's making the right choice."*

*Three years ago I had the honor of being the first Schreyer
scholar. I was able to thank Mr. Schreyer on behalf of all the
students for the wonderful gift that he gave us. Now I am getting
ready to graduate from Penn State in May with three degrees—
physics, chemistry, and Russian translation—and a minor in math.
I know that the honors education I have behind me has really been
unique, and in no other place that I can think of could I have
combined so many studies that prepared me uniquely to go into the
world of science. And I have Mr. and Mrs. Schreyer to thank for
that. I am going to graduate school with my perfect GRE score that
my honors education prepared me for. It has been an honor to be
here tonight.*

✻

*My name is Ryan Newman, and I do not have three degrees. If
you were holding your breath, you can stop because you will be
holding for some time.*

*I am from Yardley, Pennsylvania, and I went to Pennsbury
High School. Thanks to Mr. and Mrs. Schreyer's amazing support, I
had the opportunity to be the first international thesis grant recipient,
which allowed me to travel to Cameroon, Africa, and conduct
research in fertility. As a result of this research, I have been selected
to present my research at the International Mammography Conference
in Washington, D.C.*

I guarantee that because of Mr. and Mrs. Schreyer's gift, there

are many, many other students getting in line to get their thesis grants
to do the same research, the type of research that changes the world.
Thank you, Mr. and Mrs. Schreyer.

❋

Thank you, Mr. McCullough. That was a wonderful introduction. You know, at my age, when you hear something like that, it generates a rare and special kind of pleasure. So I want to assure you right up front: I do not intend to contest this decision. No recounts!

Governor Ridge, Senator Specter, Senator Santorum, Governor Thornburgh, my fellow Society members, and distinguished guests. It is a very great honor for me to receive this award from the Pennsylvania Society.

I was thinking about how I would feel as I stood here to accept this honor, and I recalled a phone conversation I had with our good friend Joe Paterno, who, as you all know, is also a Gold Medalist of the Society. I called Joe not too long ago to commiserate about the season. I figured he could use a little cheering up.

I said, "Joe, now you know how Lou Gerstner at IBM must feel. His company just fell short of its sales estimates, and do you know what happened? The stock dropped eighteen dollars per share, losing sixteen percent of its value in a single day. That decline was single-handedly responsible for dragging the Dow Jones Industrial Average below 10,000 for the first time in over six months. And analysts all over Wall Street are revising their earnings forecasts."

Joe's response was classic Paterno. He said, "Bill, look at it this way. I'm in good company!"

Well, that's exactly how I feel tonight. In very, very good company. The list of Pennsylvania Society Gold Medal Winners is a veritable who's who of accomplishment over the past century—in public service, industry, science, athletics, and the arts. People like Dr. Gertrude Barber, Andrew Carnegie and Mrs. Carnegie, Dwight Eisenhower and Mamie, Fred Waring, Arnold Palmer, and Bill Cosby, not to mention the distinguished medalists who are with us here tonight.

It's a humbling club to be part of, also a reminder of how insignificant one's own accomplishments really are. It's also a reminder of the shining ideal upon which Pennsylvania was founded—the simple ideal that people should be free to live their lives free from persecution in order to pursue their human potential to the fullest.

How well that human potential has been fulfilled over the years by people with a deep and abiding connection to Pennsylvania. My own link to Pennsylvania began with the great good fortune of being born within her borders. This connection has extended throughout my life as one long and continuous thread, interrupted on occasion by distance or absence, but never broken.

My boyhood was spent in Williamsport, and it was the happiest childhood imaginable even though we were living in the midst of the Depression. The values that I learned growing up in Williamsport have been fundamental to my life. Values like honesty and dealing straight with people. An understanding that neighbors do matter. That neighbors have an obligation to help each other. And that acts of helping, large and small, repeated day in and day out, are the definition of community.

The realization that you judge people by who they are as individuals and what they can contribute, not by their nationality, religion, or the color of their skin.

Of all the people I knew in Williamsport and remember with great affection, the one who had the most influence on me was my father. Watching him run that small Merrill Lynch office was for me like getting a graduate degree in management.

He taught me that, in fact, you don't manage people. Maybe you manage systems and processes, but you lead people. You inspire them by appealing to their highest aspirations. You guide them by example. You counsel, you convince them that by working together as a team they'll achieve far more than they ever could individually, and they'll have a heck of a lot more fun in the process. These are lessons that have served me well throughout my life.

During my career I have been privileged to meet with world leaders from so many vocational disciplines and got to know men and women who have distinguished themselves in countless aspects of human endeavor. From Williamsport, the doors to this world began opening for me when I took my first short journey west to Penn State. It was right after World War II, and many of my freshmen classmates were returning soldiers. They were a few years older than me and they knew a thing or two about life. They taught me worldly and important skills—like never mix ginger ale with good bourbon. Those undergraduate years were also the start of a lifelong passion, a dedication and loyalty to the great land grant university that is, both physically and figuratively, at the heart of Pennsylvania.

It is particularly satisfying to be recognized here tonight for an activity that I began relatively late in life. Joan and I are really enjoying the opportunity to give something back to those institutions that have really mattered to us. If we'd known how much fun this was going to be, we'd have started much sooner, except for one small problem—we didn't have the money.

But we have been fortunate to be able to support, in a significant way, the honors college at Penn State. I am glad I was given the surprise tonight and that you met two of our outstanding students. The honors college is an extraordinary resource within the university, and I want to take some time to tell you about it.

To begin with, I give a great deal of credit to Penn State's president, Graham Spanier, for his leadership in building the program. Graham has boundless energy, great imagination, and he's always doing something surprising. Who knew, for example, he would be the president to deemphasize football at Penn State!

Under Graham's leadership, along with Dean Cheryl Achterberg, the honors college has grown to become one of the largest and most comprehensive undergraduate programs of its kind in the nation. We have 1,846 students in every imaginable major—from A to Z—architecture to zoology. They come from all different backgrounds and walks of life.

But our real focus is on quality, not quantity. Forty-three percent of our incoming freshmen are in the top two percent of their high school graduating class. Average SAT scores are 1427—that's out of a possible 1600. Eighty percent of our students maintain a grade point average of 3.6 or higher. Eighty-five percent eventually go on to graduate school. And 100 percent who have applied to medical or law schools have been accepted.

These honor students, through their education at Penn State, are preparing themselves to be the global citizens of tomorrow. Last year alone, two hundred of them received grants to study abroad in some thirty-eight different countries. And they're a pretty well-rounded bunch, too. Thirty-five of our honors scholars are also varsity athletes. And together, they have logged over nine thousand hours of volunteer service to the local community last year.

I am extraordinarily proud of these young people. They will contribute greatly to Pennsylvania's reputation in the years ahead. It will not surprise me one bit when, as the twenty-first century unfolds, one of our honors graduates finds him- or herself standing right here where I'm standing tonight, accepting an award from this Society for some stunning achievement yet to be recorded, or a great contribution to mankind yet to be made.

Private philanthropy will continue to be critical in making our colleges and universities among the greatest in the world. But private dollars, as important as they are, will never be a total substitute for public support. There are many elected officials in the audience tonight. To you, I make this appeal: Please find a way to maintain and, yes, increase the level of public support that we give to our colleges and universities throughout Pennsylvania. This is not only an investment in the future; it is an investment in the here and now, the quality of life as we're living it today.

If there's a better way to create opportunity and the chance for economic advancement than opening the door to a college education, then I haven't heard of it. It works as well today as it did fifty years ago for people like me and countless others in my generation.

Now, in closing, I would like to pay tribute to one other young person who brings great credit to the Commonwealth of Pennsylvania. Some in life are called upon to exhibit great bravery and character in the face of sudden adversity, and that is certainly the case with Adam Taliaferro.

When he sustained a serious spinal injury in the final moments of the Penn State-Ohio State game, the initial prognosis was not good. But this young man is fighting back and is determined to recover. His courage is an inspiration, and I am delighted that the monetary portion of this award will go to help him.

Thank you all very much, and I remain "Bullish on Pennsylvania."

Remembrance by William A. Schreyer

A Service of Thanksgiving for the Life of
William P. Rogers, 1913–2001
January 8, 2001
The National Presbyterian Church
Washington, DC

Ladies and gentlemen, the Rogers family, fellow friends and admirers of Bill Rogers:

Our sadness at losing Bill is tempered just a little bit by the memories we have of him. Wonderful, warm memories, and some of them very funny.

When Dale called me last week and asked if I would say a few words, I thought, "Good heavens, what could I say about Bill that wouldn't already be said by someone more profoundly or more eloquently than I could?" By Secretary Baker, for example.

The public Bill Rogers—the statesman, the diplomat, the counselor to presidents, the great architect of the law—is now a well-documented part of history.

He was one of those men—those unique men—whose brilliance, whose discretion, and whose fine sense of humanity placed him center stage, for a very long time, in what has come to be known as the American Century.

But today I'd like to talk about the private Bill Rogers, and share some recollections of the man whom I and my Merrill Lynch partners knew as a trusted advisor, a confidant, and most of all, a friend.

Shortly after Merrill Lynch became a public company, Bill was asked by our chairman, Don Regan, to join our board as one of our first "outside" directors. It is hard to imagine anyone better suited for this kind of role than Bill Rogers.

And it is not possible to overstate the contributions he made to Merrill Lynch, and what he meant to me, to my predecessors, and to my successors, all of whom are here today.

He was extraordinarily sophisticated. He knew how the world worked and how to get things done. His name and his reputation opened doors all over the world. He was exceptionally intelligent, capable of unweaving the complexities of any situation, recommending a sensible course of action, and forging a consensus.

With Bill, trust was implicit. You could totally confide in him the most sensitive of matters and be absolutely certain that your trust would never be betrayed.

Bill was a great practitioner and interpreter of the law—but the advice he gave was never legalistic. It was always rooted in plain common sense. He did not spend his life "looking for loopholes," a quote that, according to Bill, was uttered by W. C. Fields when he was supposedly asked on his deathbed what he was doing reading the Bible. "Looking for loopholes."

No loopholes for Bill Rogers. Just honest, clear-eyed, solidly reasoned advice, delivered from the heart.

But there is one way that he was like every other lawyer I've ever known—every doctor, too, come to think of it—and that is this: In all the lunches and dinners we've had over the years, the subject of his picking up the check just somehow never came up.

When we roasted Bill at one of our annual Merrill Lynch "kitchen cabinet" luncheons a few years back, none of us had the nerve to kid him about this. So Bill, wherever you are up there, please forgive me. But in the interest of full disclosure, I do feel I have to mention this.

I'm kidding, of course. Bill was generous in every way that mattered. He was generous in human spirit. Regardless of how tense or difficult the situation, Bill always had the human touch. And it made so much difference—all the difference.

I'll never forget when Don Regan sent Bill and me down to Texas to sort out the mess after the Hunt brothers had tried to corner the silver market. We at Merrill Lynch were sitting there with not a small amount of exposure. After a tense day of negotiations, during which Bill exhibited all of his talents for patience and persuasion, we got back to the hotel feeling pretty beat.

Bill called me from his room and said, "Why don't you come on over? Now that we've gotten that taken care of, I'm going to make you the best martini you've ever had." He did, and it was–a darn good one!

Of all the endearing qualities of Bill Rogers–and there were many–I think the one that a lot of us cherish most fondly was his marvelous sense of humor. He wasn't a joke teller, but he was exceptionally quick-witted and shrewd in his ability to observe situations and people, and help us all see the funny side of things.

He'd come out with a remark, or an observation, or a story that would make us all laugh, but it would also do something more than that. Through his humorous commentary, a deeper truth or insight was often gently revealed.

I'll always remember the advice he gave to the late Supreme Court Justice Potter Stewart when he was coaching him on how to get through his Senate confirmation hearing. Bill said, "Potter, just say as little as possible while still appearing to be awake." That, I might add, was exactly the approach that Bill took at some of our board meetings.

Then there was the story he liked to tell about a visit to Saudi Arabia he made with Adele, early in his term as secretary of state. Befitting the stature of his office, they were received with great pomp and circumstance, and were taken by motorcade to the palace, where the king hosted a state dinner in grand style.

During the dinner, Bill noticed there were gold toothpicks at each place setting, and he told the king how much he admired them. Well, a day or so later when they got back to their airplane, an aide came up and said, "Mr. Secretary, there are four cartons of gold toothpicks delivered as a gift from the king."

Of course, Bill couldn't accept them because of government ethics rules, but Adele, being a very practical person, had even less use for them. Adele said, "Bill, for goodness sake, why didn't you tell him that you liked his limousine?!"

There's one other story Bill told that I will always remember. Bill hated long-winded speeches, and this was a dislike that he happened to share with President Eisenhower. Apparently there was another member of the cabinet who had a particular penchant for long-windedness. He would go on and on, about anything and everything.

As Bill told it, one day they were leaving a cabinet meeting, and Ike leaned over to him and said, "That fellow missed some really good opportunities to keep quiet."

What a nice way of suggesting that someone should just, well, shut up!

Today as we pay our final respects to Bill, I am going to stay mindful of his dislike of long-windedness, and take full advantage of the opportunity that now presents itself to keep quiet.

I know that I speak for all of us at Merrill Lynch when I say that our admiration of Bill and our respect for him will always endure.

Bill was a leading actor in some of the most significant historical events of our time, but he never sought the limelight.

His words and his deeds helped shape our destiny for more than half a century, but he never sought to take credit.

He was a truly great man—a greatness worn with grace, with style, and with ease. To know Bill Rogers was to revere him—a great statesman, a great counselor, a great public servant, a great mentor.

Also, a great friend. And a symbol of leadership to us all. Thank you very much.

Merrill Lynch: A Fifty-Year Perspective

Global Private Client Managers' Meeting
September 21, 2002
Santa Barbara, California

In 2002 I was asked to address two different management groups representing our capital markets and private client businesses. This is a speech I gave to a biennial meeting of several hundred of our private-client branch managers.

It was a difficult time for the company. We had just come through an ugly attack by the politically ambitious New York State attorney general, Eliot Spitzer, who, on the basis of some incredibly stupid and ill-considered e-mails by Merrill Lynch's young Internet analyst Henry Blodget, used the threat of criminal prosecution to extort a $100 million settlement from Merrill Lynch over alleged bias in our securities research–the prelude to a similar billion-dollar settlement with the rest of Wall Street.

Merrill Lynch was also embroiled in allegations by the U.S. Justice Department that some of our investment bankers had improperly abetted the financial shenanigans of the Houston-based energy company Enron, whose bankruptcy came to symbolize the financial excesses and corporate wrongdoing of the high-flying 1990s.

The setting for all of this was an historic stock market collapse that followed years of fevered speculation in new technology stocks–the so-called "tech wreck"–and that destroyed over a trillion dollars in market value and left investors, politicians, and regulators fuming and looking for scapegoats. As always, Merrill Lynch and the other Wall Street firms presented a fat target.

Market activity was depressed, both our reputation and stock price had taken a big hit, and there was a management change at the top, with Stan O'Neal succeeding David Komansky as CEO. Morale among many of our people was scraping bottom.

My purpose in delivering this speech was to put the current tough times in perspective, to remind people that the company had faced tough times before, that we had come through them then, and that with their active leadership we would come through them again. Secondarily, my goal was to share some of the culture and lore of the company, and to entertain people. I was pleased that the audience for this speech laughed often and in all the right places–including when I kidded Stan O'Neal, the first African-American CEO of a major Wall Street firm, as being "one of them. An investment banker."

As part of my introduction, they showed a tape of my "Straight Talk" TV commercial from the market crash of 1987– something that never failed to elicit an enthusiastic response from Merrill Lynch audiences.

⊛

Thank you very, very much. After that introduction and your warm response, if I was smart I would just say "thank you" and sit down.

It really is great to be back home with the leaders of Merrill Lynch, and it does very much feel like home to me. I'm sorry I could not be here for the whole meeting, because if this morning was any example, and the remarks I heard last night, then this has to have been one highly successful meeting– which doesn't come as any surprise to me.

But it just reminds me that after almost ten years of retirement from the job, just how great this place is and how great the people of Merrill Lynch are. You exemplify that, and I thank you for that very much. You know, looking at that video, it occurs to me that had I been a prizefighter back then,

I would have probably been a heavyweight. These days I'm more like a flyweight, but I look at it this way: At my age I'm just happy to be any weight.

They say old soldiers never die, they just fade away. But for some reason I'm having trouble fading. I'm careful about my diet, I watch what I eat, small portions and all of that, and of course look out for cholesterol. But the worst part is not the eating. It's having to be so darn careful about what and how much you drink. Fortunately, the one good thing about seven pleasant decades of life is that there's always a special occasion when you can bend the rules a little bit. And I've been quite successful in that principle. As a matter of fact, I consider this meeting a special occasion. I can't want to get this speech over with and go celebrate!

In all seriousness, for me, it is special to be here with all of you. And I appreciate that Dave [Komansky] and Stan [O'Neal] and James [Gorman] and Bob [Mulholland] asked me to participate. And frankly, I'm just glad they remembered me. I've always said that it's better to be gone but not forgotten than forgotten but not gone. And I hope none of you find yourselves in that latter category.

With that, the title of my talk, or reflections, today is "Merrill Lynch: A Fifty-Year Perspective." I thought that was as good a title as I could give it. I feel incredibly fortunate to have this kind of connection with a place that I love very, very much. And it's no exaggeration to say there are very few people around today who could give a speech with this title.

I joined Merrill Lynch, as Bob pointed out, in 1948. And if you count the years I spent hanging around the Merrill Lynch office in Williamsport, where my dad was the office manager, well, my connection with Merrill Lynch goes well beyond a half-century. And it has been, really...has been my life. Over that kind of time span you see a lot. A lot of change, a lot of turmoil, and a lot of good years, too. You learn a thing or two about the markets, and most important of all, if you keep your eyes and ears open, you learn a thing or two about human nature.

So, what have I learned over all these years? I'd like to make three points with you today, and the first point is this: No matter how bad it seems at any one point in time, it doesn't stay that way forever. Arthur Zeikel, the father of our asset management business, used to say that the biggest investment mistake people make is assuming that any current trend will continue indefinitely in the same direction.

The bad times are never permanent. Never. There are always better times ahead. And this is not just blind optimism coming from an old stock and bond salesman. It's reality. It's the truth.

I've seen my share of crises over the past fifty years, and had a hand in dealing with a lot of them. I think back to the early 1980s and the Hunt Silver Crisis. Some of you might remember it. The Hunt brothers from Dallas tried to corner the silver market and got themselves overextended. A good deal of their trading was with Merrill Lynch and we had a lot of exposure. Don Regan was CEO at the time, and Don is, of course, legendary in our firm, and deservedly so. Don Regan was a lot of things. One of them was that he was a very good delegator. I happened to be the "delegatee" that day.

Don sent me and Bill Rogers down to Texas to straighten things out. It was our job to explain to the Hunts that while we sympathized with their plight, we did expect them to make good on their trades with Merrill Lynch. That was one of the toughest conversations I think I've ever had. And when it was all over, the Hunts were starting to see things our way. Let me tell you, it was one of those "special occasions"!

We went back to the hotel and Bill Rogers—here you have it—the former secretary of state and one of our first outside directors, a great man, a great friend, and a great counselor to Merrill Lynch...Bill demonstrated that among his many other talents, he could mix one hell of a good martini. I don't think

I've ever tasted a better one than that one, on the day when we really settled the problem with the Hunt brothers.

And it seemed that no sooner than we got through the silver crisis, we had Baldwin United. Some of you may remember that one, too. We sold a whole lot of Baldwin United annuities, and the company then went bankrupt. Our clients were up in arms. The sales force was on the warpath. The regulators were hopping mad. It was a mess. And I'll tell you, the bonds of trust we had with our clients were sorely tested by that one. But we worked our way through it. We did right by our clients. We stood by the guarantees in those annuities. And in the end, in the vast majority of cases we were able to reestablish the trust that is so essential to what we do every day.

Then, of course, there was 1987. The year I'll certainly never forget. Things got off with a bang with the mortgage-backed securities loss. We lost north of $300 million in something called IOs and POs. I had another name for both of those.

That was a lot of money back in those days, and for that matter, it's a lot of money today. Some trader exceeded his limits and decided to hide tickets in the desk. I was CEO then, but I had learned from Regan how to delegate. I sent Tully down to clean up the problem. I always refer to that as my Chernobyl. You just know how Gorbachev must have felt when someone called him on the phone and said, "Comrade, we've got a little problem down at the nuclear plant." And he sure did, and at that point we sure did, too.

Then, of course, came October 19, 1987–the biggest one-day drop in the Dow since 1929. That day and the days that followed tested this firm like it had never been tested before. It was a dark and difficult time for Merrill Lynch. People had lost money in the market. They were mad and they were looking for someone to blame. Congress got into the act. They held hearings and made fiery speeches. Program trading by the big Wall Street firms was identified as a primary villain.

As a company we were sized for a bull market. Way over

capacity. We had to shrink the work force, close offices, and refocus a lot of our businesses. We restructured in 1989, took our first annual loss as a public company. And Tom Patrick, who you heard from this morning, who was the engineer of our restructuring over the past year or so, was the man at my side. He was CFO when we did it back in 1989. So, Tom, it was déjà vu all over again for you this time, wasn't it?

Anyhow, the press was absolutely vicious. They wrote stories questioning whether Schreyer knew what he was doing. I tell you, Schreyer was asking Schreyer if he knew what he was doing, too. Did he have a strategy? Is he going to have to sell the firm to a big bank in order to survive? And as for American investors—according to the pundits, they lost confidence. It would be a long time, if ever, before individuals would come back into the market. And by the way, does any of this sound familiar to you? Any of it?

Of course, it was all nonsense. It was nonsense then and it's nonsense now. We didn't sit around feeling sorry for ourselves; we took the bull by the horns. We made changes, we refocused our business, we pushed into new markets internationally. We continued to build relationships with the wealthiest people in America, the people with money to invest. The result was the most explosive period of growth in the company's history. From 1990 to 2000 total revenues more than quadrupled, from $11 billion to $44 billion. People who'd held Merrill Lynch stock over that period were richly rewarded.

Now, I'm not here just to tell old war stories, though it's fun doing that. I'm just trying to underscore my point. Merrill Lynch is the greatest brand in financial services. Merrill Lynch is the greatest financial services company in the world. If there's anyone here who thinks that we're not, you need to get over it.

Yep, it's frustrating and unsettling when some of our people act unprofessionally. When they send careless e-mails and make us vulnerable to attack. And when we do business with a company like Enron, which with twenty-twenty hindsight is obviously business that we'd have been better off not doing. We're all angry and upset, but we have to get beyond it. We have to take the bull by the horns again, and change what needs to be changed, and make it better.

Every great brand has had to face great problems and surmount them. I don't care whether it's Coca-Cola or Ford or IBM or Microsoft. The test of every great company is, Do you let your problems tarnish or diminish you? Or do you face them head-on and make yourselves stronger, better, a fiercer competitor than ever before? And that's exactly what's going on at Merrill Lynch. And every single person in this room can make a difference. In fact, you *will* make a difference.

And this brings me directly to the second point I want to make today. It has to do with the power and influence of everyone in this room. When you think of the role that you play at Merrill Lynch, it's important that you never underestimate the ability you have to make a positive impact on the lives and careers of the people who work for you.

I've been fortunate to know some of Merrill Lynch's greatest leaders. I had the privilege of meeting Charlie Merrill on a number of occasions in the late 1940s and early 1950s. Win Smith was an extraordinary man. Some leaders get respect, some get affection. Win Smith was that rare combination—he got both.

I was sorry, by the way, to see Win Smith Jr. leave the firm. I talked to him about it at the time. It wasn't a matter of there being nothing for him to do here. As the new operating committee was being put together, he was offered a very substantial opportunity to do what he did best, representing Merrill Lynch with our most important clients around the world. But he just decided it was a time for a change in his life. I respect that, and I know that Win will always be part of the Merrill Lynch family.

His dad was something. His dad was the kind of leader

who was quiet and unassuming, but who had an incredible ability to motivate people and get them all moving in the same direction. After I finished my training he sent me up to Buffalo to work under a partner of the firm named E. Howard H. Roth. I was about twenty-two years old at the time, and I think I had the reputation of being just a little bit cocky.

I'll never know the answer to this, but I think maybe my dad may have done some urging, and I was sent to that office. Howard Roth was an incredible individual. He was tough as nails; he was a no-nonsense branch manager. You did it his way, or else. I could spend the rest of my allotted time just telling you Howard Roth stories.

I'll never forget, I was there for about three weeks as an account executive, making cold calls, calling people on the phone. He called me into his office one day and said, "Schreyer, you know what's wrong with you?"

I said, "Well, offhand, I can't think of anything, Mr. Roth."

"You talk too goddamn much." I'm quoting him. That's exactly what he said. And that ended up where he put an egg timer on my desk, and every time when he walked by, if he saw that egg timer going through, he'd just turn it over again and stare at me, and then walk away.

And to this day I can't stand long phone conversations. I talk to my daughter on the phone, and she likes to visit a little bit. I start...she says, "You're getting nervous, aren't you, Dad?" I say, "Yep," and that's the end of the conversation.

But it made a very strong impression on me. And he said, for example, "If you ever make a trade in a client's account that you can't justify to me is in the best interest of the client, you're fired." In other words, I expect you to do business, but do it the right way. And don't make a trade for the sake of making a trade. And I could go on and on. But I've found that most successful leaders were lucky to have had an outstanding mentor, and Howard Roth was one of mine.

The things that I learned from him stayed with me

throughout my career and throughout my life. You have the same impact on the people in your respective offices. As I said a moment ago, never underestimate–*never*–your ability to be a positive influence, a teacher, and a mentor. There's nothing more satisfying. It's a critical role that you play at Merrill Lynch.

There's one final thought I want to convey to you today, and that is this. I could not, and I mean this with every ounce of sincerity in my body...I could not be more confident in the current leadership of this firm.

We are in a moment of leadership transition. Merrill Lynch has shown over and over again that we know how to handle these moments. We do it thoughtfully. We do it in an orderly fashion, with our eyes on the future. Dave Komansky has contributed tremendously to build our franchise and achieve new levels of performance during the 1990s. This on top of all the many other contributions he has made during his long and distinguished career.

He and the board have selected Stan O'Neal to be his successor, and I am absolutely convinced he is the right man at the right time to lead Merrill Lynch. He has a vision for the firm, a strategy for carrying out this vision, and he is one tough competitor. He hates to lose. And so do I.

Now, I have to admit that when they put Stan in charge of the Private Client Group back in the beginning of 2000, I had my reservations. After all, he was...one of those.

Now, don't get me wrong. I'm not talking about his race. I couldn't care less about that. "One of those"...I mean, he was an investment banker. What in the world does an investment banker know about the private client business?

Well, it turned out he knows a heck of a lot about it. The wealth management strategy he put into place is a natural evolution of fifty years of leadership in this business. The kind of leadership that only one firm can claim. Stan's team–James Gorman and Bob Mulholland and Dan Sontag–are carrying out our strategy. They have a tremendous amount of experience. And, of course, all of you are essential partners in this effort.

I've had a chance to spend some time with Stan, and I found him to be a very good listener. And I've given him lots of advice. I know he's getting advice from all of you. That's one thing you can get plenty of as a CEO. But in addition to your advice, a CEO needs your engagement, your active support, your commitment to get out there and communicate. To lead. To execute this strategy. It makes all the difference in the world.

And while we're talking about advice, I think I do want to get something off my chest. What the hell! I think it's time to get rid of this ridiculous policy of "business casual." I'm tired of coming into the Merrill Lynch office in Princeton and seeing it filled with people who look like they're headed to the nearest bowling alley! That's what they look like.

That might be fine for a bunch of nerds in Silicon Valley, but it's not the way, in my opinion, that a Merrill Lynch office ought to look, when we're out there every day trying to earn the privilege of managing other people's money. I've always found that there's a direct correlation: When you look professional, you act professional.

Geez, I feel good just getting that off my chest. And, judging from your reaction and applause, I'm obviously preaching to the choir. I'm glad you all appreciate that. You're the managers of your offices, the masters of your own destiny. Tell them to dress up!

At any rate, I have really enjoyed this opportunity to be with all of you at this beautiful resort, and Joan has, too. Every time we get together with a group from Merrill Lynch, it amazes me how much the business has changed and the firm has changed, even in just the nine years since I retired as CEO.

Certainly the change has been enormous, almost beyond comprehension, since the day fifty-four years ago when I walked through the door at 70 Pine Street as a Junior Executive Trainee. It's one of the great things about Merrill Lynch, one of the secrets of our success: The ability to constantly change. The ability of each successive generation to make their own mark. To build on the past. To leave our firm in a stronger position than where they found it.

I'm counting on all of you to do that. And I know you will do it. Most of all, I'm counting on you to bring in the profits, so the board can do the right thing and raise the dividend. A little something for those of us living on a fixed income. Fortunately, it was fixed pretty good, so I don't complain too much.

I've just got to tell you that this has really been a fantastic meeting and the feedback I've gotten has been so, so great. Well, it's just about time to go out and celebrate for that "special occasion," and have a drink. I'll be toasting all of you. I'll be wishing all of you great success.

I continue to remain bullish, not only on America, but surely on Merrill Lynch and all of you. Thank you all very, very much.

Quotations
from Chairman Bill

In 1994, Dan Tully hosted a retirement "roast" for me at the 21 Club. Paul Critchlow, Lee Roselle, Jim Wiggins, and the gang put together quite a program, including a little red book patterned after *The Quotations of Chairman Mao,* which contained some of my favorite sayings and their supposed true meaning. At least they thought it was funny. Dear reader, I reprint it here to let you be the judge.

"Don't sweat the small stuff."
(It's Tully's problem.)

"You've got to see the big picture."
(Do it my way.)

"When I come back in, I want to know what you really think."
(You better agree with me.)

"It's a dumb dog that doesn't bury a bone."
(With my Swiss bank account, I don't give a damn about you.)

"I want this first-class."
(Don't worry, I'll sign your expense account.)

"I can't do everything."
(It's a problem, so I'll let Dan deal with it.)

"It's lonely at the top."
(But a hell of a lot lonelier at the bottom.)

"No one's personal bottom line is more important than the reputation of the firm."
(Except mine.)

"In my next life I want to be Joan."
(Self-explanatory.)

"Never argue matters of little importance."
(Whatever you say, Joan.)

"Now I'm going to give you your performance evaluation."
(You've pissed me off and you'll pay.)

"May I have the other half of my first drink? Just add some ice and top it off."
(Self-explanatory.)

"Special Perrier, please."
(No water on the Tanquery Sterling.)

"Here's to us—good people are hard to find."
(Screw 'em, they're only butterflies.)

"Let's have a pop."
(It's cocktail hour somewhere in the world.)

Afterword
by Joseph V. Paterno

So there you have it: the world according to Bill Schreyer. And what a world it is. From the first page onward—a story spanning his childhood in Williamsport to his exploits on Wall Street to his current serene state of what I would call maturity and wisdom—what you get is a portrait of a guy who has really embraced life. "Living large," the kids call it. No doubt about it, Bill has lived large. But he's done much more than just that. He's enlarged life for a lot of other people, too. That's one measure of a great man—the good you do in the time you have on this earth.

What makes Bill Schreyer different? What distinguishes him from every other Wall Street bigshot who's had some success and made a lot of money? I think it begins and ends with character. His was formed early by the combined influence of his parents. He talks a lot in these pages about his dad and what that relationship meant to him. He talks less about his mother, but I think she was equally important in forming the man that Bill Schreyer would become. Through them, he developed a clear set of values—honesty, loyalty, respect for people regardless of their position in life. With these values as a foundation, the path he followed in life led

317

to a passionate devotion to three great institutions–the Catholic Church, Penn State, and Merrill Lynch. Each was made stronger by Bill Schreyer's participation.

Since Merrill Lynch is known as the firm that brought Wall Street to Main Street, it seems only fitting that his own story progressed in the opposite direction–from Main Street to Wall Street. Our lives intersected in State College, Pennsylvania, a destination we also reached from opposite directions–I from the big city, Brooklyn, by way of Brown University; he from the small town of Williamsport. While we didn't meet until we were both well into adulthood, we shared some of the same formative experiences of growing up in the thirties and forties.

Most people in America didn't have a whole lot of material things back then. Not like today. An observation about those times made by a fellow Brooklynite, the writer Pete Hamill, rings true, I think, for a lot of us growing up back then: "We were poor, but we were not impoverished." We had strong extended families, genuine neighborhoods where people looked out for each other, and there were a lot of ways that a young guy with ambition and a little bit on the ball could get a break. It was up to you to make the most of it.

So no, my dad didn't have a whole lot of money, but I was able to get an Ivy League education on a football scholarship. Bill's dad might have managed the Merrill Lynch office in town, but his family didn't have a whole lot of money, either. So Bill chose a state school rather than the more expensive, private college nearby, in order to save his dad a few bucks. What a fateful decision that would turn out to be. The day Bill Schreyer arrived on campus was one lucky day for Penn State, I can tell you that right now.

He graduated in 1948 and I arrived in 1950, as an assistant coach to Rip Engle. We didn't meet until many years later. I actually don't remember my first meeting with Bill, but by the time he became a big muck-a-muck at Merrill Lynch, we were well acquainted, and he would ask me once in a while to give a motivational speech at one of the company's events– a sales meeting or something like that. I was happy to oblige, and after all, he paid pretty well.

Bill recalls one of those events in this book, and here's where the story starts getting a little bit suspect. After reading his version of things, I decided that I needed to check the definition of the word *memoir*. According to Webster's, the original 1828 edition, this is what it means: "A *species of history* written by a person who had some share in the transactions related"–emphasis mine.

So what we have here is "a species of history." Exactly what kind of species, then, would this book be? Look in the back and you get a clue. You won't find any notes or bibliography, nothing like you would see in a painstakingly researched work of scholarship by a Penn State history professor, for example. So might that leave the author room for a little bit of, shall we say, *embellishment* in the way he describes some of the transactions in which he had a share? I think so.

Bill recalls that after I spoke at one of those Merrill Lynch meetings–this one happened to be at a fancy seaside resort– everyone hit the beach, and we chose sides for some friendly competition–tug-of-war and that sort of thing. He was captain of one team, I was captain of the other, and the way he tells it, his team defeated mine.

There's only one problem: I don't remember it that way. I don't think that's the way it happened at all. But just for the sake of argument, let's say it did go down the way he remembers it. And if it did, then Bill seems to be missing the obvious point: My guys threw the game. It was as simple as that: They let him win. I mean, think about it. What are they going to do, beat the boss? That wouldn't have been real smart, would it? I'm telling you, they just don't hire a whole lot of stupid people at Merrill Lynch.

319

STILL BULLISH ON AMERICA

I'm kidding, of course. But you don't think I'd let Schreyer get away without at least a little bit of needling in this appreciation, do you? That's the kind of relationship we have. So maybe Bill got one or two details wrong in this book. Maybe his memory was a little bit fuzzy about a couple of things. Does it matter? I think not. This is a life story written from the heart as well as from the head, and it gets to some larger truths.

Bill says he's written this book for his grandchildren, their children, and for other generations yet to come. It's a valuable gift; one that will, as they say, keep on giving. A young person can learn a lot from this book, and I am absolutely certain that these lessons will be just as valid—and valuable—one hundred years from now as they are today.

Bill writes about the importance of mentors in a person's life. He had two—his dad, who taught him how to deal with people, and Howard Roth, his first office manager in Buffalo, who taught him how to be "tough but fair" in the world of business. Bill often has said that a common characteristic of most successful people he's known is that they had the benefit of a strong mentor. What he's demonstrated in his own life is that it's a two-way street: There are mentors to be had out there, but only if you're willing to be mentored.

Courage. That's another lesson you learn from this book. Early in his tenure as CEO, when some trader lost a couple of hundred million bucks in some exotic mortgage securities, he could have cashed out right then and there and said good-bye. He was already rich beyond most people's measure, and it would have been the easiest thing for him to do. But he didn't do that. He and his partner Dan Tully hunkered down and cleaned up the mess. That required courage.

Then right on the heels of that adventure, there was the stock market crash of 1987. If you were a big player on Wall Street, your first inclination might well have been to run and hide, which is exactly what a lot of them did. Not Bill Schreyer.

Not only did he not run and hide, he went on national television to tell people that they ought to just settle down a little bit. Don't think that didn't take some guts.

I'll never forget a meeting we had right in the middle of that week, a planning session for the Campaign for Penn State. All hell was breaking loose around him, but Bill was just as cool and calm as could be. He must have been feeling at least a little bit of trepidation about the prospect of launching Penn State's first major capital campaign in the face of the biggest stock market crash since 1929, but if he was, he didn't show it. And that gave all the rest of us confidence. "Grace under pressure," Hemingway called it. When you see it on the football field or in the boardroom, it's something rare. Something to admire.

The importance of other people. That's another lesson a wise reader can learn from this book. You'll notice that a whole long section is not about Bill at all. It's about people who have been important to him, who have made a difference in his life. He is generous in his affection, because he recognizes that without these people he loves, he could not have lived the life he has led. I don't care how talented you are, how athletically gifted, how genetically well-endowed, it still comes down to the people who help you get there. Nobody knows that better than Bill Schreyer.

Finally, there's the lesson of loyalty, and the rewards that come from it over a long life. Forty-five years at one company—Merrill Lynch. Fifty years, and counting, married to the same beautiful woman. A lifelong devotion to the Catholic Church. And a passionate dedication to his alma mater, Penn State. His commitment to each of these, built and nurtured over eight decades, his given his life a richness that is just not available to those who jump from one thing to another, and hold on to nothing for very long.

When I was a young man on the verge of choosing my own path in life, the general assumption among my family was that I would go to law school. I think it came as a bit of a surprise to my father when I told him that I had decided to coach football at Penn State, but he was supportive as always, and encouraging. He said to me, "I hope you have an impact on that place." I don't know if Bill's father ever said anything similar to him, but what an impact he's had. The creation of the honors college that bears his name, along with his countless other acts of vision and generosity over the years, have strengthened the university we both love in a profound and lasting way. That's "living large," indeed.

So, here's to you, Bill. For a kid from the sticks, you haven't turned out half badly. Here's to all the good times and laughs we've had along the way. I am proud to call you my friend.

January 2, 2009
State College, Pennsylvania